ARCO

LAW ENFORCEMENT EXAMS

4TH EDITION

E. P. Steinberg

ARCO

THOMSON LEARNING

Australia • Canada • Denmark • Japan • Mexico • New Zealand • Philippines
Puerto Rico • Singapore • South Africa • Spain • United Kingdom • United States

Fourth Edition

An ARCO Book

ARCO is a registered trademark of Thomson Learning, Inc., and is used herein under license by Peterson's.

About Peterson's

Founded in 1966, Peterson's, a division of Thomson Learning, is the nation's largest and most respected provider of lifelong learning online resources, software, reference guides, and books. The Education Supersite℠ at petersons.com—the Web's most heavily traveled education resource—has searchable databases and interactive tools for contacting U.S.-accredited institutions and programs. CollegeQuest℠ (CollegeQuest.com) offers a complete solution for every step of the college decision-making process. GradAdvantage™ (GradAdvantage.org), developed with Educational Testing Service, is the only electronic admissions service capable of sending official graduate test score reports with a candidate's online application. Peterson's serves more than 55 million education consumers annually.

Thomson Learning is among the world's leading providers of lifelong learning, serving the needs of individuals, learning institutions, and corporations with products and services for both traditional classrooms and for online learning. For more information about the products and services offered by Thomson Learning, please visit www.thomsonlearning.com. Headquartered in Stamford, Connecticut, with offices worldwide, Thomson Learning is part of The Thomson Corporation (www.thomson.com), a leading e-information and solutions company in the business, professional, and education marketplaces. The Corporation's common shares are listed on the Toronto and London stock exchanges.

For more information, contact Peterson's, 2000 Lenox Drive, Lawrenceville, NJ 08648; 800-338-3282; or find us on the World Wide Web at: www.petersons.com/about

ISBN 0-7645-6099-9

Printed in the United States of America

10 9 8 7 6 5 4 3 2 1 02 01 00

CONTENTS

PART FIVE
Training

PART SIX
How to Choose

INTRODUCTION

Do you want a career in law enforcement? Have you always wanted to be a Police Officer? Do you admire the unsmiling Secret Service Agents who surround the President and wonder how you might become one of them? Does the excitement of the Customs Agent uncovering smugglers appeal to you? Or can you picture yourself as an FBI Agent catching a criminal on the "most wanted" list? All of these, and many more, are law enforcement officers. A law enforcement position offers an opportunity to serve your community and to help others. It offers diversity, excitement, and, in most cases, some personal danger. It also offers career security and growth opportunities.

Which law enforcement position is for you? Different positions have different requirements for education, experience, medical history, and physical fitness. Some require written exams; others do not. There are great variations in working conditions, time commitments, travel and relocation requirements, and the work itself.

If you are at the "career shopping" stage, this book will help you decide whether you want to consider law enforcement. Once you have decided on law enforcement, this book will help you determine the specific type of law enforcement work you would like to do and the jurisdiction—local, state, or federal—in which you would like to do it. If you choose federal law enforcement, it will help you select the agencies to which you are most suited by interest and ability. This book will also guide you in taking steps to prepare yourself to qualify for the position of your choice.

In part 3 of this book, you will find representative sample questions for a variety of local, state, and federal law enforcement examinations. These will give you a foretaste of the exam you might have to take and will assist you in making an informed choice of the particular law enforcement job for which you have the best chance. The answer explanations and advice that accompany the correct answer keys can start you on a path of directed study so you can ace your exam, earn a high position on the competitive list, and get the job you really want.

PART ONE

Law Enforcement: A Definition

CONTENTS

LAW ENFORCEMENT: A DEFINITION

A career in law enforcement offers prospects for challenge and variety found in few other areas of work. In earlier days, law enforcement agencies faced problems such as political control, low pay, and limited training. Today, they have become organizations that reflect the social, urban, and industrial complexities of our society. In viewing this career area, it is more accurate to use the term "law enforcement" than "police" because responsibility for enforcement now rests with a variety of government agencies. In the United States, there are some 40,000 separate law enforcement agencies representing municipal, county, state, and federal governments.

Law enforcement in America is fragmented and specialized primarily due to the basic distrust Americans have of the concept of a national police force. Regardless of fragmentation, all of these agencies, as representatives of the population, enforce the law by investigating, arresting, and assisting in the prosecution of persons violating the law.

In many instances, the large number of enforcement agencies in America means duplication of law enforcement activities. This often causes jurisdictional disputes among agencies with resulting confusion and complications. For example, each federal, state, and local law enforcement agency has jurisdiction in matters of illegal narcotics traffic. If their efforts are not coordinated or are unknown to each other, they may operate at cross-purposes and reduce the effectiveness of the investigations in progress. Perhaps the best way to understand our fragmented and decentralized system of law enforcement in the United States is to examine it by level of government—municipal, county, state, and federal.

At the local level, the two most important examples of law enforcement are municipal and county police agencies. Many citizens mistakenly believe that the greatest responsibility for policing the United States rests with the federal government. In fact, law enforcement is primarily a local function. The origins of law enforcement in America show that crime was treated primarily as a local problem. It follows that enforcement, for the most part, was practiced locally. Despite the development of criminal activities that crisscross local, state, and national boundaries, the main sources of crime in America can be found in local communities. More than 90 percent of all felonies occur in the jurisdictions of local police agencies. In addition, the vast majority of criminal laws are local ordinances prohibiting offenses ranging from vandalism to murder. The size of local police agencies in the United States is as varied as the number of laws they seek to enforce. Some smaller communities function with two or three officers, while large municipalities such as New York City have forces exceeding 25,000 officers. Marked differences also exist in the background, training, education, and pay of police officers throughout the country. Despite these differences, the goals of the police remain the same: the enforcement of criminal laws and the preservation of peace in the community.

Municipal Police

The entire criminal justice system in the United States starts with the police, and it is the municipal police officer who is most familiar to the average person. Municipal police departments, in both personnel and management practices, are generally organized along semimilitary lines. Police officers wear uniforms, usually blue or brown; are ranked according to a military system such as sergeant, lieutenant, captain, colonel; and are governed by specific, written rules and regulations. Highly trained police officers are found in both large and small cities. Of the more than 17,000 cities in the United States, 55 have populations exceeding a quarter of a million, and these employ about one-third of all police personnel. American cities present the greatest challenges to law enforcement, and require the highest concentration of officers.

All police agencies, large and small, have similar problems and responsibilities. Each engages in common activities that prevent crime and disorder, preserve the peace, and protect individual life and property. Police work is often thought of as confrontations between police officers and hardened criminals; this frequently is the case. In many instances, however, police officers deal with quite different and surprisingly varied situations.

Police activities can be divided into two functions: line and staff. Line functions involve activities that result directly in meeting police service goals; staff activities help administrators organize and manage the police agency. The line functions common to most municipal police departments include patrol, investigation, vice, traffic, juvenile, and crime prevention.

LINE FUNCTIONS

At the center of police law enforcement is patrol. This involves movement of uniformed police personnel, on foot or in vehicles, through designated areas. In most departments, at least half of all police personnel are assigned to patrol. Officers on patrol have a variety of duties that include interviewing and interrogating suspects and arresting lawbreakers; controlling crowds at public gatherings; enforcing laws regulating public conduct; intervening in personal, family, and public disputes; issuing warnings and citations; and providing miscellaneous services to members of the public. Although patrol officers spend more time carrying out routine police services than catching criminals, their importance cannot be underestimated. Because their primary duties are performed on the street, patrol officers are the most visible representatives of local government.

Investigation activities come into play when patrol officers are unable to prevent a crime or to arrest a suspect in the act of committing a crime. Investigative specialists, better known as detectives, help solve crimes by skillfully questioning victims, witnesses, and suspects; by gathering evidence at crime sites; and by tracing stolen property or vehicles connected with crime. Detectives investigate many types of crimes including murder, manslaughter, robbery, rape, aggravated assault, burglary, auto theft, forgery, embezzlement, and weapons violations. They spend considerable time reviewing physical evidence, clues, interviews, and methods used by the criminal that may provide a break in solving a case. In addition, investigations are coordinated using information provided by patrol officers, laboratory personnel, records clerks, and concerned citizens. All of these may lead to the identification of the guilty individual.

Vice operations in the local police agency are aimed at illegal activities that corrupt and destroy the physical, mental, and moral health of the public. Enforcement activities in vice operations are directed principally at illegal gambling, narcotics violations, traffic in liquor, prostitution, pandering, pornography, and obscene conduct. Organized crime is involved in many vice crimes, and vice crimes are directly linked to other types of street crime. For example, gambling is associated with loansharking, and prostitution and drug abuse are linked with robbery. Patrol units have the primary responsibility of enforcing vice laws and can significantly prevent such illegal activities, particularly in high crime areas. To be effective, however, there must be a continual exchange of information and a coordinated effort between vice units and all other elements of the police department as well as cooperation with federal law enforcement agencies such as the Drug Enforcement Administration and the Bureau of Alcohol, Tobacco, and Firearms.

Traffic law enforcement seeks the voluntary compliance of citizens with traffic regulations to provide maximum movement of traffic with minimum interruption. Because no shame is associated with most traffic violations and the public often breaks traffic regulations without realizing it, breaking these laws is made an unpleasant experience by enforcing penalties such as fines, loss of license, or imprisonment. In addition to vehicular traffic enforcement, uniformed police officers also engage in pedestrian control, traffic direction, investigation of accidents, and traffic education. There is an important relationship between traffic law enforcement and other police services. Stopping a motorist for a routine vehicle check or for a traffic violation often results in an arrest for a nontraffic-related reason such as weapons or drug possession, a stolen vehicle, or flight to avoid prosecution in another jurisdiction. As in the case of other police assignments, traffic officers give court testimony and are often involved in civil cases because of traffic accident investigations.

Most municipal police agencies have specific policy guidelines for dealing with juveniles. However, there may be differences in approach or philosophy among various departments depending on the needs of individual communities. In some cases, police officers are given special training and are assigned to juvenile activities on a full-time basis. In other police departments, the training in this area is minimal, and officers rely on traditional police methods in dealing with juveniles. A juvenile becomes a delinquent by committing an act that, if he or she were an adult, would be a crime. The police, however, have greater responsibilities in juvenile matters than merely enforcing laws by taking youthful offenders into custody. Police juvenile efforts are aimed at identifying neglected and dependent children, detecting and preventing predelinquent behavior, finding and investigating delinquency breeding grounds within the community, and properly disposing of juvenile cases.

The last of the basic line functions of the municipal police agency involves crime prevention. When citizens are hostile to the police agency in their community, it is as real a threat to peace and order as police indifference to the needs of the citizens. Police serve all segments of the community, but they cannot preserve law and order and control crime unless the public cooperates and participates in the law enforcement process. Hostility between citizens and police not only creates explosive situations; more importantly, it can promote crime in the community. Crime is both a police problem and a social problem that will continue to grow unless the public becomes more involved. Community relations programs, for example, can help close the gap between citizens and police by making each aware of the other's problems and by providing the impetus to settle their differences. In some municipalities, police agencies have introduced crime-prevention techniques such as neighborhood security and watch programs. These encourage citizens to take security measures in their homes and businesses and to report any suspicious persons or activities in the neighborhood.

STAFF FUNCTIONS

Staff functions are activities performed by police officers to help administrators organize and manage the police agency. Personnel recruitment, selection, and training; planning; finance; employee services; public relations; and use of civilian personnel are examples of staff work.

Staff is the costliest and most important of all the resources committed to the law enforcement process, and a police agency is only as able and effective as its personnel. To varying degrees, every police department engages in recruitment, selection, and training of personnel. It sets qualifications, recruits candidates, tests and screens applicants, and places them in training facilities. The police department also reviews performance during probation and develops salary schedules and lines of promotion for police officers. In addition, staff units are responsible for providing ongoing training to police officers at all levels in the department as a means of keeping them up-to-date on the latest developments in law enforcement. All of these factors are important because the quality of personnel and training determines the character of police performance, and in the final analysis, the quality of police leadership.

To be effective, police departments must plan and organize numerous activities that characterize around-the-clock operations. The unpredictable nature of police work, however, and the problems that arise from emergency situations sometimes make planning difficult. Work schedules, paydays, patrol assignments, uniforms, and equipment all require planning; this, in turn, involves administrative staff and line operations, extradepartmental plans, and research and development. Good planning by the police agency produces effective police service in the community.

Budgeting is an important part of the staff functions of police personnel. These responsibilities include, but are not limited to, fiscal planning and preparation of cost estimates for personnel, equipment, facilities, and programs necessary to meet the established goals of the police department.

The staff must also provide employee services to members of the police agency. They must explain benefits and help employees and their families obtain all the services to which they are entitled. For example, in cases of illness, injury, or death, specialists in employee benefits take care of matters with a minimum of inconvenience to the officers and their families.

Police personnel also engage in public relations activities. This entails the development of programs that acquaint the community with police goals and that help gain public support for police activities. Duties include providing information to the press and the public, maintaining liaison with community representatives, and working with educational organizations to improve relations with youth in the community.

A number of staff positions and auxiliary staff positions can be filled by handicapped personnel.

A widespread practice is the use of civilian personnel in certain jobs within police agencies. Civilian personnel are assigned to duties that do not require the exercise of police authority or the application of the skills and knowledge of the professional police officer. Work typically performed by civilians includes clerical or secretarial work, maintenance or sanitation work, prisoner booking, and motor vehicle maintenance. Many civilian employees develop an interest in regular police work and, if they meet the requirements for sworn status, become potential candidates for the police officer position. Some police departments will help pay for the schooling required for their civilian employees to meet the educational standards of the department. Some offer part-time training to their employees.

Besides these primary staff functions, important auxiliary staff services help line and administrative personnel meet police objectives. These services include crime laboratory, property and detention, transportation, communications, and information systems. In addition, many police departments have intelligence operations and systems of internal discipline. Brief descriptions of these auxiliary services follow.

AUXILIARY STAFF SERVICES

Crime Laboratory

Because solutions to many crimes are found through the application of physical and biological sciences, the crime laboratory is of great value to law enforcement officers. In an initial critical phase, police officers or specially trained evidence technicians identify, collect, and preserve physical evidence at crime scenes. Overlooking, contaminating, or accidentally destroying evidence can hinder the progress of an investigation. After the evidence reaches the crime laboratory, qualitative, quantitative, and interpretive analyses are performed by forensic personnel. Crime laboratory personnel are responsible for fingerprint operations, ballistics, polygraph tests, blood and alcohol tests, and examination of questioned documents. Due to the considerable expense involved with operating crime laboratory facilities, not all police agencies have them. Local and regional laboratories therefore have been established in most states to provide services to law enforcement agencies from different jurisdictions.

Property and Detention

Regardless of their size, locale, or functions, police agencies are responsible for evidence, personal property, and articles of value confiscated when carrying out police business. In addition, they must take inventory, inspect, replace, and maintain departmental property and facilities. Each police department must ensure the safekeeping of all property and evidence and make provisions for its storage, retrieval, and disposition to authorized police personnel.

Detention activities in a police agency involve temporary confinement of persons awaiting investigation or trial, as well as permanent imprisonment in city or county facilities for those sentenced by the court. Typical activities include booking, searching, fingerprinting, photographing, and feeding prisoners.

Transportation

Police mobility is crucial to crime prevention. Police officers must have the capability of moving safely and swiftly to meet their responsibilities. Police transportation activities center around the acquisition, use, maintenance, cost, and safety of a variety of vehicles. These include automobiles (patrol and unmarked), motorcycles, trucks, buses, motor scooters, aircraft (helicopters and planes), watercraft, and horses. By developing and maintaining an efficient transportation program, the police agency increases its effectiveness and its ability to enforce the law.

Communications

Communications in a police agency are the lifeline of the organization. Most police department communications systems have three parts: the telephone system, command and control operations, and radio communications. Though communications systems differ among departments throughout the country because of variations in staffing and funding, they generally operate as follows:

Telephone communications systems aim to reduce crime through rapid and accurate communication with the public. The telephone is the primary link between the police and the community, and in an emergency, the public must be able to contact the police immediately. This is vitally important because rapid police response to an emergency call can mean the difference between life and death or between the capture and escape of suspects.

Command and control means coordinating operations of radio-equipped field units through exchange of information between field units and communications centers. In its simplest form, it is the receipt, processing, and dispatching of information received in telephone complaints to field units for action. This process becomes more complex as calls increase. In large departments, the use of automated command and control equipment is widespread. Regardless of department size, rapid and accurate command and control operations are needed to ensure the safety of the community.

Radio communications, an integral part of police operations, involve the use of radio frequencies by command control and police officers both to receive and transmit information. The efficiency of radio communications, however, is often impaired because frequency ranges are limited. In recent years, frequency congestion has been the result of increased use of communication devices by the public and business. Efforts to solve this problem are receiving constant attention by law enforcement agencies at all levels. Where possible, in addition to radio-equipped vehicles, police departments provide police officers with specialized equipment such as miniature transceivers, mobile and portable radio units, and walkie-talkies. The object is to provide continuous communication among commanders, supervisors, and field personnel.

Police Information Systems

Another staff service, the information system, can also significantly affect efforts to reduce crime. Such a system consists of three components: reporting, collection and recording of crime data, and information storage and retrieval.

Reporting means thorough and precise reporting of all crimes that come to the department's attention. Included are telephone and field investigation reports and warrant information received from judicial agencies. Such information can assist in criminal investigations and is useful in other parts of the criminal justice system.

Collection and recording of crime data helps evaluate crime conditions and the effectiveness of police operations. The data are obtained from the department's reportable incident files such as precinct and field-unit activity logs, accident reports, and criminal investigation reports as well as summary dossier files consisting of fingerprints, name index to fingerprints, and criminal histories.

Information storage and retrieval, the third part of police information systems, supports police in the field by providing quick and accurate criminal information on request. Field personnel have access, for example, to arrest records, outstanding warrants, stolen vehicles, and serially identified stolen weapons and property. Development of good information systems for police officers contributes significantly to the effectiveness of the police agency.

Intelligence

Intelligence operations, still another staff service, also contribute to efficient police work. Information is gathered to keep police officials attuned to happenings in their areas of jurisdiction by providing insight into community conditions, potential problem areas, and criminal activities—all essential to law enforcement. This work deals with activities that present a threat to the community. The most common targets of intelligence investigations are organized crime and individuals or groups who cause public disorder. To be effective, intelligence activities must be continuous; the data gathered must be used to plan and carry out crime-fighting programs.

Internal Discipline

Another auxiliary staff service is internal discipline. Discipline and accountability are vital to any police agency in maintaining its integrity. Internal discipline, also known as internal affairs, involves investigation of complaints related to police department services and personnel. Complaints can be lodged by citizens or police personnel themselves. Depending on whether the charges are substantiated, complaints can lead to departmental discipline, dismissal, arrest, prosecution, and imprisonment of those found guilty. By protecting the public from police misconduct and corruption and by taking positive action against employees found guilty of misconduct, the department strengthens morale and gains the support of the community it serves.

When all the line and staff functions performed in police agencies of any size are considered, it is obvious that effective administration is not easily attained. Large agencies tend to use police officers as specialists in specific types of operations, while smaller departments use officers as generalists performing a wide variety of functions. There are merits to both systems, and their use is generally dictated by the needs and composition of the communities in which they are located.

In addition to the local police agencies in municipalities, other special-purpose public police forces are found in many cities throughout the United States. Their jurisdictions include parks, harbors, airports, sanitation departments, transit systems, housing facilities, and ports. Some of these agencies have full police officer powers within their jurisdictions; others have more limited authority.

County Police

When planning a career in law enforcement, service at the county level of government is a possibility that should be considered. A county is the largest territorial division for local government within a state. Most counties have the constitutional office of sheriff, the chief law enforcement official for that area. The County Sheriff is generally an elected official. To provide law enforcement services, sheriffs employ a force of uniformed deputies. The size of the force is most often determined by the size of the county, and as a rule, Deputy Sheriffs operate freely in unincorporated areas, that is, areas not within city or town limits. Deputy Sheriffs, although they usually patrol alone, provide police services in much the same manner as municipal police officers. They may perform extensive police services including patrol, juvenile, vice, and investigative activities, much the same as their counterparts in municipal law enforcement agencies.

In addition to sheriffs' departments, some states have developed countywide police agencies organized and administered like municipal departments. For example, although certain municipalities within a county have their own police units, their operations are coordinated with the countywide police department, which patrols and protects communities without police of their own. Typically, countywide police forces perform all major law enforcement functions—patrol, traffic, vice, juvenile, and investigative activities—carried out by the larger municipal police agencies. Patrol duties are similar to those found in municipal agencies except they are performed over a wider geographical area and in smaller communities.

In addition to countywide police and sheriff's departments, there are other local law enforcement personnel within counties. Designated as constables, marshals, or police officers, these officers enforce the law in smaller communities such as villages, towns, townships, and boroughs. The continued existence of police agencies in smaller communities is evidence of the citizens' preference for local control of police services. Also operating at the county level are special-purpose police units whose jurisdictions include tunnels, parks, bridges, freeways, and harbors. Although these agencies perform their policing duties in very limited areas of jurisdiction, they provide essential services to the public.

State Law Enforcement

Law enforcement at the state level is another area that should be considered when planning a career. Some state law enforcement agencies have general police powers, others have limited authority, and still others are regulatory in nature.

Two of the best-known state-level enforcement units are the state police and the highway patrol. There is a definite distinction between these agencies in terms of responsibility and authority. State police engage in a full range of law enforcement activities including criminal investigation. Highway patrol units are concerned almost entirely with traffic control and enforcement and have limited general police authority.

State police duties vary throughout the country. In addition to regular law enforcement responsibilities, state police officers may patrol state parks, guard executive and legislative personnel and properties, and conduct examinations for motor vehicle licenses. In some states, these officers act as fire, fish, and game wardens; court officers; and evaluators of applications for pistol permits. Very often, state police personnel are brought in during emergencies such as civil disorders, natural disasters, or situations in which a local police agency needs support. The uniformed state police force is assisted in law enforcement activities by plainclothes investigators. These detectives act on information supplied by patrol personnel when follow-up and investigation are required to solve criminal cases.

Highway patrol units enforce state motor vehicle codes and other laws relating to the operation of vehicles on the highways. They perform functions that ensure the safe, lawful, rapid, and efficient use of highway systems. Highway patrol units also use an investigative staff, usually organized as a separate agency, that is responsible for such activities as organized crime, narcotics, fraud, and gambling.

A law enforcement career at the state level is not limited to state police or highway patrol. In most states, various agencies have jurisdiction over other specialized functions that differ from the usual policing activities. Some examples of these areas of specialization follow.

Most states operate and maintain crime laboratory facilities and clearinghouses of crime information. State crime laboratories provide services to cities and counties that lack facilities of their own. Laboratory personnel examine evidence and crime scenes, identify and compare evidence, and testify in court proceedings for the prosecution. State information clearinghouses keep centralized criminal information and fingerprint files, gather and analyze crime data, and on request, provide such information to law enforcement agencies at all levels of government. In some cases, these information units are operated by the state police; in others, they are separate agencies.

Each state, to some degree, has investigation bureaus or departments that conduct civil and criminal investigations for various state agencies, departments, commissions, and in some cases, local police agencies requesting assistance. Some of these specialized investigative units often cooperate with and conduct joint operations with local and federal law enforcement units on matters of mutual concern.

The protection and conservation of natural resources, a responsibility shared by all states, has moved most states to employ law enforcement officers in parks and recreational areas, historical landmarks, and hiking and camping areas. State foresters are assigned to protect woodlands from fire, disease, and misuse. State fish and game wardens enforce the fish and game laws, license fishermen and hunters, and do whatever is necessary to protect wildlife.

Enforcement of public health and safety codes is another state employment area. State fire marshals, for example, have varied responsibilities that may include enforcing statewide fire and safety regulations, developing fire-prevention programs, and establishing licensing standards. Their efforts are closely coordinated with those of local fire officials in carrying out their enforcement responsibilities. State public health officials investigate and enforce state codes pertaining to pollution and public sanitation, communicable diseases, licensing of health facilities, and food and drug standards. They work closely with health officers from local and federal agencies in enforcing these laws.

In addition to the examples of state law enforcement jobs just mentioned, there are many others. A look at the organizational structure of any state reveals a considerable number of departments, bureaus, divisions, and agencies using investigative or law enforcement personnel to some extent. Among these state agencies are agriculture (including dairy and livestock), markets (dealing with produce, weights, and measures), liquor and racing authorities, insurance, commerce, finance, mental hygiene, labor, housing and industrial safety, investments, civil service commissions, and vocational standards agencies for licensing professionals. It is apparent that law enforcement career opportunities at the state level of government need not be limited to the traditional uniformed services.

Federal Law Enforcement

The federal government offers varied opportunities to persons considering a career in law enforcement. While the goals of federal agencies differ and their authorities cover broad geographic areas, the scope of most agencies is specific and limited. Some have enforcement duties that deal with criminal or regulatory matters; some deal with security or military affairs. Many federal law enforcement positions require extensive travel, and most entail relocation at some time during the officer's career. Federal law enforcement positions offer glamour overlaid with hard work, long hours, and in many cases, personal danger. A clearer picture of law enforcement activities at the federal level is possible if the functions of some of the major federal agencies are examined. Specific positions within some of the following agencies will be described in the next chapter.

BUREAU OF ALCOHOL, TOBACCO, AND FIREARMS

The Department of the Treasury established the Bureau of Alcohol, Tobacco, and Firearms (BATF) to enforce laws relating to alcohol, tobacco, firearms, and explosives. The objective of BATF is to enjoin voluntary compliance with these laws and to minimize willful violations. To do so, the BATF has two enforcement units—criminal and regulatory. The criminal enforcement unit seeks to eliminate illegal possession and use of firearms and explosives, to reduce traffic in illicit alcohol, and to assist state and local law enforcement agencies in reducing crime and violence. The regulatory enforcement unit helps ensure full collection of revenues due from legal alcohol and tobacco industries and aids in preventing commercial bribery, consumer deception, and improper trade practices.

DRUG ENFORCEMENT ADMINISTRATION

The Drug Enforcement Administration (DEA), an agency of the U.S. Department of Justice, has the leading role in the fight against drug abuse in our country. The DEA's mission is to control narcotic and dangerous drug abuse effectively through law enforcement, education, training, and research activities. It is responsible for enforcing statutes and laws relating to the unlawful distribution and use of such products as heroin, opium, cocaine, hallucinogens, marijuana, synthetic narcotics that can be addictive (such as Demerol and methadone), and dangerous nonnarcotic drugs (such as amphetamines and barbiturates). The aim is to bring to justice those individuals and organizations, at home and abroad, engaged in growing, manufacturing, or distributing controlled, dangerous substances destined for illegal traffic in the United States. The efforts of this agency are directed at the highest level of suppliers and toward the confiscation of the greatest quantity of illegal drugs before they reach the street pushers. In line with these responsibilities, the DEA develops overall federal drug enforcement strategies and leads the way in developing narcotic and dangerous drug suppression programs at national and international levels. The DEA also regulates legal trade in narcotics and dangerous drugs.

FEDERAL BUREAU OF INVESTIGATION

The Federal Bureau of Investigation (FBI) is responsible for investigating violations of all federal laws except those specifically within the jurisdiction of other federal agencies. The FBI deals with violations of sabotage, treason, and espionage laws as well as internal security matters. Although the jurisdiction of the Bureau in criminal matters is limited, the FBI has responsibility for enforcing numerous federal laws including those against kidnapping, extortion, bank robbery, offenses involving interstate transportation, civil rights violations, assaulting or killing a U.S. President or federal officer, and the security of personnel employed by the federal government and property owned by the government.

In addition to these traditional enforcement functions, the FBI maintains a centralized system of fingerprint identification; the National Crime Information Center (NCIC), which supplies information on known or suspected criminals; crime laboratory services, which are also available to local enforcement agencies; and training programs to increase law enforcement effectiveness at all levels of government.

GENERAL SERVICES ADMINISTRATION

The General Services Administration (GSA), one of the largest federal agencies, provides our government with the most economic and efficient methods of managing its programs and resources. These include management of property and records; construction and operation of buildings; purchase and distribution of supplies; management of communications, traffic, and transportation; and direction of the governmentwide automatic data-processing program. Within the GSA, the very large Public Buildings Service (PBS) is responsible for the protection of life and property in most federally owned or leased buildings throughout the country. In over 10,000 federal buildings, there are more than 279 million square feet of space including outside parking areas. To carry out their protective mission, PBS employs a uniformed security force staffed with Federal Protective Officers, whose duties are described in this book.

IMMIGRATION AND NATURALIZATION SERVICE

The Immigration and Naturalization Service (INS) administers our country's immigration and naturalization laws. These statutes are concerned with the admission, exclusion, and deportation of aliens and the naturalization of legal aliens. The statutes are enforced by Border Patrol Agents and Criminal Investigators, who prevent illegal entries, inspect aliens seeking entrance into the country, and determine the immigration status of persons applying for citizenship. In addition to these duties, INS personnel generally assist the U.S. Customs Service in preventing the importation of contraband.

INTERNAL REVENUE SERVICE

The Internal Revenue Service (IRS) is an important enforcement agency within the Department of the Treasury. There are two law enforcement units within the IRS. The first, Criminal Investigation Division Special Agents, investigate tax fraud including failure to file tax returns and evasion of income or miscellaneous federal taxes. The second enforcement unit, Internal Security Inspectors, investigate prospective employees' backgrounds and alleged cases of misconduct or illegal activities involving IRS personnel. IRS law enforcement personnel have powers limited by the various federal tax laws, but they cooperate with and assist local enforcement personnel in matters of mutual concern.

U.S. CUSTOMS SERVICE

The U.S. Customs Service (within the Department of the Treasury) assesses and collects duties and taxes on imported merchandise and controls carriers and goods imported into, or exported from, the United States. Customs Agents prevent smuggling and customs revenue frauds, cargo thefts, and traffic in illegal narcotics. They assist with enforcing certain environmental protection programs for other agencies. They also enforce regulations on agriculture and plant quarantine and safety laws that govern imported vehicles and equipment.

U.S. DEPARTMENT OF AGRICULTURE

The Department of Agriculture enforces numerous laws designed to protect farmers, the public, and the national forests. These include laws relating to animal disease, quarantine, meat inspection, and the entry and spread of insects in the United States. The U.S. Forest Service, one of the agencies within the Department of Agriculture, enforces federal forest-related laws and regulations. Typical violations involve stealing or damaging trees, setting fires, and operating vehicles that are hazardous to fire safety. In general, when they are not on federal lands or are not dealing with forest-related violations, Forest Rangers have very limited powers of enforcement. However, they may call in law enforcement personnel from other agencies when circumstances warrant it.

U.S. DEPARTMENT OF DEFENSE

The Department of Defense is responsible for the major branches of the Armed Forces—Army, Navy, Marine Corps, and Air Force—each of which engages in law enforcement of various kinds. Their activities include investigating crimes within their own jurisdictions, providing and controlling security for classified projects, and gathering intelligence and operating counterintelligence.

U.S. DEPARTMENT OF HEALTH AND HUMAN SERVICES

The Department of Health and Human Services has among its responsibilities the task of protecting the health of our nation. Two agencies within the department that enforce laws related to this goal are the Public Health Service and the Food and Drug Administration. Federal Public Health Officers inspect or direct the inspection of public facilities for health hazards and for adherence to accepted standards. They also have the power to impose quarantines and to prohibit the sale of unsafe milk or dairy products. Federal Food and Drug Inspectors enforce legal standards set down in federal laws regarding purity, potency, safety, and proper labeling of essential commodities used by the public.

U.S. DEPARTMENT OF THE INTERIOR

As custodian of the natural resources of our country, the Department of the Interior uses some law enforcement personnel. They are stationed in places such as fish and wildlife preserves, historic sites, territories, reservations, and island possessions of the United States. The National Park Service, for example, employs Park Rangers, who enforce laws on federal lands and perform other duties including search and rescue, visitor assistance, and park management.

U.S. Park Police Officers enforce federal law in the District of Columbia, Gateway National Recreation Area in New York and New Jersey, and Golden Gate National Recreation Area in San Francisco.

U.S. DEPARTMENT OF LABOR

The Department of Labor has among its many duties the responsibility of enforcing laws that protect American workers from abuses, that improve and make safe their working conditions, and that ensure equal opportunities in securing employment. The department employs personnel to investigate violations and to pursue criminal and civil court actions for illegal acts under the labor laws. Other laws enforced are in the areas of occupational safety and health, wages and hours, employment and training, employment security, veterans' programs, and worker's compensation, to name a few.

U.S. MARSHALS SERVICE

The U.S. Marshals Service operates under the general authority of the U.S. Attorney General in the courts of the various federal districts throughout the United States. In each of the 94 U.S. judicial districts, a U.S. Marshal is appointed by the President of the United States to be responsible for directing the activities of Deputy U.S. Marshals and supportive staff. Marshals are present at federal court proceedings and carry out such responsibilities as maintaining order, removing unruly persons, accompanying and guarding prisoners, serving orders of the court, and generally assisting the court in carrying out decisions.

U.S. POSTAL SERVICE

The U.S. Postal Service's investigative agency is the oldest federal law enforcement unit in existence. Postal Inspectors engage in more than 250 different types of investigations pertaining to postal operations and illegal activities involving the mail. They conduct criminal investigations of mail thefts and losses caused by damage or destruction of postal property. Other responsibilities include providing security for post office personnel and recovering mail, money, or other properties lost or destroyed. In addition, Postal Inspectors determine whether postal revenues are being protected and whether the Postal Service is operating according to postal laws and regulations.

U.S. SECRET SERVICE

The U.S. Secret Service, created in 1865, is one of our nation's oldest law enforcement agencies. It was originally formed as a bureau of the Department of the Treasury and was given the responsibility of eliminating the counterfeiting of our currency as well as the forging and cashing of government checks, bonds, and securities. During that period (after the Civil War), about one-third of all money in circulation was counterfeit, and the prospects of economic chaos moved Congress to create this agency. The Secret Service distinguished itself by waging a successful battle against counterfeiters and forgers, hundreds of whom were seized, arrested, and imprisoned. Even today, the effectiveness of this agency can be judged by the minor losses sustained by the public from counterfeit money or government obligations.

The Secret Service is perhaps best known for its protection of the President of the United States. After the attempted assassination of President Truman, Congress granted the U.S. Secret Service its permanent protection authority.

U.S. DEPARTMENT OF TRANSPORTATION

Within the Department of Transportation are agencies that enforce federal laws: The Federal Aviation Administration enforces federal regulations related to air safety and has jurisdiction in such matters as the manufacture, registration, safety, and operation of aircraft. The U.S. Coast Guard, except when operating as part of the Navy in wartime, performs duties within the Department of Transportation and assists in the enforcement of federal laws on the high seas or on seas within U.S. jurisdiction. It also develops and carries out port security programs.

In viewing law enforcement as it exists at each level of government—local, county, state, and federal—it is apparent that few careers in public service present such variety or prospects for challenge. The role of law enforcement officers is changing rapidly in response to the needs of society and will continue to do so as law officers carry out their primary tasks of maintaining peace and order within the framework of the law.

In the following section, law enforcement occupations representative of those found at the local, county, state, and federal levels are presented in detail.

PART TWO

What the Jobs Are

CONTENTS

WHAT THE JOBS ARE

Local Positions

By far, the greatest number of law enforcement officers is employed by local, municipal departments. Law enforcement personnel at the local level can count on working close to home throughout their careers. Local law enforcement officers are seldom called upon to travel and, when reassigned within the department, do not have to uproot and relocate their families. A local law enforcement officer who proves effective in early assignments can look forward to promotion to positions of greater responsibility or to specialized assignments.

The cornerstone of the local law enforcement unit is the Police Officer. Although it is possible to enter the local law enforcement department through civilian auxiliary staff positions, the most common entry point into the local law enforcement system is as a Police Officer.

POLICE OFFICER

Duties of the Job

The fundamental purpose of the police throughout America is crime prevention through law enforcement; to most citizens, the most visible representative of this effort is the uniformed Police Officer. There is no more important police function than day-to-day patrol activities, for the effectiveness of police agencies depends on it. After their basic training, most Police Officers are assigned to patrol duty, and their specific duties and responsibilities are numerous and varied. Unlike the specialist, **Patrol Officers** must perform well in a variety of tasks. Regardless of police department size, these officers have two basic responsibilities: to prevent criminal activities and to furnish day-to-day police service to the community. Patrol Officers protect the public, interpret and enforce the law, control traffic, and perform preliminary investigations. They frequently face situations that require swift yet sound decisions. For example, they must decide whether to take no action in an incident or to offer advice, whether to warn or to arrest persons, perhaps using firearms or substantial force. In some situations, they must determine the difference between crime and bizarre behavior or between disturbing the peace and legitimate dissent by citizens. Regardless of the circumstances, their first duty is protection of constitutional guarantees, and their second duty is enforcement of the law.

Police Officers patrol assigned sectors in motor vehicles or on foot, working alone or with a partner, paying close attention to area conditions and inhabitants. During patrol, Police Officers observe suspicious behavior, conditions, or illegal activities in their sector and report incidents by radio to a superior officer prior to taking action. They investigate incidents and question the individuals involved to determine violations of the law. They respond to radio calls sent by police dispatchers or superior officers ordering them to the scene of incidents such as burglaries, bank robberies, homicides, rapes, suicides, assaults, and crimes in progress. They make preliminary investigations, question victims and witnesses, recover stolen property, and take evidence into possession. Where indicated, they arrest suspects at crime scenes or after pursuit and use physical force and firearms to subdue them. When making arrests, they advise suspects of their constitutional rights, as required by law, and transport them in police vehicles to police booking and detention facilities prior to court arraignment. At the time of trial, Police Officers testify in court to provide evidence for prosecuting attorneys.

Traffic control is an essential part of police patrol activities. Police Officers direct and control pedestrian and vehicular traffic in high-density areas to ensure safe and rapid movement, observe parked and moving vehicles for evidence of traffic violations, and issue citations for violations of traffic regulations. Other responsibilities include maintaining order and traffic flow during public gatherings; demonstrations; and emergencies such as riots, fires, explosions, auto accidents, and natural disasters; using crowd control and traffic-direction techniques to carry out such assignments. They administer first aid to victims of accidents or crimes and arrange for the dispatch of medical units to the scene. In cases of traffic accidents, they investigate circumstances and causes and record findings for subsequent use by the parties involved and their attorneys.

Assignment to patrol duty requires the performance of a number of miscellaneous tasks. Police Officers check entrances and exits of commercial facilities for security during hours of darkness. In some police departments, officers inspect residential buildings for safety and suggest methods of improving security such as installing special locks, alarms, or improved lighting in entry areas. They inspect premises of public, licensed business establishments to enforce laws, local ordinances, and regulations concerning their operation. Police Officers also provide information and assistance to inquiring citizens, help settle domestic disputes when called to the scene, and may lend assistance in cases of emergency childbirth. They note conditions that are hazardous to the public such as obstructions, potholes, inoperable street lamps, and defective traffic signals and report them for appropriate action. At the conclusion of each daily work tour, a Police Officer prepares a written activity report that describes arrests, incidents, and all relevant information gathered and submits it to a superior officer, usually a Police Sergeant.

As noted previously, Police Officers on patrol duty are generalists who perform a number of police functions well. Many aspects of modern police service are complex, however, and require use of specialized personnel. The degree of specialization within a police agency varies with the size and resources of the department and the needs of the community. Small communities usually require less specialization, while highly populated areas make specialists a necessity. In small police agencies, specialists are generally used on a part-time basis, while the larger departments usually employ full-time specialists. The following are some examples of the various specialized assignments carried out by Police Officers.

Specialized Assignments

Bomb Squad Officers are highly trained police personnel who respond to incidents of bomb threats and report to locations where bombs have been detonated. Sophisticated equipment and specially trained dogs may be used to locate and disarm explosive and incendiary devices, many of them real and others cleverly constructed hoaxes.

Community Relations Officers help develop and maintain contact between the police department and community groups, organizations, and schools in the area. Their objectives are to promote understanding of the police role in the community, to develop closer working relationships, and to keep open the lines of communication between citizens and the police department. These officers meet with members of the community and assist in developing police-sponsored programs to help reduce crime. Other duties include conducting tours of police facilities and addressing student and civic groups on relevant topics such as drug abuse, crime prevention, and traffic safety.

Canine Officers team with specially trained dogs to provide assistance to other police units within the department. For example, they are called to different scenes where their special skills are used to conduct building searches, to track suspects in wooded or mountainous terrain, to locate lost persons, or to help in crowd-control operations. Canine Officers personally train their dogs with the help of professional instructors and are responsible for the animals' general care as well.

Crime Prevention Officers conduct security surveys of multiple-dwelling and commercial establishments and suggest methods of improving security such as the use of burglar alarms, window gates, and better locking devices. Speaking before civic groups to inform citizens of crime-prevention and safety methods and presenting slides and movies that demonstrate various crime-prevention programs may be other job duties. In some departments, Crime Prevention Officers analyze information contained in police reports for indications of crime patterns or trends. They then alert police units to potential problem areas and methods of operation used by perpetrators. This often effects a reduction in criminal activities.

Emergency Service Officers are highly trained police personnel who are brought into situations that other Police Officers are not equipped to handle. Examples of problems dealt with range from people threatening to jump from bridges or high buildings to persons trapped in automobile wreckage or threatened by a dangerous animal. Such cases require a special expertise, and these officers have the equipment and training needed to do the job.

In some police agencies, Police Officers are assigned to **Fugitive Search Units** in which they are responsible for conducting investigations to locate and return fugitives for prosecution by criminal justice agencies. Data received from national, regional, and state crime information centers are examined, and employers and other law enforcement agencies are contacted to develop leads. Once a fugitive is located, these officers obtain the legal documents necessary for custody and may be required to travel to other criminal justice agencies throughout the country to return prisoners wanted for unlawful flight.

Harbor Patrol is a specialized unit in which Police Officers are responsible for patrolling municipal harbors to detect and apprehend criminals and to aid persons in distress. Patrol is usually in power launches and may involve rescuing drowning victims, recovering bodies, or assisting ships in distress. These officers also cooperate with other law enforcement agencies in an effort to apprehend criminals and to prevent smuggling or entry of illegal aliens.

Hostage Negotiation Teams are another area in which some Police Officers may specialize. Members of these units are specially trained officers who have the difficult task of rescuing hostages from their captors without bloodshed or violence. This is hardly easy because people holding hostages are often nervous and desperate. Such situations require cool, calm, and logical actions on the part of each officer.

Police Officers in certain police departments are members of **Intelligence Units**. These units gather and compile information about community conditions, potential problems, organized crime, and lawlessness in the form of civil disorder. To obtain this data, officers often work undercover to infiltrate organized crime and terrorist groups or seemingly legitimate businesses used as fronts for criminal activities. They coordinate their activities with other law enforcement agencies and furnish current information about the location and activities of members of organized crime and subversive groups to local, state, and federal agents.

Police Officers assigned to **Juvenile Units** have the responsibility of conducting juvenile investigations, providing assistance to field officers in matters involving juvenile problems, and coordinating efforts with other agencies such as courts, schools, and social service and counseling agencies. Juvenile Officers investigate not only juvenile offenses but also cases of lost or runaway children to discover their whereabouts and to locate their parents. They take into custody delinquent or neglected children and refer cases involving serious offenses to the juvenile court system. They also patrol neighborhoods where youths gather, investigate reports of large gatherings that might indicate trouble, and enlist the help of the community in preventing potential juvenile problems.

Mounted Police Officers are specially trained officers who patrol their assigned areas on horseback or motorcycle. Officers on horseback perform the basic duties of the Patrol Officer, but their skills are particularly effective in crowd-control activities. Through skillful handling of their mounts, these officers preserve order where large crowds congregate (such as at parades and sporting events) and, in cases of riot or civil unrest, disperse unruly crowds. Officers patrolling on motorcycles perform important traffic-control duties in congested areas by helping to facilitate the flow of traffic. In many cases, patrol cars are unable to reach the scene of disturbances or accidents, and motorcycle officers, first on the scene, provide assistance to sick or injured persons, direct traffic around fires or explosions, and perform general police work by keeping order and apprehending criminals.

Another specialized assignment that may be available to Police Officers is the **Property Unit**. Property Officers are responsible for property confiscated as evidence, removed from suspects, lost or stolen, or purchased by police department officials. Work also involves keeping detailed records of all properties under their control and, when authorized, releasing property to arresting officers for use as evidence in legal proceedings. They return personal property to suspects being released from custody and contact owners of lost or stolen property to claim articles upon proof of ownership. Property Officers keep extensive records of articles confiscated during arrests (such as narcotics and firearms) and arrange for their transfer to official disposal sites when required by law. Responsibility may also include receiving and examining property purchased by the department to verify the completeness and satisfactory condition of these purchases against invoices or other records.

Aviation programs in which Police Officers are trained as **Police Pilots** provide another area of police specialization. Because aircraft are not restricted by roads or traffic congestion, larger areas can be patrolled, and aircraft can be used for aerial surveillance missions, high-speed transportation, and police rescue missions. Police Pilots may fly helicopters, conventional fixed-wing aircraft, or Short Takeoff and Landing (STOL) aircraft in carrying out their assignments. Helicopters are very effective in urban patrol as part of helicopter-automobile patrol teams. They can shorten response time to crime scenes, hover, or patrol at slow speeds to observe ground activities or to illuminate an area at night. Conventional fixed-wing aircraft are very effective in highway speed enforcement as part of air-ground teams and in search and surveillance operations. Unlike the helicopter, however, they cannot hover or cruise at reduced speeds needed in urban areas. STOL aircraft combine some of the characteristics of the helicopter with those of conventional, fixed-wing aircraft. These aircraft can take off and land in distances shorter than those required for other fixed-wing aircraft. Faster than most helicopters, they can cruise at slower speeds than other fixed-wing craft and can stay airborne without refueling twice as long as rotary-wing aircraft. Regardless of the type of aircraft they fly, Police Pilots play a crucial role in law enforcement activities.

In some departments, cases of rape and sexual assault are the responsibility of Police Officers assigned to **Sex Crimes Units**. These crimes create special problems for both victims and the criminal justice system. Fear of harassment or humiliation during police investigations and medical examinations makes victims reluctant to report such crimes and to go through the ordeal of a trial. Sex Crimes Units are staffed with both male and female officers who are specially trained, are sensitive to the plight of victims, and can provide needed support during medical examinations, interviews with police and public prosecutors, and subsequent investigations. In some departments, rape victims, if they so desire, can deal exclusively with other women who act both as interviewers and as criminal investigators. These officers can also provide referrals to community agencies that give special help to victims of sex crimes.

Anti-Crime or Street-Crime Units are a successful innovation being used by many departments throughout the country. Police Officers assigned to these units work in high-crime areas, out of uniform, and pose as unsuspecting citizens from various walks of life. Their objective is to present themselves as targets for assaults and robberies and to apprehend suspects who attempt to commit such crimes. These decoys team with backup units in the area so that a response is made when suspects attempt to carry out crimes against the decoy officers. Members of these units also conduct surveillance activities on stakeouts.

Many police agencies have developed **Tactical Forces**—highly mobile units that can be deployed rapidly against special crime problems. Normally made up of Police Officers from within the police agency and varying in size from a few officers on small forces to several hundred on larger forces, these units are motorized and assigned to areas where patterns of serious crimes are occurring. The work can be varied, and officers may find themselves working in plainclothes on a robbery detail and then being abruptly assigned to work in uniform on a different type of assignment. When no specific crime problems occur in a particular area, these officers are deployed over a wider area and then, if needed, can be called back quickly to work as a unit on a particular case. In some police agencies, these officers are members of specially trained units such as sniper-suppression teams and special weapons attack teams (SWAT), which are used during specified emergency situations. The overall purpose of Tactical Forces is to strengthen the regular patrol force and help the line units meet their goals.

Police Instructors are another example of the varied specializations into which Police Officers may move. These training officers instruct police recruits in basic phases of police work and in the duties and responsibilities of the Police Officer. They conduct lectures, discussions, and demonstrations and use audiovisual materials to teach basic core skills to new personnel. Subject matter of the training sessions includes criminal law, traffic regulations, human relations, criminal investigation, patrol techniques, report writing, firearms, and physical training. In addition to training police recruits, Police Instructors train veteran officers through inservice courses and refresher sessions. Some instructors specialize in one area of training, and the educational and background qualifications for this position vary among departments.

Traffic Officers are members of specialized police units whose aim is to produce voluntary obedience to traffic regulations and to provide maximum mobility of traffic with a minimum of interruption. These enforcement units operate in preselected locations where high rates of vehicular and pedestrian accidents, auto thefts, and traffic-law violations occur. Traffic enforcement is closely related to other police activities because, in many instances, persons stopped for traffic violations are found to be involved in criminal activities or are fugitives wanted in another jurisdiction.

In addition to the Police Officers who work in local and county police agencies, there are others who are employed by special-purpose public police forces in many cities throughout the United States. Some typical examples include park, harbor, airport, sanitation, transit, housing, and port police forces. Some of these agencies have full peace-officer powers within their limited jurisdictions; others have limited authority. In New York City, for example, there have been at various times as many as three major public police forces besides the New York City Police Department itself. These are now or have been the independent forces of the Port Authority, the New York City Transit Authority, and the New York City Housing Authority.

The Port Authority of New York and New Jersey Police is responsible for policing and providing security in bus, rail, and air terminals; in tunnels and bridges of the Port Authority; and in any buildings, properties, or facilities operated by the Port Authority. As the name implies, the Port Authority is a joint agency of the states of New York and New Jersey. Since the Port Authority is an entity unto itself, its directors set job descriptions and qualification requirements for all its employees. As is typical of all police officers, Port Authority Officers enforce the law and apprehend and arrest suspects, using physical force or firearms if necessary. Other responsibilities include controlling traffic and crowds and handling emergency situations occurring within their jurisdiction. Because of the bi-state nature of the Port Authority, the Port Authority Police will always maintain its integrity as a separate police force.

Transit Authority Officers, whether part of an independent Transit Police Department (as they were until April 1995) or as the Transit Bureau of the New York City Police Department, enforce the law and provide security services for the New York City Transit System, which includes nearly 500 subway stations. The officers patrol subway stations, trains, and buses, particularly during the high-crime hours of 8 P.M. to 4 A.M. They apprehend and arrest suspects and use physical force and firearms if necessary to carry out their duties. The jurisdiction of Transit Authority Officers, even when the police force was independent, has never been limited to Transit Authority property; these officers have full police powers to enforce all local and state laws anywhere in New York City. In eras during which the philosophy is that a dedicated force intensively trained for more limited policing is more effective, the Transit Police Department is a separate force. In eras during which the philosophy is to cut costs by avoiding duplication of administrative services and to give greater coverage to "hot spots" by maintaining an integrated, flexible police force under centralized command, the Transit Police is constituted as a division of the City Police Department.

Housing Authority Officers patrol grounds, cellars, roofs, stairwells, and elevators of public housing projects. Officers are assigned to housing projects around the clock based on the incidence of crime in various locations. They conduct investigations of all crimes and disturbances on properties within their jurisdiction and apprehend and arrest suspects, using physical force or firearms if necessary. As with the Transit Police, the independence or integration of the Housing Police depends on the philosophy of the city administration at the time. In any event, all police agencies cooperate closely; the New York City Police Department provides records, booking, laboratory, and detention services for all divisions or departments.

Working Conditions

Police Officers work in locations ranging from boroughs, townships, and counties to urban areas of varying sizes. Working conditions vary considerably according to location, size, organization, and jurisdiction of the police agency. Officers who work in small towns and rural communities most certainly face problems that differ from those met by their counterparts in the inner cities of larger urban areas. There are definite differences in pace, types of criminal activities encountered, and availability of manpower and services needed to provide adequate police protection to the public. But all Police Officers, regardless of where they work, share certain problems. They constantly deal with human suffering, yet they must always maintain self-control and act in a calm, efficient manner. They face danger, difficulty, and frustration, perhaps daily, but can do little to prevent it from happening. They also share the problems of long, irregular hours and, in some communities, a lack of public support for Police Officers.

As a rule, most Police Officers, while conducting patrols or carrying out other assignments, work outdoors in all types of weather. Some officers on special duty may perform their duties indoors at police facilities. Depending on the size of the department, Police Officers may work alone or may have a partner. Because police agencies operate 24 hours a day, officers are usually required to work five-day rotating shifts including holidays and weekends. Police Officers are on call at all times and, during periods of emergency or manpower shortages, are required to work additional tours of duty. All Police Officers, regardless of where they work or the size of the employing police agency, *must live with the very real threat of physical injury or death.* The apprehension of suspects who may be armed and dangerous, situations involving high-speed chases, or the rescue of individuals attempting suicide are some of the possibilities that make this work *hazardous.* Such hazards should be fully considered by individuals thinking about a police career. In most police agencies, Police Officers have fringe benefits that include some or all of the following: paid vacation, sick leave, and holidays; overtime pay; life, medical, and disability insurance; uniform allowances; tuition-assistance or -refund programs for college studies; and retirement pension. In some departments, officers may retire after 20 years of service if they are between 50 and 55 years of age. In departments with different standards, Police Officers may retire after 20 years of service regardless of age.

Training and Promotion Opportunities

Following the completion of training, new officers are assigned to work under the supervision of a veteran officer. The experienced officer evaluates their work performance from time to time during the probationary period, which may last one year to 18 months. New officers may also team with experienced officers who provide them with practical instruction and field experience. After successfully completing the probationary period, these officers become permanent licensed or certified law enforcement officers; they are sworn in and are awarded a badge.

Once entry into this work is made, promotional prospects are generally good and are usually governed by merit or civil service system regulations. Police Officers as a rule become eligible for promotion after a specified number of years (three to five in most police agencies). Promotions are made according to the officer's position on a promotion list, which is determined by scores on a written, competitive examination as well as ratings of on-the-job performance. The first promotional level for uniformed Police Officers is the position of Sergeant. Thereafter, they are eligible to compete for other positions such as Lieutenant, Captain, or higher command positions, the titles of which vary among police agencies throughout the country. A Police Officer might instead opt for lateral promotion into the Detective division. The officer would then begin as a Police Detective and move up the ranks to Detective Sergeant, Detective Lieutenant, Detective Captain, and even beyond as merited by education, performance, and scores on competitive examinations.

POLICE DETECTIVE

Duties of the Job

Police Detectives, key members of the police law enforcement team, conduct investigations to prevent crime, to protect life and property, and to solve criminal cases, which can range from misdemeanors to homicide. As a rule, crimes are initially investigated by uniformed Police Officers who are dispatched to crime scenes to apprehend suspects, question witnesses, and preserve evidence. If arrests are not made or the crime remains unsolved, Detectives take over the criminal investigation. Working in plainclothes, Detectives assigned to a case report to the scene, where possible, and determine the nature of the incident, the exact location and time of the occurrence, and the probable reason for the crime. They obtain reports from uniformed Police Officers; question witnesses, victims, and suspects if they have been apprehended; and arrange for official statements to be given at a police station or headquarters. In addition, they search the area carefully to detect clues and to gather evidence for use in the investigation. Detectives then direct Evidence Technicians to examine the scene to locate and lift latent fingerprints and to photograph the scene and any evidence obtained for eventual use in preparing the case for court. In some police departments, Detectives trained in fingerprinting and photography perform these duties themselves.

In seeking solutions to crimes, Detectives use all the resources of the police agency such as ballistics experts, police chemists, laboratory technicians, computers, and speedy communication systems. Once all the available information has been compiled, they analyze the results to determine the direction the investigation will take. Detectives study the files and records of suspects, if any, evaluate police laboratory findings, and prepare detailed reports including descriptions of evidence, names and statements of witnesses and victims, circumstances of the crime, and statements made by suspects. In an attempt to develop leads, copies of fingerprints found at the crime scene may be transmitted to the State Crime Information Center (S.C.I.C.) and the National Crime Information Center (N.C.I.C.) for comparison with those found at scenes in other localities. Information may also be given to police artists in their own departments or in state and local law enforcement agencies for use in preparing composite sketches of suspects. Members of police patrol units are advised about crimes occurring in various areas and about the methods of operation used by perpetrators. In many instances, Police Detectives question informants on their knowledge of a crime or on their information about the personal habits, associates, characteristics, and aliases of crime suspects.

As evidence begins to develop, court-approved wire tapping or electronic surveillance methods may be used to gather data pertinent to the investigation. Detectives conduct surveillance of suspects on foot or in vehicles to uncover illegal activities; they participate in stakeouts at specific locations to gather evidence or prevent commission of crimes. When all investigative efforts have been made, each Detective prepares a written progress report of the case assigned and submits it to the Detective Sergeant or other superior officer for criticism and suggestions. At this point, the Detective usually plans what action is to be taken to resolve the case based on the evidence gathered and the recommendations of supervisory officers. Police Detectives arrest, or participate in the arrest of, suspects based on this evidence and as authorized by appropriate legal warrants.

During the process of arrest, Police Detectives are authorized to use firearms and/or physical force when necessary to subdue suspects. At the time of arrest, they advise suspects of their constitutional rights and escort them to the police station or headquarters for booking, interrogation, and detention. Suspects are turned over to designated police personnel for fingerprinting, photographing, recording of personal effects, and checking of their records by the records section of the department against outstanding warrants in other jurisdictions.

An important responsibility of Police Detectives involves the preparation of criminal cases scheduled for trial. This entails preparing a written summary of facts gathered during the investigation including evidence obtained and official statements made by witnesses, victims, Police Officers, and defendants. Prior to trial, Detectives usually review the case summary with the prosecutor to detect legal flaws; they may have to supply supplemental data to strengthen the case for the prosecution. Detectives spend many hours in court testifying as arresting officers and appearing as witnesses for the prosecution. In instances of unsolved cases, Detectives usually forward copies of the fingerprints gathered during the investigation to the Federal Bureau of Investigation (FBI) for comparison with prints that will be recorded during future arrests made nationwide by other law enforcement agencies.

The duties just described are common to Police Detectives in most local, county, and state investigative units. The increasing complexities of police work, however, have caused many agencies to use Detectives as specialists in various types of investigations. The size and resources of the department plus the needs of the community determine the extent of such specialization. Detectives in small police agencies tend to specialize less and are usually generalists who investigate a wide range of crimes. Detectives in large departments in heavily populated urban or suburban areas are more likely to specialize. The following are examples of some of the specialized assignments carried out by Police Detectives.

Specialized Assignments

Bombing/arson cases are those in which Detectives investigate incidents of suspected arson or the use or presence of explosive devices. Arson is the intentional or attempted destruction, by fire or explosion, of the property of another, or of one's own property, with the intent to defraud. Bombing incidents involve detonation or attempted detonation of an explosive or incendiary device for a criminal purpose or with disregard for the safety and property of others. In some departments, Detectives supervise or actually remove suspected explosive devices to safe areas, using special skills and equipment to reduce the risk to police personnel and public safety.

Detectives assigned to **Burglary/Robbery Units** specialize in the investigation of such incidents to solve current criminal cases and to prevent future crimes of this sort. Burglary is the actual or attempted entry of a structure, with or without force, with the intent to steal or commit a felony (serious crime). Robbery is the unlawful taking or attempted taking of property in the immediate possession of another person by force or threat of force, with or without a deadly weapon.

Detectives, Fraud and Embezzlement, specialize in crimes involving embezzlement, fraud, forgery, and counterfeiting. Embezzlement is the illegal appropriation of entrusted property with the intention of defrauding the legal owner or beneficiary. Fraud involves deceit or intentional misrepresentation with the aim of illegally depriving a person of his or her property or legal rights. Forgery is the creation or alteration of a written or printed document with the intention to defraud by claiming it is the act of an unknown second party. In a check forgery, for example, the forged signature is accepted as being legitimate, and the transaction is completed. Counterfeiting involves manufacture of a copy or imitation of a negotiable instrument with value set by law. Examples include currency, coins, postage, food stamps, and bearer bonds. The investigations into these "white-collar crimes" bring Detectives into close association with representatives of banks, brokerage firms, hotels, and retail establishments as well as other law enforcement agencies.

Homicide Detectives investigate criminal homicide cases in which one person is killed by another or cases in which death appears imminent as the result of aggravated assault. Criminal homicides are those that involve the death of another person without justification or excuse and include acts such as murder and voluntary, involuntary, and vehicular manslaughter.

Detectives assigned to a **Juvenile Section or Division** specialize in investigating cases involving juveniles (youths under 18 years of age who are subject to the jurisdiction of juvenile court). These Detectives investigate all cases of juvenile crimes. They maintain surveillance in areas where youths gather to keep abreast of happenings and to develop case leads and arrest juveniles suspected of violating the law. Cases involving serious offenses are referred to Juvenile Court, and parents or guardians are notified to advise them of circumstances in the case. Meetings may also be held with parents or guardians of juveniles in detainment, but not arrested or charged, to stress the need for increased supervision to prevent development of delinquent behavior.

Narcotics Detectives conduct specialized investigations to identify and apprehend persons suspected of illegal use or sale of narcotics and dangerous drugs. Narcotics Detectives examine physicians' and pharmacists' records to determine the legality of sales and to monitor the distribution of narcotics and the quantity of drugs in stock. They must often perform undercover work to investigate known or suspected drug suppliers and handlers who have been identified through surveillance or informants. Detectives purchase narcotics from suspects for use as evidence and arrest individuals identified as distributors, suppliers, and pushers. Narcotics Detectives also work on a cooperative basis with other police agencies involved in narcotics investigations and with federal agencies such as the Drug Enforcement Administration (DEA).

Detectives in some police agencies are part of **Organized Crime Activities Units** and specialize in investigating such activities. They gather data about members of organized criminal groups through the use of informers, surveillance, and infiltration by undercover officers. Not only are cases involving members of organized crime solved by such efforts, numerous criminal acts are prevented from occurring at all. Often, participation in the Federal Organized Strike Force Programs and work with members of law enforcement agencies from all levels of government is part of these Detectives' assignments.

Motor vehicle theft and truck hijacking are another type of investigative specialization. Detectives question salvage and junkyard operators, motor vehicle and motor parts dealers, owners of retail stores, and pawnbrokers to uncover possible leads. They check inventories and records to make certain that stocks are legitimate. They maintain surveillance of known thieves and fences who illegally dispose of stolen property, they use informers, and they take suspects into custody when sufficient evidence has been gathered. Other duties include identification of stolen property and making arrangements for its return to owners.

Investigation of establishments and persons suspected of violating morality and antivice laws pertaining to liquor, gambling, and prostitution is the concern of **Vice Squad Detectives.** They monitor places where liquor is sold to check on hours of operation, underage patrons, and general adherence to the law. Establishing surveillance of suspects and locations to gather evidence of gambling and/or prostitution activities and working undercover to gain access are also part of the job. When sufficient evidence is gathered, necessary legal warrants are obtained, raids on suspects' establishments are conducted, and accused persons are taken into custody. In addition to the situations just mentioned. Detectives may, in some police agencies, specialize in the investigation of sex offenses, kidnappings, bank robberies, and missing-person cases.

Working Conditions

Local, county, and state police agencies employ Detectives. Working conditions differ widely according to the size, location, organization, and jurisdiction of the police agency. During investigations, considerable time is spent in office work such as reviewing files, gathering data, evaluating and preparing reports, meeting with other Police Officers, and making telephone inquiries. A good deal of time is also spent away from police offices working in a variety of locations and in all kinds of weather: reporting to crime scenes, questioning suspects and witnesses, conducting surveillance and stakeouts, and making arrests. Detectives drive unmarked police vehicles. They may work alone or with partners. Their basic work schedule is rotating shifts of five days a week, eight hours a day, including weekends and holidays. At times they work long, irregular hours; a considerable amount of overtime may be necessary during the investigation of certain cases. As with other Police Officers, Detectives are on call at all times and may be recalled to duty during periods of emergency. *Although detective work is a challenging career, there are times when it is tedious, routine, andfrustrating.* Furthermore, *detectives are often exposed to the risks of bodily injury and death* during the course of criminal investigations.

In most police agencies, Detectives receive fringe benefits including some or all of the following: paid vacation, sick leave, and holidays; overtime pay; life, medical, and disability insurance; tuition-assistance or -refund programs for college studies; and retirement pension. In some departments, Detectives can retire after 20 years of service if they are in the 50-to-55-year age bracket. Other departments have different standards in which Detectives may retire after 20 years of service regardless of age.

Training and Promotion Opportunities

After successfully completing their training, new Detectives remain on probation. They are assigned to work with experienced investigative personnel who provide practical guidance and assistance under actual field conditions. After demonstrating the ability to perform this job on an independent basis, newly hired Detectives are permanently assigned.

Advancement prospects for Detectives are governed by work performance as well as by the personnel practices and size of the agency. Promotional opportunities are usually good and are made according to merit system or civil service regulations. Detectives are, as a rule, eligible for promotion after satisfactory service for a specified period of time, say two to four years. When skills are developed through training, experience, and further education, it is possible to compete for the position of Sergeant, the first step in the promotion ladder. Subsequently, qualified candidates can compete for such positions as Lieutenant, Captain, and other high-level jobs known in different parts of the country by various titles such as Inspector, Major, Lieutenant Colonel, and Colonel.

County Positions

County law enforcement is another aspect of local law enforcement. The jurisdiction of county law enforcement officers varies greatly from state to state, but it generally includes all areas that are not the domain of municipal or town law enforcement departments except for areas patrolled by the state police.

The county law enforcement officer can work close to home with a minimum of extended travel. The amount of daily travel is dictated by the size of the county and the officer's specific assignment. The county law enforcement officer need not fear relocation nor uprooting of his or her family.

DEPUTY SHERIFF

The majority of counties throughout the United States have the constitutional office of Sheriff, which, in varying degrees, has responsibility for county policing, jails, and court activities. Most sheriffs' agencies provide full police services, but in some counties where Sheriffs do not have patrol and investigative functions, these functions are performed by either independent county police forces or state police agencies. Depending on the size of the county and the extent of its legal obligations, county sheriffs' departments employ forces of uniformed Deputy Sheriffs to meet these responsibilities.

Duties of the Job

Deputy Sheriffs are county law enforcement officers who patrol assigned districts within their jurisdictions to enforce federal, state, and local laws, to investigate crimes, and to maintain the peace. While patrolling assigned areas, they observe persons and conditions for evidence of suspicious or criminal activities based on their observations or in response to radio calls from superior officers. They detain and question suspects or apprehend and arrest suspects at crime scenes or after pursuit, either alongside or with the assistance of backup units and with the use of physical force or firearms when necessary. They advise suspects of their constitutional rights at the time of arrest and escort them to department headquarters for booking and confinement to jail prior to arraignment in court. Deputies may also transport suspects between courtrooms, jail, district attorneys' offices, and medical facilities or may act as extradition officers escorting wanted persons back across state lines to stand trial. Investigating, assuming control at scenes of accidents, administering first aid to the injured, and radioing for ambulance and emergency vehicles are also part of the job. Other duties include issuing citations for traffic violations on county roads, performing traffic control duties in designated geographic areas, and maintaining order during public demonstrations and parades and in emergency situations such as natural disasters, riots, or civil disorders. Some Deputies are given criminal investigation assignments in which they work as plainclothes officers and investigate cases involving vice, narcotics and dangerous drugs, juvenile offenses, fugitives from justice, burglaries, stolen vehicles, assaults, homicides, and missing persons. Some Deputies also enforce laws in county and state parks and game reserves, including environmental, fish, and game laws. Specially trained Deputies may also be part of special weapons attack teams, hostage-negotiation teams, search-rescue units, and sniper-suppression teams used during specified emergency situations. Occasionally, they may perform the duties of radio dispatcher and broadcast orders to patrol units in the various sectors to investigate complaints received from the public as well as instructions from the watch commander to patrol units in the field. Regardless of assignment, all Deputy Sheriffs are required to prepare daily written reports of work activities during tours of duty, maintain accurate police records, and be prepared to testify during court proceedings if necessary.

In addition to patrol, criminal investigation, and traffic duties, some Deputy Sheriffs have unique responsibilities related to the county court system. They serve civil papers and orders of the court such as subpoenas, garnishments, property executions, arrest orders, and show-cause orders to individuals. They serve warrants, evict persons from property, and confiscate real or personal property as designated by court order. In addition, assignments dealing with security in county jails and courts involve guarding court facilities, searching the premises, and questioning people entering jails and courts to verify credentials. In instances in which the law is broken, Deputies arrest individuals and summon patrol units to assume custody of prisoners.

Working Conditions

Deputy Sheriffs work primarily outdoors, in all types of weather conditions, while on patrol duty in county areas. Deputies assigned to duty at county jails and courts spend the majority of their time indoors. Some work in sprawling rural areas with low populations; others perform their duties in heavily settled suburban counties. Depending on the size of the department, Deputies may work alone or with a partner; while *not directly supervised,* they do maintain radio contact with their communications center and with superior officers to report in and to receive new or revised orders. Generally, sheriffs' departments operate 24 hours a day, and Deputies are usually required to work 5-day rotating shifts including holidays and weekends. As with other law enforcement officers, Deputy Sheriffs are on call at all times and, during periods of emergency, may work extended tours of duty. The apprehension of suspects who may be armed and dangerous or situations involving high-speed chases subject Deputy Sheriffs to the *hazards of serious physical injury or death.* Such possibilities should be given much thought when an individual is considering this work as a career possibility. In most county sheriffs' departments, Deputies receive fringe benefits that include paid vacation, sick leave, and holidays; overtime pay; life, medical, and disability insurance; uniform allowances; and retirement pension.

Training and Promotion Opportunities

The training program for Deputy Sheriffs is followed by a probationary period ranging from 6 to 18 months. During this time, probationary Deputies work with experienced Deputies and develop their skills. Since Deputy Sheriffs must often work alone, they will not be hired as permanent members of the force until they have demonstrated their ability to work independently. Once hired, an individual's advancement prospects depend on the size of the agency as well as its personnel policies. Qualified Deputies with the proper experience, training, and education may advance through the ranks to the positions, where available, of Sergeant, Detective, Lieutenant, Captain, or Chief Deputy.

State Positions

State law enforcement spans a bridge between local law enforcement and federal law enforcement. The duties of the State Police Officer are general law enforcement duties. In this respect, they are similar to the duties of Local Police Officers and County Police Officers. Unlike federal law enforcement officers, who tend to specialize in narrow areas of investigation, control, prevention, or protection, state law enforcement officers do whatever must be done including traffic control, assisting accident and crime victims, controlling large assemblies, preventing violations, and apprehending suspects.

On the other hand, the State Police Officer does not have the security of the location of his or her workplace that is enjoyed by local and county officers. Even in tiny states such as Rhode Island or Delaware, reassignment to a barracks at the other end of the state may entail relocating one's residence. Manpower needs do shift from one area to another, and if superior officers expect the need for increased manpower at a particular location to be a long-term need, permanent reassignments will fill that need.

STATE POLICE OFFICER/STATE TROOPER

Duties of the Job

State Police Officers provide police services to the public by patrolling state and interstate highways, turnpikes, and freeways and by enforcing motor vehicle and criminal laws. Powers of the State Police vary widely among the states. Some forces have full police powers throughout the state; others are restricted to highway patrol and traffic regulation. Regardless of these variations, the officers perform a vital service in ensuring the safety of all citizens. The following are typical work activities of State Police Officers.

In most cases, State Police units are organized into posts or troops within specified geographic areas. Each troop or post is housed in a headquarters building that contains a communications center, barracks, lockup, crime laboratory, pistol range, and motor pool. The workday begins at the headquarters location where State Police Officers report daily for roll call, inspection, and duty assignment. The vast majority of these officers use specially equipped patrol cars in performing their assignments, but there are a small number who use motorcycles, fly helicopters, or light fixed-wing aircraft on special duty. When patrolling assigned sectors, State Police Officers carefully observe conditions, strictly enforce motor vehicle codes and criminal laws, watch for traffic violations, and issue warnings or citations to offenders. Where justified, arrests are made for violations of motor vehicle regulations and safe driving practices, and offenders are escorted to headquarters for detainment.

Other duties include monitoring traffic to detect vehicles reported stolen and arresting drivers whose ownership credentials are lacking or questionable. Often, State Police Officers provide assistance to motorists on the highway, furnish road information and directions to drivers, and may give details about restaurants, lodging, or tourist attractions in the area. At accident scenes or where vehicles are disabled, State Police Officers radio for emergency equipment such as ambulance or towing vehicles and give first aid to injured parties until help arrives. They prevent further accidents, damage, or injuries by directing traffic around the accident, by using road flares at night, and by removing debris and vehicles from the roadway. They investigate the causes of each accident and prepare detailed written reports including information such as names and addresses of parties involved, scale drawing of the scene, road and weather conditions at the time of the accident, description of damage, and estimated speed of the vehicle or vehicles involved in the accident. This report is legal evidence that the officer may be called upon to present in court.

State Police Officers are also responsible for providing help to victims of fires, floods, or other disasters and for controlling traffic in such circumstances. In some states, job duties include weighing commercial vehicles, stopping vehicles for spot check of driver's licenses, and conducting driver-training sessions in public schools. State Police Officers may also test applicants for driver's licenses, inspect motor vehicles for safety, and on occasion, serve as escorts for parades, military convoys, and funeral processions.

In many states, besides being involved with highway activities, State Police Officers have responsibilities similar to municipal and county police, particularly in areas that do not have local police forces. In such cases, these activities include investigation of burglaries, robberies, assaults, domestic disturbances, drug traffic, and liquor violations; taking part in roadblocks to apprehend suspects or escaped criminals; and helping city and county police agencies in cases of riot or civil disturbance. They seize and arrest lawbreakers using physical force and/or firearms when the situation warrants, patrol business and residential areas, and check the security of buildings in the district. Some State Police Officers are given special training and serve as radio dispatchers, instructors at police academies, or pilots of police aircraft. They also may work with canine and mounted units or may be assigned to protect governors and legislators. All State Police Officers are required to prepare written reports of their work activities, must maintain accurate police records, and may be called upon to testify in court proceedings.

At present, every state, with the exception of Hawaii, has a State Police force. The largest of these is the 5,000-member officer force in California, while the smallest is the 100-member unit in North Dakota.

Working Conditions

The conditions under which State Police Officers work vary according to assignment. For the most part, they work outdoors in all types of weather while patrolling highways and roads in their sectors. Officers work alone or with a partner and *do not receive direct supervision because of the nature of their duties.*

They do, however, stay in constant touch with their communications centers to report to superior officers and to receive new or revised orders. Since the State Police operate around the clock, officers are subject to rotating shifts usually consisting of a 5-day, 40-hour workweek, including weekends and holidays. In addition, they are on call at all times and may work for extended periods during emergencies. *Certain aspects of this work are dangerous.* State Police Officers risk serious injury or death from high-speed pursuits and from the apprehension of criminals who may be armed and dangerous.

Fringe benefits that State Police Officers receive usually include paid vacation, sick leave, and holidays; overtime pay; life, medical, and disability insurance; uniform allowances; tuition-refund programs; and retirement pension.

Training and Promotion Opportunities

As is the case with nearly all law enforcement positions, prospective State Police Officers do not achieve permanent status until they have successfully completed the probationary period that follows training. Probation may last from six months to a year depending on the state. During the probationary period, the new officer gets valuable experience at the side of a veteran officer.

Advancement opportunities in State Police agencies are based on merit, and promotional examinations are scheduled periodically. All qualified personnel can compete for promotional opportunities, and the first level of advancement is to Sergeant. Thereafter, qualified officers may advance through experience and education to the positions of First Sergeant, Lieutenant, Captain, Major, Inspector, Deputy Superintendent, and Superintendent.

Federal Positions

Federal law enforcement positions are diverse in their job descriptions and in the demands they make of people who fill them. While there is a great deal of overlap among some federal agencies, as well as with state and local law enforcement agencies, there are also real differences between the jobs in the different agencies.

The advancement route also varies from federal agency to federal agency. In some agencies, advancement is simply to more responsible work and supervisory duties within the same job title. In other agencies, a person may advance to a different job title, perhaps with more exciting duties. The distinguishing features of each position are highlighted by italics in each of the following job descriptions.

BUREAU OF ALCOHOL, TOBACCO, AND FIREARMS INSPECTOR

Duties of the Job

An important part of the Bureau of Alcohol, Tobacco, and Firearms (BATF) law enforcement effort is its inspection force. BATF Inspectors are constantly alert to the possibility of fraud, negligence, or other illegal activities. When evidence of criminal activities is uncovered, they turn it over to BATF Special Agents responsible for criminal investigations. Although BATF Inspectors are not criminal investigators, they frequently work with BATF Special Agents who conduct criminal investigations for the Bureau. The Federal Alcohol Administration Act, for example, governs the production, storage, processing, packaging, labeling, importation, exportation, distribution, and advertising of distilled spirits, beer, and wine. Other regulations similar to these apply to tobacco products, firearms, and explosives and to the use of distilled spirits for scientific, medical, and industrial purposes.

BATF Inspectors carry out their duties in a variety of work settings. Inspections may take them to such locations as breweries; wineries; distilleries; plants that manufacture distilled spirits for industrial, scientific, and medical use; and laboratories conducting scientific research projects. Other locations include wholesale liquor establishments, cigar and cigarette manufacturing plants, firearms and explosives retailers, and manufacturers and importers.

When BATF Inspectors are given their work assignments, they visit business establishments alone or as part of an inspection team. They contact and interview company representatives and gather basic data about procedures and operations. They acquire financial statements as well as business and public records to verify information and to make certain that required taxes have been paid. In addition, they determine that the business has the various special licenses, permits, and other authorizations required by federal law. Another important aspect of this job involves observation of conditions to judge whether facilities and equipment meet legal standards and whether manufacturing processes and operations are being conducted in accordance with the law. If violations are detected, BATF Inspectors advise company representatives and arrange for correction of these conditions. In cases in which criminal violations such as fraud, tax evasion, or falsified inventories are uncovered, detailed summaries of evidence assist agents in preparing cases for criminal prosecution. BATF Inspectors prepare written reports of their work activities, may serve legal papers on persons in violation of federal laws, and sometimes testify as government witnesses during court proceedings.

Working Conditions

BATF Inspectors may be assigned to work stations anywhere in the United States and are required to travel when performing field inspections. Working hours are usually regular and average 40 hours per week. The fringe benefits that BATF Inspectors receive include paid vacations, sick leave, overtime pay, low-cost medical and life insurance, and retirement annuities.

Promotion Opportunities

BATF Inspectors are chosen from the top of the list of eligible candidates meeting the entry standards of the Bureau of Alcohol, Tobacco, and Firearms. Prospects for advancement in this work are generally favorable. Promotions are not automatic; rather, they're based on satisfactory performance and the recommendations of supervisory staff. As BATF Inspectors show the ability to assume more complex assignments, they are recommended for promotion in line with such responsibilities. If they so desire, BATF Inspectors may choose an alternative advancement route by becoming BATF Special Agents. Many of the experience requirements for Special Agents can be fulfilled by years of satisfactory service as a BATF Inspector. Federal agencies give preferential treatment to job applicants from within the agency.

BUREAU OF ALCOHOL, TOBACCO, AND FIREARMS SPECIAL AGENT

Duties of the Job

An essential part of the federal government's law enforcement effort is the U.S. Treasury Department's Bureau of Alcohol, Tobacco, and Firearms (BATF). BATF Special Agents, stationed in hundreds of offices throughout the United States, contribute greatly in the battle against crime and violence in our country. *The work of these Agents is far from routine* because they face ever-changing situations while carrying out their duties. The major responsibilities of BATF Special Agents are twofold. First, they enforce federal laws concerned with the sale, transfer, manufacture, import, and possession of firearms and explosives. They also inspect the records and inventories of licensed firearms or explosives distributors to check compliance with federal laws and to uncover possible evidence of unlawful activities. Throughout their investigations, BATF Agents rely on their extensive knowledge of firearms and explosives. They probe a variety of cases involved with illegal transport of firearms and explosives across state lines. Their efforts are particularly directed at organized criminal elements and at terrorist groups operating in this country. Agents seek to eliminate or substantially reduce the illegal possession of items such as handguns, sawed-off shotguns, fully automatic or rapid-fire weapons, dynamite, and plastic explosives. In addition, Agents investigate and solve bombing incidents and attempt to prevent repetition of such occurrences.

The second major responsibility of BATF Agents involves the difficult task of enforcing federal liquor and tobacco regulations. They investigate and uncover illicit distillery operations and are empowered to seize and destroy contraband and illegal production facilities. They work to reduce contraband cigarette smuggling and bootlegging of untaxed tobacco products by locating and eliminating sources of supply as well as distribution networks. Activities of reputable distillers, breweries, and manufacturers are also investigated to make certain that regulations pertaining to alcohol and tobacco products are being followed.

Regardless of the type of case assigned, BATF Special Agents, working alone or in teams, gather all available data and plan the conduct of the investigation. They make use of the technical resources of their own bureau as well as those of other law enforcement agencies in obtaining additional information relevant to the case. They interview, observe, and interrogate suspects, informants, and witnesses connected with the investigation to gather facts and evidence of federal violations. In addition, Agents engage in surveillance activities on foot, in vehicles, or at stakeouts and, if necessary, use court-approved electronic methods. Agents also assume other identities and work undercover. They associate with criminals, purchase contraband, observe illegal activities, and gather intelligence information through these investigative methods. After sufficient evidence is gathered, it is evaluated by BATF Special Agents to determine what actions should follow. Where indicated, Agents seize, search, and arrest suspects and gather contraband and other evidence as authorized by appropriate legal warrants. In carrying out these tasks, Agents work in teams or as part of a larger group of Agents conducting raids of suspected locations. BATF Special Agents are trained in self-defense tactics as well as in the use of various types of firearms, and they employ these skills as needed during the course of an investigation. Agents prepare detailed, written summaries of all facts and evidence assembled in each investigation. They assist the U.S. Attorney in preparing the case before trial and in presenting it before the court. BATF Special Agents often make court appearances to testify for the prosecution during criminal proceedings.

Working Conditions

Special Agents *may be assigned to work locations anywhere in the United States and travel frequently* during the course of their investigations. They are also *subject to transfers* and work assignments based on the needs of the Bureau. The *working hours of Special Agents are often irregular* and in excess of 40 hours a week. In addition to working under *stressful and dangerous conditions,* the *work is often physically strenuous* and is performed in all kinds of environmental conditions. These factors should be weighed carefully when considering this career. The fringe benefits available to BATF Special Agents include:

(1) The opportunity to join group health and life insurance plans with the government sharing the costs. Immediate family members of Special Agents are included in health and benefit plans.
(2) Sick leave earned at the rate of 13 days a year that may be accumulated without limit.
(3) Annual leave earned at the rate of 13, 20, or 26 days a year, based on the length of government employment.
(4) Eligibility for retirement at age 50 with 20 years' service in the criminal investigative field.

Promotion Opportunities

Employees hired as BATF Agents usually enter duty at the GS-5 level (the General Schedule—or GS—is a pay schedule for federal employees). Promotions are contingent upon satisfactory work performance at each level and require the recommendations of supervisory personnel. As Agents demonstrate their capabilities, they are given progressively more responsible assignments and promotions commensurate with those responsibilities.

The journeyman level for a Special Agent is GS-11. Selections for promotion to positions above the GS-11 level are made as vacancies occur and in accordance with the Bureau's merit promotion procedures.

The minimum waiting period in each grade is one year. Periodic within-grade "step increases" are provided for Agents who remain at the same grade level. It is the policy of this agency to advance and develop employee potential within reasonable periods of time. Prospects for upward mobility are favorable, and Agents who demonstrate the capability to assume more difficult and responsible assignments are recommended for promotion by supervisory personnel.

DRUG ENFORCEMENT ADMINISTRATION SPECIAL AGENT

Duties of the Job

The illegal manufacturing and distribution of drugs is a worldwide problem that can only be resolved through the international efforts of all countries. The primary mission of the U.S. Department of Justice Drug Enforcement Administration (DEA) is to enforce the drug laws and regulations of the United States of America. The DEA is charged with bringing to justice organizations, and principal members of organizations, involved in the illegal growing, manufacture, or distribution of drugs in the United States. The DEA also recommends and supports nonenforcement programs aimed at reducing the availability of illegal drugs on the domestic and international market.

The DEA's primary responsibilities include investigation and preparation for prosecution of major violators of the drug laws of the United States; regulation and enforcement of the laws governing the legal manufacture and distribution of drugs; management of a national narcotic intelligence system in cooperation with federal, state, local, and foreign officials to collect, analyze, and distribute significant information; coordination and cooperation with state and local law enforcement officials on drug enforcement efforts by expanding these investigations beyond local jurisdictions and resources; operation of all programs associated with drug law enforcement officials of foreign countries; providing for training, research, scientific, technical, and other support services that enhance the DEA's overall mission; being a liaison with the United Nations and other organizations on matters relating to international drug control programs; and coordination and cooperation with other federal, state, and local agencies and with foreign governments in programs designed to reduce the illicit availability of illegal abuse-type drugs on the United States market using nonenforcement methods such as crop eradication, training of foreign officials, and the encouragement of knowledge and commitment against drug abuse.

DEA Special Agents are the backbone of this agency and represent half of its total workforce. A Special Agent's career within the DEA represents an *opportunity for diversified experience,* international posts of duty, and assignments at numerous posts of duty within the United States. The job is not without frustration or danger. It does *provide a unique role in combating a serious national and international problem.*

The primary mission of DEA Special Agents is to enforce laws dealing with narcotics and dangerous drugs by investigating the alleged or suspected criminal activities of major drug traffickers on both the national and international scene. They concentrate their efforts on locating and eliminating illegal sources of supply and distribution that quite often involve secret manufacturers of drugs and sources of drugs diverted from legitimate channels. When a case assignment is received from DEA supervisory personnel,

Special Agents, working alone or in teams, review and analyze all the available data the agency has on file and make preliminary plans about the ways in which the investigation will be conducted. Additional facts and evidence are obtained by interviewing, observing, and interrogating witnesses, suspects, and informants with knowledge of the case. In many instances, Agents must carefully examine and evaluate financial and inventory records or other sources of information to verify facts previously obtained or to uncover new evidence indicating criminal activities. Very often, hard facts and evidence about activities of illegal drug dealers cannot be obtained by traditional investigative methods. In such cases, Special Agents undertake the very risky job of assuming other identities and working undercover. This is a *stressful, demanding activity requiring long hours and close association with some of society's most undesirable elements.*

An important part of the Special Agent's job involves surveillance activities. This is done in a number of ways, such as on stakeouts, in vehicles, or on foot, and may involve the use of electronic methods authorized by appropriate court orders. Information concerning illegal drug trafficking by individuals and organized groups is collected, analyzed, and distributed as intelligence data so that investigations may be conducted in a systematic fashion and duplication of effort may be avoided. These data are also used in the planning and development of DEA strategies and in the continuous exchange of information among federal, state, and local law enforcement agencies and appropriate foreign governments. When investigations have been concluded, Special Agents evaluate all the available facts and evidence and consult with supervisory personnel to determine what legal actions should follow. Special Agents have full police power to enforce all federal laws anywhere in the United States. When sufficient evidence exists, they arrest, take suspects into custody, and seize evidence and contraband as authorized by appropriate legal warrants. These actions are carried out by teams of Special Agents or by groups of Agents who are part of a strike force unit. DEA Special Agents are well trained in the use of firearms and self-defense methods and employ these skills as needed during arrests. Agents prepare detailed, written reports of each case in which they take part. These reports include all data, evidence, statements of witnesses and defendants, and other relevant information useful during court proceedings. They assist government attorneys in trial preparations and testify for the prosecution during trials and grand jury proceedings.

The Drug Enforcement Administration is also responsible for regulating the legal trade in narcotic and dangerous drugs, and Special Agents must have the versatility to conduct accountability investigations of drug wholesalers, suppliers, and manufacturers. Activities include establishing import-export and manufacturing quotas for various controlled drugs, registering all authorized handlers of drugs, inspecting the records and facilities of major drug manufacturers and distributors, and investigating instances in which drugs have been illegally diverted from legitimate sources. In addition to their enforcement responsibilities, DEA Special Agents use methods of training and education in their fight against narcotics and drug abuse. In overseas operations, for example, DEA activities are aimed at developing international awareness of the criticality of the illegal drug problem and obtaining support for drug trafficking suppression measures. Agents also work to secure cooperation between nations in sharing information and intelligence about drug-related activities. On the domestic scene, Special Agents train federal, state, local, and foreign law enforcement officers in drug identification techniques and narcotic and dangerous drug control methods. Special training is also available through DEA in forensic drug chemistry for chemists employed by law enforcement agencies and for key personnel in the legal drug industry. Agents give lectures, make speeches, and serve as panel members for civic, social, community, and other types of organizations expressing concern and interest in the drug abuse problem.

Working Conditions

Special Agent positions are located in most major cities throughout the United States and in certain large cities overseas. The work involves *frequent travel* as well as *irregular hours and overtime*. Special Agents work a considerable amount of administratively uncontrollable overtime for which they are well compensated. Special Agents must be available for assignment at any time; they are usually *required to transfer to different locations, at government expense,* based on workload requirements and the needs of the agency. Special Agents must be willing to accept assignment to duty stations *anywhere* in the United States upon appointment and at any time thereafter, including foreign assignments. In fact, applicants are required to sign a statement to this effect prior to appointment.

This job involves *hazardous duty,* working under stress, and the possibility of physical injury during dangerous assignments. The fringe benefits that DEA Special Agents receive include paid vacation and holidays, sick leave, overtime pay, low-cost medical and life insurance, financial protection in the event of job-related injury or death, and a liberal retirement pension. Agents with 20 years of service in criminal investigation activities are permitted to retire at age 50.

Training and Promotion Opportunities

The training program that DEA Special Agents must undergo is so rigorous that many applicants do not make it to the first cut. Candidates must sign a statement of understanding prior to appointment that continued employment with DEA is contingent upon successful completion of this training.

Most Special Agents are given special appointments approved for DEA by the Office of Personnel Management. Agents given these appointments may be converted to career appointments after three to four years of fully satisfactory service. Once hired, prospects for upward mobility are generally good. Special Agents are eligible for promotion after one year of satisfactory work performance at the entry level. Promotions are not automatic and are based on the Agent's job performance, demonstrated ability to perform the duties of the higher-level job, and the recommendations of supervisory personnel.

Most Special Agents are appointed at grade 7. A limited number of appointments may be made at grade 9. The Special Agent position has promotion potential to GS-12. Promotions are not automatic; they are based on merit. Promotions beyond GS-12 are made through DEA's Merit Promotion Plan.

FBI SPECIAL AGENT

Duties of the Job

The Federal Bureau of Investigation (FBI) is probably the best known of the several major agencies that are part of the U.S. Department of Justice. The FBI is responsible for the investigation of more than 200 different types of cases resulting from violations of federal laws within its jurisdiction. The FBI is a fact-gathering agency, and its Special Agents function only as investigators. This agency does not prosecute cases; it turns over facts and evidence to a U.S. Attorney who makes the decision regarding legal action.

In addition to its investigative activities, the FBI provides important supportive services to law enforcement units at the federal, state, and local levels. Bureau personnel assist these various units by providing access to extensive files of fingerprints, firearms, document examinations, typewriter faces, handwriting, nicknames of criminals, heelprints, tire treads, paper watermarks, and automotive paint samples, to name just some of the subject areas. In addition, the FBI has the world's largest crime laboratory, which provides such skilled services as microscopic and chemical analysis, spectrography, and cryptography. The FBI also conducts specialized training programs at its National Academy for selected members of police agencies throughout the country in a continuing effort to increase the effectiveness of law enforcement at all levels.

The FBI's Special Agents are responsible for enforcing a wide variety of federal laws within their jurisdiction, dealing with such matters as kidnapping, bank robbery, thefts of government property, organized crime activities, espionage, sabotage, civil rights violations, and white-collar crimes such as bank embezzlements or bankruptcy fraud. Special Agents can be assigned to any of these various cases;

however, where possible, Agents with specialized backgrounds, such as accounting or science, are given cases in which their skills can best be used.

The most important function of these Agents is gathering evidence in cases in which specific federal laws have been violated and presenting their findings to the office of a U.S. Attorney. Agents carry out their assignments and conduct their investigations thoroughly using the considerable resources of the Bureau. When a case assignment is received, Agents, working alone or in teams, review and analyze all the available data and plan the scope and direction the investigation will take. They gather facts and evidence by interviewing, observing, and interrogating suspects, informants, and witnesses involved in the case. In addition, Agents examine and evaluate records and other pertinent information to uncover evidence or to discover facts that confirm evidence already obtained.

Under certain circumstances, Agents assume other identities and work undercover to observe suspects and to gather evidence needed to build or solve a case. Surveillance activities are another important part of an FBI Agent's work. Surveillance is carried out in different ways such as on foot, in vehicles, or on stakeouts, and it includes the use of court-authorized electronic methods when necessary. When the Agents assigned to a case have completed their investigations, facts and evidence are evaluated to determine what actions will be taken. When indicated, Agents seize, arrest, and take suspects into custody as authorized by appropriate legal warrants. Such actions may be carried out by teams of Agents or, in some cases, by large groups of Agents participating in raids. FBI Agents are skillful in the use of several types of firearms as well as in hand-to-hand defensive tactics. They use these skills as needed when seizing and arresting suspects.

FBI Agents are *required to prepare detailed, written reports* on all aspects of cases in which they are involved. Included in these reports are all facts, evidence, statements of witnesses and other pertinent case data that can be used in future legal proceedings. Agents also confer with and assist the staff of U.S. Attorneys' offices in preparing cases for trial and appear as witnesses during trials and grand jury hearings.

Working Conditions

Most FBI Special Agents are assigned to one of the 59 divisional offices located in cities throughout the United States and Puerto Rico. The remainder work in FBI headquarters in Washington, D.C., or in FBI resident agencies scattered across the nation. *Work in excess of 40 hours a week is common,* and Agents may be called upon to *travel* during the performance of duties. They must be available for assignments at any time and are on call 24 hours a day. In addition, *transfer to different work locations is usually required at some point during their careers. Hazardous duty,* working under stress, and the prospect of physical injury resulting from participation in dangerous assignments are essential aspects of this work. The fringe benefits Agents receive include paid vacations, sick leave, life insurance, full medical insurance, overtime pay, and retirement annuities. FBI Agents with 20 years or more of service are required to retire at age 55. All Agents are covered by the Retirement and Insurance Division of the U.S. Office of Personnel Management.

Training and Promotion Opportunities

Newly appointed FBI Special Agents serve a one-year probationary period before achieving permanent status. Once permanently appointed, these Agents enjoy job security. There is no automatic promotion machinery, but supervisory and administrative positions are filled by Agents from within the organization, and promotions are based on demonstrated leadership qualities and work expertise.

FEDERAL PROTECTIVE OFFICER

Duties of the Job

Federal Protective Officers are uniformed, armed personnel who are authorized to enforce all laws and regulations that pertain to protection of life and property and who have powers of arrest and seizure in locations under the control of the General Services Administration. To maintain law and order and to preserve the peace on federal property, officers use a number of security and enforcement techniques. Some assignments involve patrol of assigned areas on foot, in vehicles, or on roving patrols to probe parking areas, loading platforms, building interiors, and public entrances for evidence of trespass or hazardous conditions. Other officers are assigned to fixed posts or control desks where they monitor and regulate such equipment as automated security and fire-protection systems and devices such as intrusion alarms, electronic sensing instruments, and entry-control devices. Monitoring telephone and radio communications within the location, relaying messages, keeping logs, and helping to dispatch personnel and equipment in cases of emergency are other duties. Officers assigned to entrance-control posts are responsible for examining personnel identification credentials, issuing keys, controlling access to various locations, and conducting patrols of the building complex. In some cases, officers are given traffic-control posts where they control and direct pedestrian and vehicular traffic, investigate and report accidents, and issue citations for violations of the law.

In protecting federal properties and their occupants, Federal Protective Officers are trained and ready to act in emergency situations such as fires, explosions, civil disorders, bomb threats, natural disasters, and potential or actual attack by enemies of the United States. To cope with incidents like these, officers follow established plans of action under the direction of supervisory personnel. In cases of fire or explosion, for example, they utilize standardized firefighting control methods and evacuation procedures to reduce danger to life and property and to facilitate the safe removal of occupants from buildings.

In addition to responsibilities of protection, Federal Protective Officers have enforcement responsibilities as well. These duties entail preventing specified crimes on federal property, enforcing laws and regulations, and apprehending persons committing illegal acts. The crimes with which they are concerned are felonies and misdemeanors. A felony is a crime punishable by death or by imprisonment in a penitentiary for more than one year. A misdemeanor is a lesser offense punishable by fine or by confinement in a jail or workhouse for one year or less. Some examples of felonies include murder, manslaughter, robbery, burglary, arson, mayhem, malicious destruction, sabotage, and espionage. Misdemeanors include breaches of the peace, assault, disorderly conduct, riot, unlawful assembly, and petit larceny.

When any of these crimes is committed or incidents occur that disrupt the normal conduct of government business, Federal Protective Officers take action. These officers may be at the scene in mobile response units or in special tactical forces dispatched to the trouble spot. At the scene, they conduct a preliminary investigation, gather information from witnesses or victims, if any, and prepare a report of findings. In cases of injury, officers may administer first-aid or lifesaving assistance to victims. If Federal Protective Officers respond to a crime in progress, they may pursue, apprehend, and arrest those engaged in the illegal activities. Officers are authorized to use whatever force is needed, including firearms, to carry out their responsibilities. They do not enforce any laws outside their jurisdiction; they leave such matters to the appropriate local or federal police agency.

Federal Protective Officers may be called upon to testify as witnesses or arresting officers in a case. They must be prepared to inform the court of pertinent facts surrounding the case and to provide such information as the time, date, place, and identity of persons involved in the incident.

Working Conditions

Federal Protective Officers may be assigned to work locations in any areas of the country where the General Services Administration is responsible for federal properties. These include federal buildings housing U.S. District and Appellate Courts, federal buildings located in the various states housing the offices of U.S. Senators and Congressmen, and buildings housing the Selective Service System at any time during which it is operative.

Federal Protective Officers *often work under stressful conditions* and are subject to physical injury when performing their duties. The fringe benefits these officers receive include paid vacation, holidays, and sick leave; free uniforms and equipment; overtime pay; low-cost medical and life insurance; and liberal retirement annuity.

Training and Promotion Opportunities

Uniformed Federal Protective Officers enter the force at the level of GS-4 or GS-5, depending on the quality of training and previous law enforcement experience. After training and a year's probationary appointment, they are eligible for permanent status. They also are eligible to participate in a management training program, a career advancement program, or a technical advancement program. The prospects for advancement in this work are generally favorable. Promotions are based on satisfactory work performance, demonstrated abilities in handling more complex tasks, and supervisory recommendations. Qualified Federal Protective Officers may advance in rank in the following order: Corporal, Sergeant, Lieutenant, Captain, Major, and Lieutenant Colonel.

BORDER PATROL AGENT

The Immigration and Naturalization Service (INS), an agency of the U.S. Department of Justice, administers and enforces laws that govern the admission, exclusion, deportation, and naturalization of aliens. Through a variety of law enforcement activities, the INS protects the national security of the United States and the welfare of persons who live in this country legally. An essential part of the INS law enforcement effort is carried out by a group of highly trained officers known as the Border Patrol. This organization offers interesting career prospects to those who qualify. The following are some of the typical work activities of Border Patrol Agents.

Duties of the Job

The Border Patrol is a highly mobile, uniformed enforcement organization whose primary responsibilities are to detect and prevent the illegal entry or smuggling of aliens into the United States and to detect, take into custody, and arrange for the deportation of those living illegally in this country. Border Patrol Agents perform their work along the more than 8,000 miles of land and coastal areas that make up the international boundaries of the continental United States. In many cases, these borders are barely visible lines located in rugged and uninhabited mountains, canyons, and deserts. Agents patrol designated areas to uncover attempted or actual illegal entries into this country. To be effective, Border Patrol Agents use special techniques and equipment in meeting their responsibilities. These include electronic communication systems, electronic sensing devices, pursuit vehicles, jeeps, fixed-wing aircraft, helicopters, and patrol boats. Electronic sensors, for example, are concealed at strategic points along the borders and are monitored at headquarters. When these devices are tripped, a signal is received and Agents are sent to the scene to investigate. Agents perform line-watch duties at points that provide good visibility and use binocular devices to scan areas for illegal entrants. They also use an age-old technique called "sign cutting." Smoothing the surface of specified sandy areas along points commonly used for attempted entries creates "sand traps." When these traps are examined, they can indicate, by means of footprints, the direction taken and the number of possible illegal entrants in the area. These tracks are then followed until the aliens are apprehended. Another method used to enforce immigration laws is jeep-plane teams. These teams coordinate aerial surveillance or search activities with ground operations over wide expanses, such as agricultural areas, to pinpoint the location of possible lawbreakers.

In addition to their duties in the more remote areas, Border Patrol Agents investigate other possible means of illegal entry into this country and use their foreign language skills where appropriate. They stop vehicles at traffic checkpoints on roads and highways leading from the border and determine the citizenship of occupants. They also make inquiries into the immigration status of farm and ranch employees. Agents inspect and search trains, buses, trucks, aircraft, ships, and passenger and cargo terminals to locate illegal aliens. During these searches, Agents sometimes uncover evidence of smuggling activities. When illegal aliens are discovered, Border Patrol Agents are authorized to arrest them without warrant, using firearms and physical force if necessary. These individuals are then held for possible criminal prosecution or deportation. Border Patrol Agents make detailed written reports of cases in which they are involved and may be called upon to give testimony during court proceedings.

Working Conditions

Newly hired Border Patrol Agents are *assigned initially to duty stations in the southern border states* of California, Arizona, New Mexico, and Texas. Many of these work locations are situated in *small, isolated communities.* Some of these areas may have poor schools and medical facilities. It is *sometimes difficult to transfer to a preferred area.* If your heart is set on living in a specific location, you may be disappointed.

A Border Patrol Agent is required to work overtime and may work long hours. *Sixty-hour weeks* and 10- to 16-hour days are not uncommon. An Agent works *irregular rotating shifts* every two to four weeks. These shifts are subject to change, often on short notice. Agents may earn from 10 percent to 25 percent *additional pay for the performance of extra duty time.* Border Patrol Agents work under *stressful* and *dangerous* conditions and are subject to the *hazards of physical injury* during the performance of their duties. Fringe benefits that Border Patrol Agents receive include paid vacation (13 days per year for the first three years, 20 days per year after three years of service up to 15 years, 26 days per year after 15 years of service), holidays, and sick leave of 13 days per year that may be accumulated if not used. Agents are also eligible for low-cost medical and life insurance, and they receive an annual $480 uniform allowance. Note, however, that the *new Border Patrol Agent must make the initial outlay of about $1,275 (tax deductible) for uniforms for the first year,* $300 before entering the training academy.

Border Patrol Agents who have at least 20 years of service are eligible for special retirement with a good pension at age 50. This special provision also applies to other law enforcement officers and certain supervisory personnel who have been promoted from law enforcement positions. *Retirement is mandatory at age 55,* allowing the Agent to pursue a new career or hobby while collecting retirement pay.

Promotion Opportunities

Initial appointment is at grade GS-5. Career progression generally follows at one-year intervals to GS-7 and journeyman GS-9. Promotions and salary increases occur even during the three-year conditional appointment period. The prospects for advancement are excellent. Border Patrol Agents may compete for other assignments within the Border Patrol or for supervisory-level positions, or they may apply for other positions within the Immigration and Naturalization Service.

IMMIGRATION INSPECTOR

An integral position in the Immigration and Naturalization Service uniformed officer corps is the Immigration Inspector. Approximately 300 million people enter the United States annually. The Immigration Inspector is usually the first United States official a person meets when entering this country.

Duties of the Job

The key responsibility of the Immigration Inspector is to prevent the entry of people who are ineligible to enter the United States and to properly admit those who are eligible to enter. The work is performed primarily at land ports of entry, airports, seaports, and other places where people enter the United States from other countries. The trainee Immigration Inspector performs certain phases of inspection work under fairly close supervision and assists higher-grade officers in other inspectional processes.

Working Conditions

The Immigration Inspector *must wear an official uniform* while on duty, *must enforce laws and regulations that may conflict with personal beliefs,* must work in pressure situations in which complaints and criticism from the public are frequent, and must work *long, irregular hours* under constantly varying conditions. Overtime is frequently required, and Immigration Inspectors *may earn substantial overtime pay* for the performance of extra duties.

Promotion Opportunities

Initial appointments are at grade GS-5. Career progression to grade GS-7 and journeyman grade GS-9 generally follows at one-year intervals. Promotions to higher-graded positions are made through the competitive procedures of the Federal Merit Promotion System.

CRIMINAL INVESTIGATOR, IMMIGRATION AND NATURALIZATION SERVICE (SPECIAL AGENT)

The Immigration and Naturalization Service (INS), an agency of the U.S. Department of Justice, administers and enforces laws that govern admission, exclusion, deportation, and naturalization of aliens. Its responsibilities include determining whether aliens may enter or remain in the United States, evaluating the applications of aliens seeking U.S. citizenship, reviewing applications for visas, guarding against illegal entry into this country, and representing the U.S. government at official immigration hearings. To meet the new and varied problems and challenges that these responsibilities create, the Immigration and Naturalization Service employs a force of highly trained officers known as Criminal Investigators. This force, made up of nonuniformed enforcement officers, has the mission of investigating and gathering facts in all cases falling within the jurisdiction of INS. Most cases involve administrative proceedings and criminal prosecutions.

Duties of the Job

The primary responsibility of Criminal Investigators in the INS is investigation of alleged or suspected violations of federal immigration and naturalization laws. When they receive their assignments, Criminal

Investigators, working alone or in teams, identify the charges or issues involved and evaluate all the available information concerning each case. Based on this evaluation, they plan the preliminary direction, scope, and timing of the investigation. In conducting their probes, investigators obtain data and evidence in a number of ways. They interview, observe, and interrogate suspects and witnesses who are parties in a case. They cultivate and make use of informants to obtain leads to relevant information. Investigators examine various types of legal records and immigration documents to see if they are genuine and to uncover evidence of fraud, conspiracy, or other immigration law violations. These examinations may also serve to confirm the accuracy of information and evidence gathered from other sources. Quite often, traditional methods of investigation are not sufficient to obtain hard facts and evidence about the deliberate illegal activities of persons or groups who break immigration and nationality laws. In such cases, Criminal Investigators may assume other identities and work undercover. This is an often risky and demanding activity that involves *long and irregular hours* as well as *close association with criminal elements. Undercover activities, however, have their positive side and can be a satisfying experience, particularly when evidence is uncovered that builds or breaks a case.*

Surveillance activities, an important part of this work, are carried on in different ways such as on foot, in vehicles, or on stakeouts and include use of electronic methods. Information gathered during the course of an investigation is analyzed and distributed within INS to aid in planning and to avoid duplicate effort. In cases in which evidence is uncovered about illegal actions in the jurisdiction of other agencies, Criminal Investigators relay this information and may coordinate their activities with the agency in question. When INS Criminal Investigators decide that sufficient evidence has been gathered to justify action, they are authorized to seize, arrest, and take suspects into custody and to seize evidence using court-obtained warrants where required. Investigators may carry out these actions alone, in teams, or as part of a large group. Criminal Investigators are skilled in the methods of self-defense as well as in the use of firearms, and they use these skills as required.

Investigators write comprehensive reports of each case for which they are responsible. Reports consist of evidence, statements of witnesses and suspects, and all other relevant data that can be used during administrative or criminal proceedings. Investigators may assist INS attorneys in the preparation of cases and may be called upon to testify in court.

Working Conditions

INS Criminal Investigator positions are located throughout the United States. The larger field offices are usually in metropolitan areas. The work may involve *irregular hours, travel, and overtime* as part of normal duties. Certain parts of this job involve *hazardous duty,* working under stress, and the possibility of physical harm. Benefits available include paid vacation, sick leave, and holidays; overtime pay; low-cost medical and life insurance; financial protection in the event of death or injury; and a retirement annuity. Criminal Investigators with 20 years of federal law enforcement service are eligible for retirement at age 50. Retirement is mandatory at age 55.

Promotion Opportunities

Initial appointments are at grade GS-5. Career progression to grades GS-7, GS-9, and journeyman GS-11 generally follows at one-year intervals. Thereafter, promotions are made through the competitive procedures of the Federal Merit Promotion System. Investigators who demonstrate the skills required to perform complex assignments may compete for supervisory or other high-level positions.

DEPORTATION OFFICER

The Immigration and Naturalization Service, in its responsibility to administer and enforce immigration and nationality laws, maintains liaison with numerous federal, state, local, and foreign officials. The Deportation Officer plays an important role in these activities.

Duties of the Job

The job of the Deportation Officer is to provide for the control and removal of persons who have been ordered deported or required to depart from the United States. This is accomplished by closely monitoring deportation proceedings from initiation of the proceedings to the removal of the person from the United States. Close liaison with foreign consulates and embassies is required to facilitate the expeditious issuance of passports and travel documents required for deportation. The Deportation Officer must ensure that no avenues of relief have been overlooked for the person being deported, offering every assistance possible such as recommendation for release on bond or recognizance. Deportation Officers compose letters to foreign consulates and other agencies and write formal responses to congressional inquiries and to applications for relief.

Working Conditions

Overtime is required and Deportation Officers *earn overtime pay* for performance of extra duties beyond the normal working day. Federal employment provides many benefits including vacation and sick leave, life and health insurance, and a liberal retirement plan.

Promotion Opportunities

Initial appointments are at grade GS-5. Career progression to grades GS-7, GS-9, and journeyman GS-11 generally follows at one-year intervals. Thereafter, promotions to higher grades and to supervisory levels are made through the competitive procedures of the Federal Merit Promotion System. Deportation Officers who have at least 20 years of service are eligible for special retirement at age 50. This special provision also applies to other law enforcement officers and certain supervisory personnel who have been promoted from law enforcement positions. Such retirements are mandatory at age 55.

INTERNAL SECURITY INSPECTOR, INTERNAL REVENUE SERVICE

The Inspection Service, an essential part of the Internal Revenue Service (IRS), carries out responsibilities of great importance to America and its citizens. It has the mission of ensuring that high standards of honesty exist and are maintained at all levels of operation in the Internal Revenue Service.

The Inspection Service's two basic operations are Internal Audit and Internal Security. Staff members in these units are responsible for making sure that the IRS maintains a reputation as one of the most efficient government agencies with personnel who meet high standards of honesty, loyalty, and conduct. Members of Internal Audit review and appraise operations of the Internal Revenue Service at all levels of management to be sure that responsibilities are handled effectively. Internal Security, the law enforcement part of the Inspection Service, conducts investigations of various types. It is in this unit that Internal Security Inspectors are employed to carry out the following duties, which are aimed at maintaining the reputation of the Internal Revenue Service.

Duties of the Job

Internal Security Inspectors make up the IRS' own investigative unit, and their duties are varied and often complex. Part of their work requires conducting detailed character and background investigations of prospective IRS employees including applicants or appointees to technical or nontechnical jobs and those involved with handling funds; public accountants and former IRS employees who apply to represent taxpayers at IRS hearings; and those involved in charges of unethical conduct by lawyers, accountants, or others involved in IRS proceedings. Of primary importance to these Inspectors are complaints or information that indicate possible wrongdoing by IRS employees. Attempts made to bribe or corrupt employees to obtain improper advantage in tax matters threaten the integrity of IRS, and swift action is required to gather evidence, resolve the accusations, and take whatever measures are necessary to protect trust in the agency.

Internal Security Inspectors also investigate attempts to influence or interfere with the administration of IRS statutes through the use of threats, assaults, and similar methods. They are often assigned as armed escorts responsible for protecting IRS employees and government witnesses in legal proceedings. Other duties performed by Inspectors include investigation of cases in which federal tax information was illegally disclosed, either by IRS personnel or by preparers who were given this information in confidence; accidents involving IRS employees or property that result in civil law suits; and the conduct of special investigations, studies, and inquiries when directed by the Secretary of the Treasury, the Commissioner of the Internal Revenue Service, or other high-level officials. Internal Security Inspectors work cooperatively with law enforcement personnel of other agencies and at times may assist in providing security for the President of the United States and other American of foreign dignitaries.

By its very nature, *the job of the Internal Security Inspector is often more difficult than many others in the investigative field.* Since most of the Internal Security Inspector's criminal investigations involve secret or concealed crimes, he or she must first learn that the crime has been—or is going to be—committed. The Internal Security Inspector must discover where and how it occurred—or will occur—and who is involved. Upon accomplishing this, he or she must secure all the necessary evidence, arrange the apprehension of those responsible, and prepare the material that will lead to successful prosecution. The average criminal investigator rarely has so complex a problem. In burglary or homicide, for example, someone usually reports the crime, and thus there is evidence that the crime did occur. The sole remaining problems are to find out who did it and to prove it. Much of the critical evidence remains at the scene of the crime.

Internal Security Inspectors are faced with extremely heavy workloads as the following excerpt from the Commissioner's Annual Report of 1982 attests. In reading the record of indictments and convictions, keep in mind that the majority of investigations lead to innocent persons.

> The internal security division's investigations to protect the integrity of the IRS resulted in the arrest or indictment of 95 taxpayers and tax practitioners and 272 current or former IRS employees. There were convictions or guilty pleas in the cases of 121 individuals arrested or indicted in 1982 or earlier. Of these convictions, 18 were for bribery and 21 for assault, while the rest involved conspiracy to defraud the government, embezzlement, impersonation of a federal officer, narcotics, and other offenses.
>
> The internal security division completed 5,495 background investigations of employees during the year and conducted police record checks on all persons considered for temporary appointments. These investigations and record searches resulted in the rejection of 72 job applicants and administrative actions against 332 employees. Internal security also conducted 902 investigations of alleged employee misconduct, with 74 resulting in exoneration of the employees involved.

To summarize, the investigative jurisdiction of the Inspection Service includes bribery, perjury, embezzlement, fraud, assault, conspiracy, collusion, extortion, forgery, unauthorized disclosure of information, and any acts that threaten the proper administration of IRS regulations. Internal Security Inspectors, using physical force or firearms when necessary, apprehend and arrest suspected individuals. It is interesting to note that more bribery cases have been successfully prosecuted by the Internal Revenue Inspection Service than by all other federal investigative agencies combined.

Working Conditions

Internal Security Inspectors may be assigned to work stations at the National Office of the Internal Revenue Service in Washington, D.C., or to one of the regional or district offices found throughout the United States. There are 58 IRS district offices with at least one in each of the 50 states. Regional offices are located in the following cities: San Francisco, Dallas, Cincinnati, Chicago, Atlanta, Philadelphia, and New York. Internal Security Inspectors *work irregular schedules in excess of 40 hours a week* and *may have to travel* to carry out their duties. They often work under *stress* and are subject to *personal risks* during certain assignments. Fringe benefits associated with this work include paid vacation and holidays, overtime pay, sick leave, low-cost medical and life insurance, financial protection in the event of job-related injury or death, and a retirement pension. Internal Security Inspectors who have 20 years of service in criminal investigation activities are eligible to retire at 50 years of age.

Promotion Opportunities

Generally, the prospects for advancement in this field are favorable, and those who demonstrate the ability to assume more difficult and responsible tasks may compete for higher-level technical, supervisory, and managerial positions.

INTERNAL REVENUE SERVICE SPECIAL AGENT

Duties of the Job

Criminal violations of the Internal Revenue Code, with the exception of those relating to alcohol, tobacco, and firearms, are the responsibility of Special Agents of the Criminal Investigation Division (CID). Attempts to evade or defeat a tax and willful failure to file returns are the principal violations with which Agents are concerned. Their investigations center primarily on income, employment, and excise taxes and are carried out to the extent necessary to determine whether violations of federal tax laws have occurred. If violations took place, Special Agents must then gather sufficient evidence to prove guilt beyond a reasonable doubt. Tax fraud occurs in a variety of occupations and income groups. Examples of those who may be recommended for prosecution are attorneys, accountants, politicians, proprietors of businesses, tax protesters, corporate officers, narcotics dealers, and physicians. Tax evaders often use clever methods to avoid tax payments, and their criminal acts often take place over a period of years. As a result, investigations are made difficult by the numerous transactions taking place during those years plus the sizeable number of records requiring analysis.

The investigation process begins when the Criminal Investigation Division in a particular tax district receives reports about alleged tax violations. Typical sources of this information include IRS Agents, Tax Technicians, and Revenue Officers; IRS Special Agents working on related cases; officers of other federal, state, and local law enforcement agencies; and informants. The information is evaluated by supervisory personnel, and if criminal violations are indicated, the case is assigned to a Special Agent of the Criminal Investigation Division. Initially, Special Agents attempt to determine the true taxable income of the subject and whether a deliberate attempt was made to understate income or to avoid filing a tax return. They do this by interviewing the subject, key witnesses, and other parties to the case. Any evidence gathered is carefully recorded, evaluated, and organized. In certain instances, individuals involved in a case may be hostile or reluctant to give information, or they may give false testimony to protect the taxpayer in question. Special Agents, however, are quite skilled at spotting tax frauds and uncovering unreported income or hidden assets. In cases in which taxpayer records are withheld, lost, destroyed, or altered, Special Agents are faced with the difficult task of reconstructing these records by locating alternative sources of information. They do so by investigating the subject's personal and financial history and by examining such items as bank records and cancelled checks, brokerage accounts, property transactions, and tax returns filed in past years. These activities require a sound knowledge of accounting and tax-law procedures, rules of evidence, and the constitutional rights of individuals involved in the case.

In addition to gathering data, Special Agents engage in surveillance of suspects and are authorized to conduct searches and arrest individuals using physical force or firearms as necessary to protect human life. Once a case assignment is concluded, Special Agents prepare detailed reports of all information gathered during the investigation process. These reports contain a history of the investigation, evidence of additional income and intent to defraud, the subject's explanation and defense of actions, and any evidence that either proves or disproves the subject's defense. In addition, the report contains the agents' conclusions about the case as well as recommendations about criminal prosecution and civil penalties. If the subject of the investigation is brought to trial, Special Agents assist the U.S. Attorney in preparing the case and usually appear as principal witnesses for the government.

An important function of IRS Special Agents involves investigations of organized crime activities. Under federal law, income from illegal sources such as bootlegging, prostitution, and narcotics sales is subject to tax. Such income is used by members of organized crime to support other illegal activities or to infiltrate legitimate businesses. As a result of IRS investigations, many crime figures have been prosecuted and convicted of tax evasion, resulting in substantial blows to the financial resources of criminal groups. As part of this effort, the Internal Revenue Service participates in the Federal Organized Crime Strike Force Program and works on a cooperating basis with other law enforcement agencies at all levels of government.

Working Conditions

Special Agents may be assigned to work locations at the National Office of the Internal Revenue Service in Washington, D.C., or to one of the regional or district offices located throughout the United States. Regional offices are situated in the following major cities: New York, Philadelphia, Atlanta, Chicago, Cincinnati, Dallas, and San Francisco. There are 58 district offices with at least one in each of the 50 states. Special Agents *may be required to travel* during the course of investigations, and *working hours are sometimes irregular and in excess of 40 hours a week.* In addition, they often work under stress and are exposed to the risk of physical harm when participating in arrests. The fringe benefits that IRS Special Agents receive include paid vacation, sick leave, overtime pay, low-cost medical and life insurance, financial protection in the event of job-related injury or death, and a liberal retirement annuity. Special Agents with 20 years of service in criminal investigation activities are permitted to retire at 50.

Promotion Opportunities

Prospects for advancement in this work are generally good. Individuals who demonstrate the skills needed to assume higher-level duties may eventually move into supervisory or higher managerial positions.

CUSTOMS AID

Duties of the Job

Customs Aids perform semi-technical duties that require the application of a specialized knowledge of certain provisions of customs laws and regulations. A Customs Aid can work at small ports, performing entry receipt and cash-processing functions, or at docks, serving as general assistant to Customs Inspectors supervising the unloading of vessels and examining merchandise (a small number of Customs Aids also perform marine duties in assistance to Marine Officers); at regional offices, receiving and acting on entries before final liquidation takes place; and at airports, assisting Customs Inspectors and other specialized personnel in carrying out a variety of duties including security functions in some cases.

Working Conditions

The Customs Aid enjoys all the benefits of Customs employment. These include liberal vacation and sick leave; low-cost group hospitalization, medical, and life insurance plans; government-paid financial protection in the event of job-connected injury or death; and a Civil Service retirement plan. If an employee enters the Armed Forces after taking a position at Customs, the position will be waiting for the employee on his or her return. The Customs employee may also receive pay raises and be promoted in absentia. If a Customs employee is a member of a military reserve unit and must attend annual training, he or she will receive up to 15 days of military leave with full pay.

Promotion Opportunities

Entry-level appointments to Customs Aid positions are made at the GS-4 and GS-5 levels, with opportunities for advancement to the GS-7 level. Some positions at the GS-5 and GS-6 levels and most positions at the GS-7 level include the responsibility for supervising the work of a group of Customs Aids in lower-graded positions. For qualified individuals, advancement opportunities to higher grade levels exist in other occupational series.

CUSTOMS INSPECTOR

Duties of the Job

Customs Inspectors, as members of the U.S. Customs Service law enforcement team, play a key role in enforcing numerous customs regulations through precise and thorough methods of examination, inspection, and questioning. Their responsibilities include cargoes and baggage; articles worn or carried by individuals; and vessels, vehicles, and aircraft entering or leaving the United States. When carriers such as ships, aircraft, or motor transport enter our borders, Customs Inspectors are authorized to go aboard to inspect, search, and determine the exact nature of the cargo. Cargo manifests and baggage declarations are reviewed, cargo containers are examined, and unloading activities are overseen to prevent smuggling, fraud, or cargo thefts. Customs Inspectors may weigh and measure imported merchandise to make certain that customs, neutrality, and commerce laws are followed. For example, to protect U.S. distributors of certain trademarked, imported merchandise, restrictions are placed on the amounts that may be brought into the country. Business magnates, captains of ships, and importers are the Inspectors' daily contacts as they review manifests, examine cargo carried by container on specially designed vessels, and control shipments transferred under bond to ports throughout the United States.

Customs Inspectors are also responsible for the examination of crew and passenger lists, health clearances, stores' lists, and ships' documents and for issuing required permits. They seal the holds of ships and compartments containing sea stores used by crew members as a means of preventing the illegal sale or smuggling of dutiable merchandise into the United States. In certain cases in which wrongdoing is suspected, they conduct body searches of crew members to check for contraband.

When assigned to baggage examination stations at points of entry into the United States, Customs Inspectors perform a variety of tasks. They classify, assess, and collect duties on articles being brought into the country, and they advise tourists about U.S. Customs regulations. For example, some tourists entering the country bring in more items than are permitted under duty-free regulations. In such instances, when informed of the regulations, tourists usually change their Customs declarations and pay the duty before baggage inspection. However, if undeclared items are discovered in baggage, the Customs Inspector must determine whether this is merely an oversight or deliberate fraud on the passenger's part. In most instances, these matters are settled immediately, but occasionally the articles are held, and a U.S. Customs hearing is scheduled to decide the case. Customs Inspectors are sometimes alerted by peculiarities in an individual's appearance, such as an unusual bulge in a traveler's pocket. In such cases, the traveler is asked to empty the pocket and display the contents on the counter for examination. Sometimes this reveals a poor attempt to hide a dutiable item; other times the item may turn out to be gloves or a scarf. Penalties are levied against persons caught trying to evade duty payments.

Customs Inspectors often question suspicious-looking individuals. They explain Customs procedures and laws to tourists or others unfamiliar with them. When the situation warrants, Customs Inspectors are authorized to search suspected individuals and to seize contraband and undeclared merchandise. In addition, they may arrest or detain these individuals using physical force or firearms if necessary. In carrying out their responsibilities, Customs Inspectors often work in cooperation with other government agents such as Special Agents, Customs; Customs Patrol Officers; Import Specialists; Special Agents, FBI; Special Agents, Drug Enforcement Administration; Agents of the U.S. Immigration and Naturalization Service and the Food and Drug Administration; and public health and agricultural quarantine inspectors. Customs Inspectors prepare reports to submit to supervisors regarding findings, transactions, violations, and arrests that take place during their work tour. They are also called upon to testify in court as government witnesses in cases in which they have been involved.

Working Conditions

The Customs territory of the United States is divided into nine regions made up of the 50 states, the District of Columbia, Puerto Rico, and the U.S. Virgin Islands. Customs Inspectors may be assigned to any of the nearly 300 ports of entry along our land and sea borders or may work overseas. These work locations include airports and seaports, waterfronts, border stations, customs houses, and in some cases, the U.S. Customs Service Headquarters in Washington, D.C. *When possible, Customs Inspectors are placed in the work location of their choice.* The typical work schedule is eight hours a day, five days a week, but it includes *rotating shifts and weekend duty.* The hours of the typical seaport or airport are often long and irregular, and *remoteness characterizes the many one-man border ports where Customs Inspectors must often perform immigration and agricultural inspections in addition to regular duties.*

For all this extra effort, however, Customs Inspectors are liberally compensated by *special overtime privileges* enacted by congressional legislation. The possibility of physical injury exists when Customs Inspectors seize and arrest persons suspected of serious Customs violations. The fringe benefits a Customs Inspector receives include paid vacations and sick leave; military leave; low-cost group hospitalization, medical, and life insurance; and retirement annuities covered by the Bureau of Retirement of the Office of Personnel Management.

Promotion Opportunities

After achieving permanent employment status, Customs Inspectors who qualify may compete for promotions to higher-level positions within the U.S. Customs Service. These may be supervisory positions or simply those at a higher grade level in the agency.

IMPORT SPECIALIST

Duties of the Job

The U.S. Customs Service is a major revenue-producing agency whose primary functions are to assess and collect duties and taxes on imported merchandise, to control imports and exports, and to combat smuggling and Customs revenue frauds. The member of the Customs Service team responsible for meeting these objectives is the Import Specialist. Import Specialists enforce regulations of the U.S. Customs Service through the precise examination, classification, and appraisal of imported merchandise. Guided by federal revenue laws, they translate the language of trade into the legal terms of Customs regulations. As required by import regulations, they examine and appraise merchandise and accompanying documentation based on such factors as legal restrictions, country of origin, import quotas, and current market values. Next, Import Specialists perform the critical task of determining the unit value of the merchandise—often a difficult task—when calculating the amount of money due the government. They interview importers or their representatives and, after a thorough check of import entry documents, make certain that the imports match the description contained in itemized lists. They classify merchandise according to U.S. tariff schedules and determine the exact duties and taxes payable to U.S. Customs.

In some instances, Import Specialists detect serious problems or violations related to import shipments. They may then call for a formal inquiry by Customs Special Agents or may notify agents of other government agencies responsible for import inspections. Examples of such situations include evidence of intent to cheat the government of the United States and violations of copyright, trademark, and marking laws that apply to specified products in international trade. Once the importer meets all the various U.S. Customs requirements, Import Specialists issue the permits authorizing the release of merchandise for delivery within the United States. Importers who fail to obey U.S. Customs requirements are denied these permits until they qualify under Customs law. In cases in which merchandise is seized by U.S. Customs personnel or is left unclaimed, Import Specialists appraise its value before its sale at public auctions.

As a result of ongoing training and experience gained on the job, Import Specialists develop technical expertise in specific categories of merchandise such as wines and spirits, electronic equipment, and industrial machinery. In addition, they must keep up with ever-changing tariff regulations. As a means of keeping their expertise current, they physically examine selected commodity shipments at arrival points, importers' premises, and industry trade exhibitions. The professional judgment of Import Specialists is of special importance to international trade experts, importers, and customhouse brokers who rely on the Specialists to authorize the lowest allowable duties on merchandise to encourage legitimate international trade. Import Specialists may be called upon to provide technical assistance to the Department of Justice in defending the U.S. government's position in Customs cases. They assist federal attorneys in the preparation of cases for Customs Court by supplying technical information and advice and by securing qualified witnesses and evidence. They give testimony in court and may be called upon to defend merchandise appraisals during appeals proceedings requested by importers.

Working Conditions

The Customs territory of the United States is divided into nine regions made up of the 50 states, the District of Columbia, Puerto Rico, and the U.S. Virgin Islands. Import Specialists may be assigned to any of the nearly 300 ports of entry along our land and sea borders. Work stations include airports and seaports, waterfronts, border stations, and customs houses. *When possible, Import Specialists are placed in the work location of their choice.* The typical work schedule is eight hours per day, five days per week, but it *may involve weekend duty and rotating shifts.* At times, the working hours at certain stations are irregular or involve overtime hours. The fringe benefits that Import Specialists receive include overtime pay, paid vacations, and sick leave; military leave; low-cost group hospitalization, medical, and life insurance; and retirement annuities covered by the Bureau of Retirement of the Office of Personnel Management.

Promotion Opportunities

Entry-level appointments to the position of Import Specialist are made at grades GS-5 and GS-7. After a one-year probationary period, employees may achieve permanent status. Import Specialists have excellent advancement potential, with opportunities to apply for supervisory and management slots at grades GS-13 and above.

SPECIAL AGENT, CUSTOMS

Duties of the Job

The U.S. Customs Service, part of the Department of the Treasury, enforces not only its own but some 400 laws and regulations for 40 other federal agencies. Playing a crucial part in carrying out these responsibilities is a highly trained group of plainclothes investigators called Special Agents. They make certain that the government obtains revenue on incoming goods and that contraband and controlled substances, including marijuana, narcotics, and dangerous drugs, do not enter or leave the country illegally. Special Agents investigate smuggling, currency cases, criminal fraud against the revenue system, and major cargo thefts. Their targets include professionals and amateurs alike: international crime syndicates, importers undervaluing goods to avoid duties or taxes, and tourists giving false information on baggage declarations. Through investigation of individuals, of transporters, and of merchandise arriving in or departing from the United States, they protect both government and business community interests as well as the health and safety of our citizens.

Special Agents, of course, cannot function without assistance in their investigations and sometimes require the aid of other law enforcement officers. For example, information supplied by Customs Patrol Officers, Customs Import Specialists, and Customs Inspectors often eventually leads to the undoing of persons engaged in illegal acts. In addition to coordinating efforts with the Customs Service personnel, Agents also work along with representatives of other law enforcement agencies such as the Federal Bureau of Investigation, Immigration and Naturalization Service, and the Drug Enforcement Administration. Special Agents gather information from different sources including informants, public and private records, surveillance activities, and questioning of suspects. At times, other identities are assumed and work is performed undercover to collect evidence of illegal activities. In some instances, Agents make use of support services such as complex radio communications networks; Customs Dog Handlers, whose specially trained canines can detect hidden quantities of narcotics; or Customs Pilots, who patrol designated areas to detect questionable or illegal activities.

After gathering and analyzing all available facts and evidence in a case, Special Agents plan what investigative, seizure, and arrest activities should follow. These Agents have special powers of entry, search, seizure, and arrest when enforcing customs laws and regulations. They are authorized to board common carriers and search both property and people, using firearms or other means to gain access. Customs Special Agents have the broadest powers of search of any law enforcement personnel in the United States. Probable cause is not needed to justify search or seizure near a border or port of entry. Probable cause, but not a warrant, is necessary to conduct a search in the interior of the United States. In cases in which arrests take place for violations of Customs laws, Special Agents play an active role in starting criminal or civil proceedings along with seizing contraband, vehicles, aircraft, or seacraft suspected of carrying smuggled merchandise. They write detailed reports of all facts and evidence gathered during investigations and assist prosecuting attorneys in readying cases for prosecution. Special Agents are frequently called upon to testify for the prosecution during court proceedings. In addition, they investigate applications for duty refunds to determine whether they are legitimate, and they make recommendations regarding increases or reductions in penalty payments owed to the U.S. Customs Service.

Working Conditions

The Customs territory of the United States consists of the 50 states, the District of Columbia, Puerto Rico, and the U.S. Virgin Islands. Special Agents are generally assigned to any of the nearly 300 ports of entry as well as land and sea borders in these areas, but some are given overseas assignments. Agents *often work shifts and weekends in excess of 40 hours a week* and *may be required to travel* during investigations. *At some point in their career, relocation to other work stations may also be required.* Persons considering this career should note that *hazardous duty,* working under stress, and the risk of physical injury are typical conditions of this work. The fringe benefits of work as a Special Agent include paid vacation and sick leave, low-cost group hospitalization plans, low-cost life insurance plans, military service leave, and a retirement plan covered by the Bureau of Retirement of the Office of Personnel Management.

Promotion Opportunities

Entry-level appointments from the TEA register are made at grades GS-5 and GS-7. Applicants with sufficient specialized law enforcement experience or education should establish eligibility on the Mid-Level Register for appointment at grades GS-9, GS-11, and GS-12. Positions offer extensive opportunities for paid overtime and have excellent advancement potential, with slots at GS-13 and above available on a competitive basis to those who qualify.

U.S. PARK POLICE OFFICER

U.S. Park Police Officers serve as law enforcement officers at a number of urban federal parks. U.S. Park Police Officers have arrest authority under Federal law. In addition, they have state arrest powers within and outside of federal parks.

Working Conditions

U.S. Park Police Officers are assigned to patrol federal parklands in San Francisco and in Washington, D.C. All other U.S. Park Police Officers are located in the New York City area at the Statue of Liberty, the Ellis Island National Monument, and the Gateway National Recreation Area in Brooklyn, Queens, and Staten Island.

Along with excellent pay ranging from $29,082 to $48,553 as of 1995, U.S. Park Police Officers earn a 10 percent premium for night work, a 25 percent premium for Sundays, and a full range of federal benefits.

DEPUTY U.S. MARSHAL

The Judiciary Act of 1789 authorized creation of the federal court system and, with it, the office of U.S. Marshal. As officers of the court, U.S. Marshals became responsible for carrying out the orders of federal courts. In the early years of the nation, and particularly in the frontier areas of the West, U.S. Marshals and Deputy U.S. Marshals faced the difficult task of executing their duties as federal peace officers under hostile and often dangerous conditions. Most Americans are familiar with historical accounts describing the hardships, adventures, and heroics of these officers. Since the first 13 U.S. Marshals were appointed, duties of the office have broadened to a substantial degree. Today, 94 Marshals appointed by the President of the United States direct the complex work activities of Deputy U.S. Marshals in each of the U.S. Judicial Districts.

Duties of the Job

Under the direction of U.S. Marshals, Deputy U.S. Marshals perform a variety of duties, primarily of a law enforcement nature. Deputies are charged with primary responsibility for providing security to the federal courts and for ensuring the personal safety of judges, jurors, and attorneys as well as the physical security of court buildings and facilities. They remove disorderly spectators from court premises and, in some cases, repel attempted attacks by intruders during federal judicial proceedings. During crucial court cases, Deputies conduct surveys of federal court buildings to determine the adequacy of security and, where necessary, recommend the use of fixed and mobile security units. Specially trained Deputies furnish 24-hour protection to federal judges and their immediate families when threats, whether real or apparent, are made as a result of decisions rendered by the court. The Marshals Service has primary responsibility for investigating violations of certain federal fugitive statutes. Deputies perform investigative duties in the execution of arrest warrants for federal probation, parole, mandatory release, and bond default violators and in the apprehension of federal escapees. Under the Organized Crime Act of 1970, the U.S. Marshals Service provides protection to state and federal witnesses who testify for the government in cases against organized crime. The protection of these witnesses, and members of their families whose lives may be jeopardized by court testimony, can extend from the initial court appearance through the completion of the trial and includes the use of modern electronic communication and security equipment. Deputy U.S. Marshals have the added responsibility of maintaining custody of federal prisoners from the time of arrest to their sentencing or release from confinement. They also transport federal prisoners between court and prison facilities as directed by legal warrants and the Bureau of Prisons.

The Marshals Service also performs specialized law enforcement functions for the U.S. Attorney General. The service's Special Operations Group (SOG) is frequently called upon to perform such tasks. A specially trained mobile force of Deputy U.S. Marshals, SOG's mission is to provide swift federal assistance in emergency situations that have national impact such as terrorist activities, major civil disturbances, riots, and mob violence situations. Membership in the elite SOG is part-time work and is purely voluntary. Normally, only one out of every two persons who apply will be accepted for the program. To be eligible, Deputies must be in superb physical condition and must successfully complete the special operations training course. The SOG furnishes backup support to U.S. Marshals in the various judicial districts. It can assemble a fully operational force anywhere in the United States within a period of six hours. The duties require physical stamina to resist assaults, repel unruly crowds, or subdue and arrest lawbreakers. Deputies must also be capable of running considerable distances to reach emergency scenes, enduring extended exposure to varying types of weather conditions, and standing for extended periods of time. In addition to these activities, Deputy U.S. Marshals carry out their traditional duty of serving a variety of civil writs and criminal warrants issued by federal courts. Their assignments may involve seizing and disposing of property according to court orders or performing other special enforcement duties as directed by federal decree or by the U.S. Department of Justice. In executing their responsibilities, Deputies deal with persons from all levels of society and apply extensive knowledge of federal and state laws under which they have jurisdiction. They are further responsible for the custody and control of property, money, and evidence confiscated under federal law.

Working Conditions

Positions for Deputy U.S. Marshal are located in the 94 U.S. Judicial Districts of the U.S. Marshals Service centered in the 50 states, the District of Columbia, Puerto Rico, and the Virgin Islands. For the most part, jobs are located in or near larger metropolitan areas. Openings that occur outside of the 48 contiguous states (Alaska, Hawaii, Puerto Rico, Virgin Islands) are filled by residents of those areas. Newly hired Deputy Marshals must be willing to accept an *initial assignment to any duty location* and must be available for *transfer to different work locations* based on the needs of the U.S. Marshals Service. This work involves *frequent travel for extended periods of time* as well as *irregular work schedules and overtime.* It also may involve *personal risk,* working under both physical and mental stress, and the possibility of physical injury during the performance of duties. Fringe benefits of this work include paid vacation and holidays, sick leave, overtime pay, low-cost medical and life insurance, injury compensation, and a retirement pension. Deputy U.S. Marshals with 20 years of law enforcement service may retire at age 50 if they so choose.

Promotion Opportunities

All Deputy U.S. Marshals enter the service at grade GS-5. Once appointed, they may progress to the GS-9 level. Positions above this level are filled through service-wide competition. These higher-level jobs often require reassignment to another district at government expense.

POSTAL POLICE OFFICER

A Postal Police Officer provides a full range of security services at major post offices and at other postal installations and facilities. The Postal Police Officer may work inside postal buildings or outdoors at loading docks and in parking lots. A Postal Police Officer may be armed.

Duties of the Job

Postal Police Officers perform all the functions of municipal police officers but within the limited jurisdiction of postal property. Their assignments tend to be concentrated in and near population centers where postal buildings are large and heavily trafficked and where many postal vehicles are garaged and dispatched.

Within postal buildings, Postal Police Officers maintain security against ordinary hazards and sabotage. They assist postal patrons and employees in giving simple directions and when called upon in cases of accident or emergency. While security against fraud within the postal community is the province of Postal Inspectors, Postal Police protect the mails and postal resources against theft.

In other postal facilities—garages, warehouses, equipment repair shops—Postal Police provide the full range of security services, guarding against burglary, hijacking, and other illegal acts.

As the nature of criminals and their crimes has become more sophisticated, the work of the Postal Police Officer has become more complex, more challenging, and more dangerous.

Working Conditions

Full-time employees work an eight-hour day, five days a week. Both full-time and part-time employees who work more than eight hours a day or 40 hours a week receive overtime pay of one-and-one-half times their hourly rate. In addition, pay is higher for those on the night shift.

Postal employees earn 13 days of annual leave (vacation) during each of their first three years of service including prior federal civilian and military service, 20 days each year for three to 15 years of service, and 26 days after 15 years. In addition, they earn 13 days of paid sick leave a year regardless of length of service.

Other benefits include retirement and survivorship annuities, free group life insurance, and optional participation in health insurance programs supported in part by the Postal Service.

Promotion Opportunities

Advancement opportunities are available for most postal workers because there is a management commitment to provide career development. Also, employees can get preferred assignments, such as the day shift, as their seniority increases. When an opening occurs, employees may submit written requests, called "bids," for assignment to the vacancy. The bidder who meets the qualifications and has the most seniority gets the job.

Postal Police Officers can advance through police ranks—Sergeant, Lieutenant, Captain—in a manner similar to Municipal, County, or State Police Officers. They may also advance into the ranks of the Postal Inspection Service and become Postal Inspectors.

POSTAL INSPECTOR

Protection of the U.S. mail system is the primary mission of the Postal Inspection Service, a separate department of the U.S. Postal Service. The Inspection Service is a major federal law enforcement agency whose professional staff of Postal Inspectors carry out the security, investigative, audit, and enforcement responsibilities that keep the postal system sound and stable. It has jurisdiction in all criminal matters related to the integrity and security of the mail and the safety of all postal property, valuables, and personnel. The Inspection Service plays a key role in maintaining effective postal operations by helping establish safe and efficient systems, investigating criminal matters, and making certain that the mails are not used to encourage criminal activities.

Duties of the Job

Postal Inspectors perform a variety of duties and have jurisdiction over 85 postal-related laws. Their responsibilities can be divided into three broad areas: criminal investigations, audit investigations, and security/administrative functions.

Criminal investigations deal with illegal acts committed against the U.S. Postal Service, its property, and its personnel. The following are some examples of cases in the jurisdiction of the U.S. Postal Inspection Service: post office burglaries (robberies of postal facilities, vehicles, or mail carriers);

embezzlement by postal employees; and thefts from house, apartment, or U.S. Postal Service mailboxes. Postal Inspectors also investigate cases of fraud involving use of the U.S. mail. These acts, which cheat citizens from all walks of life, include land, charity, and advance-fee schemes; chain letters and lotteries; nonaccredited correspondence schools; and insurance, banking, and credit-card frauds. The result has been the elimination of many fraudulent or borderline operations that cheat the public.

Illegal narcotics traffic is another target of Postal Inspectors who investigate cases of suspected movement of drugs, narcotics, and other controlled substances through the U.S. mail and who work closely with other federal agents in efforts to halt such traffic. Postal Inspectors also probe incidents involving bombs or incendiary devices dispatched through the mail system or directed at properties of the U.S. Postal Service as well as investigate extortion attempts, illegal transport of concealable firearms, and obscene materials sent through the mail.

Once assigned to a case, Postal Inspectors collect, assemble, and evaluate all available data and determine a course of action. Employing professional investigative techniques, they question witnesses and victims to develop leads and identify suspects. Crime laboratory services are used to analyze certain types of evidence that may help in tracing or identifying suspects. Suspects are sometimes kept under surveillance, or stakeouts may be used to locate others involved in a case. Postal Inspectors are armed and empowered by law to apprehend, interrogate, and arrest suspects. They are also authorized to serve warrants and subpoenas to persons involved in a case. All of these powers are restricted to the enforcement of laws covering illegal use of the mail, properties of the United States in the custody of the U.S. Postal Service, or other postal offenses. However, these powers are valid even if the Postal Inspector is not on U.S. Postal Service property. Postal Inspectors make comprehensive oral and written reports of data and evidence gathered in a case and submit them to supervisory personnel for evaluation. They work closely with U.S. Attorneys in preparing and prosecuting cases and are often called upon to give testimony during court proceedings.

The next area of responsibility dealt with by Postal Inspectors involves audits, which are investigations aimed at evaluating postal operations and identifying problems within the system itself. Using thorough investigative methods, Postal Inspectors determine whether the Postal Service is operating according to postal laws and regulations and in the best interests of the public. They also determine whether postal revenues are adequately protected and used economically. The results of these audits are often beneficial: They lead to reductions in operating costs and increases in management effectiveness in such areas as customer service, mail handling, financial operations, data systems, and work methods and procedures.

Security and administrative functions make up the last area dealt with by Postal Inspectors. Background and security investigations of designated personnel make certain that postal service standards are met. Effectiveness of fire, safety, and security systems used in postal facilities are evaluated, and surveys are conducted to determine whether improvements can be introduced. In cases of disaster such as floods, fires, and air or train wrecks, Postal Inspectors direct activities of mobile response units composed of postal security personnel responsible for recovering mail and providing security against theft or looting.

Working Conditions

People considering this career area must be willing to accept certain basic features of the work. *Initial work assignments are not made in the applicant's locality,* and the individual *must be willing to accept an appointment wherever the greatest need is at any time throughout his or her career.* Because Postal Inspectors must respond to emergency situations, they are *subject to call at any time and often work irregular hours.* In addition, the work involves a substantial amount of *travel and time away from home.* In extreme cases, Postal Inspectors may remain on extended duty but are *not eligible for overtime, night differential, or other types of premium pay.* However, in the absence of special circumstances, they are assigned customary work schedules. Postal Inspectors often work under *stressful and hazardous conditions* and may be subject to physical injuries during the seizure and arrest of suspects. The fringe benefits of Postal Inspectors include paid vacations and sick leave, job security, and life and health insurance benefits. Postal Inspectors with 20 years of investigative work experience are eligible to retire at age 50.

Promotion Opportunities

Postal Inspectors are appointed at EAS-17 with nearly automatic promotion to EAS-21 within two-and-a-half years. Further promotion is possible to Specialist at EAS-23 and Team Leader at EAS-24. In addition, Postal Inspectors receive a cost-of-living allowance and are eligible for merit increases.

The advancement potential for Postal Inspectors is excellent, and those who qualify can compete for promotions to supervisory or administrative positions.

U.S. SECRET SERVICE UNIFORMED DIVISION OFFICER

The U.S. Secret Service Uniformed Division was begun in 1922. In September of that year, the Congress of the United States, at the urging of the President, authorized the creation of a uniformed security unit to be known as the White House Police Force, working under the supervision of the President's military aide. In 1930, supervision was transferred to the Director of the Secret Service. This force was given the responsibility of protecting the President and his family when in residence at the White House and maintaining security for the Executive Mansion and grounds in the District of Columbia or any buildings in which White House offices are located. In 1970, the name of this police force was changed to the Executive Protective Service. Its staff was increased, and it was given the added responsibility of maintaining security at the foreign diplomatic missions located in the Washington, D.C., metropolitan area. In November 1977, President Carter signed into law a bill that changed the name of the Executive Protective Service to its present title of U.S. Secret Service Uniformed Division.

Duties of the Job

Currently, the Secret Service Uniformed Division is composed of two main sections: the White House and Foreign Missions branches. Officers assigned to the White House branch help protect the President and family members, provide security throughout the White House complex, and safeguard other locations housing presidential offices. Officers in the Foreign Missions branch provide protection and security for foreign diplomatic missions located in the District of Columbia or in any areas of our nation, its territories, or possessions specified by order of the President. In addition, Uniformed Division Officers help protect the Vice President and family members as well as their official residence in Washington, D.C.

Vital functions carried out by the Uniformed Division Officers are continuous—24 hours a day, seven days a week. They are authorized to enforce all laws related to their protective responsibilities. To carry out their assignments in an effective manner, these officers employ sound professional law enforcement practices. They engage in continuous patrol activities on foot or in mobile units such as motorbikes or automobiles, according to the nature and location of their duty posts. During these patrols, they thoroughly check the security of buildings, grounds, and alarm systems. Some Uniformed Division Officers are assigned to fixed security posts rather than continuous patrol. Such posts may be points of entry or exit at foreign embassies or in the White House complex. Officers examine visitors' credentials, prevent unauthorized entry or exit, and maintain order within their assigned areas.

Uniformed Division Officers are fully trained for all types of assignments and are ready to respond to a variety of situations. For example, in cases of bomb threats, the delivery of suspicious parcels, or suspected intruders on government or embassy properties, the Uniformed Division may call in canine teams to assist in solving the problem. These dogs and their Uniformed Division handlers are skilled in methods of search, scouting, and apprehension as well as in the techniques of detecting explosive devices, whether real or false. In certain instances, the Secret Service Uniformed Division, at the request of the U.S. State Department, assigns officers to duty at foreign embassy functions to provide extra security and to direct traffic control activities. Uniformed Division Officers have full authority to detain, search, and arrest individuals suspected of breaking laws falling within the jurisdiction of the U.S. Secret Service. This includes use of firearms and physical force if the situation justifies. However, the Secret Service Uniformed Division does not routinely enforce laws outside its jurisdiction, leaving such matters to the local police department or appropriate federal law enforcement agencies. In addition to their law enforcement and security activities, Uniformed Division Officers, upon request, speak before foreign embassy personnel to describe in detail the administration, purposes, and jurisdiction of the Uniformed Division of the U.S. Secret Service.

Working Conditions

Officers of the Uniformed Division are *generally assigned to work locations in the metropolitan areas of Washington, D.C.* At times, however, assignments may be made to other areas of the United States, its territories, or possessions, according to presidential directive. Officers must be available for weekend duty and *rotating shifts* and may be required to work in excess of 40 hours a week. They often perform their duties under *stress* and are subject to potential *physical hazards* throughout their careers. The fringe benefits Uniformed Division Officers receive include paid vacation and sick leave, paid holidays, *free uniforms and equipment,* overtime pay, low-cost medical and life insurance, retirement credits for prior military or federal civilian service, and retirement pension after 20 years of service.

Promotion Opportunities

The U.S. Secret Service Uniformed Division offers its officers favorable career-development prospects and provides opportunities for participation in advanced in-service training programs. Officers who exhibit the desire and competence to engage in more complex assignments can compete for supervisory or higher-level positions.

SECRET SERVICE SPECIAL AGENT

Duties of the Job

The primary responsibility of the Secret Service is protection of the President of the United States. In addition, Special Agents are authorized by law to protect the Vice President, the immediate families of the President and Vice President, the President-elect and Vice President-elect and their immediate families, a former President and his wife during their lifetime, the widow of a former President until her death or remarriage, minor children of a former President until age 16, major Presidential and Vice Presidential candidates, and visiting heads of foreign governments.

The protective measures used by the U.S. Secret Service are, for the most part, basically the same for all individuals being safeguarded. When Special Agents are assigned to protect a particular person, their first task is to plan, organize, and put into effect security arrangements well in advance of the person's arrival. These advance agents and other agency staff work closely with the Special Agent in charge of the district field office in devising all of the projected security arrangements. These arrangements are never exactly alike and depend on such factors as the identity and number of persons to be protected; the time, location, and length of visits; and the itinerary and methods of transportation. Creation of security perimeters, for example, is a vital element in security operations. This blanket security results from the work of advance teams of Special Agents who thoroughly inspect the area and determine the manpower and equipment needed to carry out the assignment. These security arrangements may include the use of police patrols on the streets parallel to, adjacent to, or with access to the route to be taken, or the deployment of helicopters for surveillance purposes. If the person being protected is traveling on or near water routes, U.S. Coast Guard and police patrol craft are used. Special Agents assigned to advance-team duty are also responsible for briefing and assigning personnel to duty posts and for selecting sites, such as hospitals, evacuation routes, and relocation areas, to be used in emergency situations.

Special Agents assigned to protective duty receive essential support from the Intelligence Division of the Secret Service. Intelligence Agents provide this support by collecting, evaluating, storing, and distributing protective-security information to Agents responsible for protection activities. Agents assigned to intelligence activities gather much of their information by developing and maintaining contacts with state and local law enforcement agencies as well as with such federal agencies as the Federal Bureau of Investigation, Central Intelligence Agency, Treasury Department, Department of State, Department of Defense, Drug Enforcement Administration, U.S. Postal Service, and General Services Administration. Some examples of information sought by Intelligence Agents from law enforcement agencies and concerned citizens include facts about individuals who advocate the violent overthrow of our government; persons or groups making direct threats against or displaying intent to harm anyone under Secret Service protection; persons with a history of violent behavior, grudges, or strong grievances against public officials; and activities of persons or groups who advocate interference with, harassment of, or harm to public officials. However, the Secret Service does not seek information about individuals or groups voicing legitimate criticism of or opposition to government policies or public officials. In addition, Special Agents involved with intelligence gathering are responsible for overseeing electronic-security operations and keeping current with new developments in security measures.

Prior to the arrival of the person under protection, the Secret Service conducts detailed briefings of all staff involved with the assignment. The subject areas covered at these meetings include work locations and areas of responsibility, protective-intelligence data, contingency plans, and the official identification methods to be used by agency personnel during the assignment. Security operations during each protective assignment are coordinated and controlled by Secret Service personnel in a central command post. This post functions as a vantage point and communications center in which intelligence data and orders are received and sent to Special Agents on protective details. Special Agents assigned to the permanent Secret Service detail that protects the President have a difficult and complicated mission. While charged with providing the Chief Executive with maximum protection, they have the impossible task of guarding against all the perils that can develop, particularly when national or international travel is involved. Presidents are often reluctant to follow any security measures that hinder their work activities or limit their contact with the general public. Providing maximum security without affecting the President's customary routine makes the work of these Special Agents a complex and challenging assignment.

In addition to their protective responsibilities, Special Agents of the Secret Service have investigative functions as well. They investigate all cases that involve counterfeiting of U.S. currency and securities and forgery of U.S. government checks, bonds, and securities. In most instances, these are stolen items that fail to reach the payees and are forged and cashed by the thieves. Each year, Special Agents seize and arrest thousands of people engaging in such illegal activities.

Regardless of the type of case assigned, Special Agents, working alone or in teams, collect and evaluate all the available data from other law enforcement agencies, informants, and the general public and plan the conduct of the investigation. They interview witnesses and suspects to obtain useful information and evidence in the case. When necessary, they work undercover, keep suspects under surveillance, and use court-approved listening devices to gather evidence and uncover others involved in the case. After gathering and analyzing all available data and evidence, Special Agents determine what investigative, arrest, and/or seizure activities are in order. When the evidence indicates, they seize, search, arrest, and take suspects into custody, as authorized by appropriate legal warrants. They carry out these activities in teams or as part of a group of agents conducting raids on suspected establishments. Special Agents are highly skilled in the use of various types of firearms as well as in hand-to-hand defensive tactics, and they use these skills as needed when apprehending suspects. Agents prepare detailed, written reports of all cases in which they take part and assist U.S. Attorneys in the preparation of cases for trial. They are also called upon to give court testimony in cases in which they participated.

Working Conditions

The Secret Service has district field offices throughout the United States; its headquarters are in Washington, D.C. Special Agents may be *assigned to work locations anywhere in the United States* and *travel frequently* while performing their duties. In addition, they are usually *subject to transfers and work reassignments throughout their careers.* Agents must be available for assignments at any time and *often work more than 40 hours per week.* They work under *stress* and are exposed to *potential physical harm* during the course of their protective or investigative duties. The fringe benefits for which Special Agents are eligible include low-cost medical and life insurance, financial protection in the event of job-related injury or death, paid vacations, sick leave, overtime pay, and retirement annuities. Agents with 20 years of service may retire at age 50. Retirement is mandatory at age 55.

Promotion Opportunities

Secret Service Special Agents start at grade GS-5 or GS-7. The advancement prospects of Special Agents are quite favorable, and those who demonstrate the ability to assume greater responsibilities are eligible to compete for supervisory or higher-level positions.

OTHER OPTIONS

We have described a representative sampling of federal law enforcement positions, but there are many other opportunities available. To learn about the many specialized federal law enforcement careers, read Arco's *Federal Jobs in Law Enforcement.*

PART

THREE

How to Qualify

CONTENTS

HOW TO QUALIFY

Each city or town, each county, each state, and each federal agency sets its own standards for the law enforcement officers it employs. The only requirements that *all* federal and almost all state and local jurisdictions have in common are United States citizenship and a high school education.

Beyond these two basics are many variations. Some jobs require an associate's or bachelor's degree; others require graduate or professional degrees. Some require specific training or expertise. For some positions, a certain number of years of experience in a related field is necessary.

Not only do education and experience requirements vary, medical and physical requirements differ as well. Some law enforcement positions may be filled by the handicapped; others require perfect vision and excellent hearing. Some law enforcement positions require demonstration of physical strength, agility, and endurance; others do not.

For some law enforcement positions, you must pass a written examination before you can be admitted to the training program. For many federal positions, not only those with the Treasury Department, this exam will be the Treasury Enforcement Agent Examination. Other federal agencies devise their own exams or require none at all. Most state and local law enforcement agencies have developed their own exams.

All these requirements lead the applicant to qualify for training, not for the job itself. All law enforcement agencies offer some sort of training to new recruits. This training may be given in a formal school setting or may consist of on-the-job training in the form of an apprenticeship. The training period is always followed by a period of supervised probation, generally ranging from one to three years. Only after the new law enforcement officer has successfully completed training and has worked effectively through this probationary period will he or she receive a permanent appointment to the force.

Because of the variations, we will go through the positions one by one as we did in the preceding section, detailing the requirements, training, and probationary period for each.

Important Note: If you are a veteran of the United States Armed Forces, be sure to make this fact known. Veterans receive some form of employment preference when they apply for *any* government position—local, state, or federal. The veteran's preference sometimes takes the form of points added to the examination score. For some positions, the maximum age of entry is raised by the number of years served. Service-connected disability, if it is not disqualifying for the job, can add still more weight to the application. Even if your experience in the Armed Forces was such that it cannot be counted toward the experience requirements of the position, be sure you get credit for the very fact of that service.

Local Positions

POLICE OFFICER

Entry requirements for Police Officers vary to a certain degree among police agencies throughout the country. As a rule, however, applicants must be U.S. citizens between the ages of 20 and 35 at the time of appointment to service. Time served in the military is usually deducted from a candidate's chronological age in meeting the upper age requirement. Most police agencies require completion of high school or its equivalent as the educational minimum, although some insist on completion of a specified number of college credits and, in some instances, a college degree. Secondary and postsecondary courses helpful in preparing for police work include government, English, psychology, sociology, American history, physics, and foreign languages. In addition, more than 1,000 junior colleges, colleges, and universities offer programs in police science or criminal justice. The vast majority of police agencies in the United

States operate under civil service systems and select candidates accordingly. Candidates must pass a competitive examination and obtain a qualifying rating on an interview conducted by senior police officers. Each applicant must pass a comprehensive medical examination, which in some agencies includes psychological and psychiatric evaluations to determine emotional stability and acceptability for police work. Performance tests designed to gauge strength, agility, and stamina must be passed, and departmental standards with regard to height, weight, and eyesight must also be met. Because good judgment and a sense of responsibility are essential in police work, a thorough background investigation is conducted to assess general character, past history, honesty, and general suitability for this work. As a rule, possession of a valid driver's license is also required prior to employment by the police agency. Meeting the preceding requirements is the typical way of beginning a police career. In some localities, however, young high school graduates or law enforcement students in college can enter this field as police cadets or interns. These individuals, hired as paid civilian employees of the police agency, perform nonenforcement duties and attend classes to learn basic police skills. Those who successfully complete this type of program and meet the basic entry requirements for Police Officer may be appointed to the regular force at age 21.

Newly hired Police Officers enter training on a probationary basis prior to being assigned to duty. Programs vary widely with regard to length and content. In small departments, there is less formal instruction and a greater degree of on-the-job training as a means of developing skills. In large police agencies, formalized programs of instruction are the rule and may last from several weeks to six months, depending on department policy and availability of training facilities. Newly hired officers receive instruction in a variety of subjects including criminal law; motor vehicle codes; arrest, search, and seizure procedures; constitutional law; civil rights, methods of patrol, surveillance, and communications; traffic control; accident investigation; laws of evidence; crime prevention and criminal investigation procedures; pursuit driving; armed and unarmed defense tactics; use of various types of firearms; physical conditioning; crowd control; first aid; community relations; preparation of reports; court procedures; use of legal warrants; police ethics; and departmental regulations. Some departments combine this formal training with field experience to reinforce concepts learned in the classroom.

Following the completion of training, new officers are assigned to work under the supervision of an experienced officer. The experienced officers with whom probationary officers are teamed provide them with practical instruction and field experience and evaluate their work performance from time to time during the probationary period. Probation may last from a year to 18 months, after which the new officer becomes a permanent member of the force.

POLICE DETECTIVE

"Detective" is a promotional title in most police agencies; in some, however, this job is at the same grade and salary level as a Police Officer. Regardless, the job of Detective has status within police circles, and competition for openings is always keen. Opportunities for entry into the job vary, depending on the size of the department.

Detectives in most local, county, and state police agencies are selected internally from the ranks of Police Officers who meet specific requirements. The duties and varied problems encountered on patrol are considered to provide a sound training ground for investigative work. The basic requirements for this work usually include a minimum of three years' experience as a uniformed Police Officer, demonstrated investigative talent, and in some agencies, the completion of a specified number of college credits. Police executives sometimes assign Police Officers with demonstrated investigative skills to detective work without a written examination. Others administer departmental examinations to aid in the selection process; still others are required to use civil service examinations. The personal qualifications for this job are hard to gauge, but most successful Detectives are energetic, patient, persistent, imaginative, and show initiative. In addition, they are streetwise, able to reason logically, and able to retain information and exercise sound judgment in reaching conclusions about people and events. These are the qualities that police executives look for when interviewing and evaluating candidates for this position.

Most new Detectives receive formal instruction in a police training facility. Length of training varies among departments throughout the country and can range from two weeks to a few months or more. Where formal training is not available, candidates are trained on the job. Whether the training is formal, on the job, or a combination of both, new Detectives are instructed in most or all of the following: criminal and civil law; local laws and ordinances; rules of evidence; courtroom procedures; warrant and subpoena procedures; media relations; investigation techniques; analysis of crime scenes; collecting, recording, and analyzing information; collection, preparation, classification, and use of fingerprints; police photography; capabilities of crime laboratories; methods of interrogation and interview; surveillance and undercover methods; information sources and informants; and identification of suspects by witnesses or victims. In progressive police departments, Detectives continue to receive periodic in-service training. Detectives with special assignments, such as arson/bomb disposal or narcotics, receive additional intensive training to develop skills in these areas.

Even if they have already served as permanent members of a police force, newly trained Detectives serve a period of probation under their new titles before being permanently appointed as Police Detectives.

County Positions

DEPUTY SHERIFF

The entry requirements for Deputy Sheriffs vary significantly among counties throughout the country. Generally, however, candidates must be U.S. citizens between the ages of 21 and 29 at the time of appointment. In most cases, time spent in military service can be deducted from the candidate's chronological age in meeting the upper age limit. Most sheriff's agencies require completion of high school as the educational minimum, but increasing numbers are asking for college credits as well. Courses considered useful in preparing for police work include civics, sociology, government, English, history, science, and language study. The selection and employment of Deputy Sheriffs is controlled by established regulations or programs that differ from one county to another. Among these regulations are state and county civil service laws, merit board regulations, and formal work agreements or contracts. Each is unique but usually involves some kind of test-selection activity, whether written or oral, or an evaluation of prior work experience. In addition to meeting prescribed physical requirements (including standards of height, weight, and vision), candidates must also pass a comprehensive medical examination that may also include psychological evaluation. All candidates undergo a thorough background investigation to determine past history, character, stability, and general suitability for law enforcement work. Possession of a valid driver's license is necessary to appointment to a sheriff's agency.

Newly hired Deputies receive some type of formal training before being assigned to duty, but there are wide differences in its length and extent among the various sheriffs' departments around the country. Deputies in large agencies are likely to enter training academies where programs range from two to six months in length. Those in smaller agencies may not receive such formal training but, where possible, may be sent to state or municipal training academies at a future time to develop their skills further. Regardless of how or where the training takes place, Deputies usually receive instruction in such subjects as criminal law; arrest, search, and seizure procedures; methods of patrol, surveillance, and communications; accident prevention and traffic control; motor vehicle codes; laws of evidence; crime prevention and criminal investigation procedures; pursuit driving; methods of self-defense; use of various types of firearms; crowd control; first aid; community relations; preparation of reports; agency regulations; and police ethics. After training is successfully completed, candidates are placed on probation for a period ranging from six to 18 months, depending on agency policy. They are assigned to work with experienced Deputies and, when skilled enough to work independently, are hired on a permanent basis.

State Positions

STATE POLICE OFFICER/STATE TROOPER

Candidates for the position of State Police Officer are selected according to civil service regulations that vary from state to state. Generally, applicants must be U.S. citizens between the ages of 21 and 29 at the time of appointment; service in the military may be deducted from the candidate's chronological age in meeting this requirement. As a rule, most state police agencies demand completion of high school or its equivalent, but persons with college training have a distinct advantage. Secondary and postsecondary courses considered useful in preparing for this work include government, English, psychology, geography, American history, physics, chemistry, and foreign languages. It is necessary to receive a passing mark on a written civil service examination as well as a qualifying rating on an interview conducted by a police board of examiners. The board evaluates candidates for such factors as verbal communication skills, tact, physical appearance, and the ability to exercise sound judgment. Each applicant must pass a comprehensive medical examination, and some state police agencies require candidates to undergo psychological and psychiatric testing to determine emotional stability and suitability for this work. In addition to meeting the physical requirements (including standards of height, weight, and vision), applicants are given performance tests designed to measure strength, agility, and stamina. A thorough background investigation is also made to determine general character, honesty, past history, and overall suitability for the job. Finally, possession of a valid driver's license is necessary prior to employment by the state police agency.

Candidates who meet all the entry requirements of the state police agency are placed on a certified civil service list of eligibles and are selected from this list as vacancies occur. The annual number of openings for this work varies within each state and is dependent on such factors as budget limitations and legislative actions.

When a number of vacancies occur or appear to be imminent, a group of prospective State Police Officers is selected from the civil service list. These recruits enter training school on a probationary basis. They must complete an intensive training program of approximately 12 to 16 weeks. Instruction is given in a variety of subjects such as criminal law; state motor vehicle codes; laws of evidence, arrest, search, and seizure; methods of patrol, surveillance, and communications; arrest, search, and seizure procedures; accident prevention and traffic control; crime prevention and criminal investigation methods; police ethics; pursuit and defensive driving; armed and unarmed defense tactics; use of various types of firearms; physical conditioning; safety education; first aid; community relations; photography; written and oral communications; and agency rules and regulations. Candidates who successfully conclude this training are assigned to duty on a probationary basis for a period ranging from six months to one year or longer, depending on state police policy. They work with experienced troopers until they are skilled enough to function independently and receive permanent employment status after completing a probationary period.

Some state police agencies have cadet programs for high school graduates under the age of 21 who are interested in a law enforcement career. They work as civilian employees performing nonenforcement duties but also receive instruction in the various facets of police work. Some of these cadets attend colleges offering programs in law enforcement and criminal justice as preparation for a police career. Cadets who successfully complete this program may receive an appointment as State Police Officer upon reaching the age of 21.

Federal Positions

BUREAU OF ALCOHOL, TOBACCO, AND FIREARMS INSPECTOR

Candidates for the position of BATF Inspector must be U.S. citizens and be at least 18 years old. Basic requirements for this position are a bachelor's degree from a four-year college or university, three years of relevant work experience, or credentials as a Certified Public Accountant (CPA). Education beyond the high school level may be substituted for work experience at the rate of one year of study for nine months of experience. Applicants must earn a competitive score above 70 on the Administrative Careers with America (ACWA) exam. This exam, while no longer part of a centralized Office of Personnel hiring program, is administered by the Office of Personnel Management (OPM) for the benefit of the Bureau of Alcohol, Tobacco, and Firearms to assist in the selection of BATF Inspectors. Possession of a valid driver's license is also necessary. When the requirements are met, the applicant's name is placed on a certified list of eligibles by the Office of Personnel Management. Candidates selected from this list by the Bureau of Alcohol, Tobacco, and Firearms undergo a qualifying medical examination to determine physical and mental fitness and freedom from any conditions that would prevent performance of normal work activities. Finally, a background investigation is conducted to determine the candidate's suitability for this work.

Newly hired BATF Inspectors undergo intensive training during their first year. This 12-month program combines one month of classroom instruction with on-the-job training by experienced inspection personnel. The program of study includes such areas as bureau rules and regulations; inspection methods and procedures; report writing; legal procedures; federal laws that regulate the production, storage, processing, packaging, labeling, importation, exportation, distribution, and advertising of distilled spirits, wine, and beer; and federal statutes pertaining to firearms and explosives. After successful completion of the first year of training, new BATF Inspectors gradually assume more responsibilities until they are able to work independently.

BUREAU OF ALCOHOL, TOBACCO, AND FIREARMS SPECIAL AGENT

Applicants for the job of BATF Special Agent must be U.S. citizens between the ages of 21 and 37 at the time of appointment to duty. Other requirements include a bachelor's degree in a field of major study from an accredited college or university or three years of work experience including at least two years of criminal investigation activity. In some cases, academic study beyond the high school level may be substituted for work requirements at the rate of one year of study for nine months of specialized experience. In addition, applicants must get a qualifying score of at least 70 on the Treasury Enforcement Agent Examination. Individuals who have completed accredited courses in police science or police administration may have extra points added to their qualifying score on this examination. Those who qualify are placed on a certified list of eligible candidates. *Persons with the highest scores* are then further evaluated by personnel of the Bureau of Alcohol, Tobacco, and Firearms. Extensive panel interviews take place, during which ratings are given for such factors as appearance, poise, communication skills, interpersonal skills, and analytical ability. A qualifying medical examination determines physical and mental fitness for normal work and training activities. Distant vision without correction must test at least 20/40 in each eye. No waiver on these requirements will be granted. Weight must be in proportion to height. Finally, a comprehensive background investigation of each candidate is made to assess general character, honesty, stability, and overall suitability for this position.

Newly hired Special Agents enter an intensive training and development program that provides the special knowledge and skills demanded by the Bureau of Alcohol, Tobacco, and Firearms. The program combines classroom study with closely supervised on-the-job training. New Agents first receive about eight weeks of intensive training at the consolidated Federal Law Enforcement Training Center in Georgia. This general program of study includes subject areas such as use of firearms, methods of self-defense, arrest and surveillance techniques, undercover operations, courtroom procedures, rules of evidence, scientific investigative devices, techniques of investigation, and bureau rules and regulations. Later, new Special Agents enter the Special Agents Basic School where they receive specialized instruction related to their responsibilities. Courses are given in firearms and explosives identification and nomenclature, search techniques at bomb scenes, illegal liquor and tobacco investigations, case report preparation, and federal laws enforced by the Bureau of Alcohol, Tobacco, and Firearms. After successfully completing training, new Special Agents are assigned to BATF field offices where they work under the guidance of experienced BATF Special Agents.

DRUG ENFORCEMENT ADMINISTRATION SPECIAL AGENT

Candidates for appointment at the GS-7 level must present three years of general experience and one year of specialized experience. General experience must have been progressively responsible experience that required the ability to work and deal effectively with individuals or groups of persons, skill in collecting and assembling pertinent facts, the ability to prepare clear and concise reports, and the ability and willingness to accept responsibility. Specialized experience must have been progressively responsible criminal investigative experience or comparable experience that demonstrated the initiative, ingenuity, resourcefulness, and judgment required to collect, assemble, and develop facts and other pertinent data; the ability to think logically and objectively, to analyze and evaluate facts, evidence, and related information, and to arrive at sound conclusions; skill in written and oral reports and presentation of investigative findings in a clear and concise manner; and the tact, discretion, and capacity for obtaining the cooperation and confidence of others.

It is possible to substitute education for experience according to the following formulae:

- *General Experience:* (1) Study successfully completed in an accredited college or university may be substituted at the rate of one academic year of study for nine months' experience. Completion of all requirements for a bachelor's degree will substitute for three years of general experience. (2) Possession of a certificate as a Certified Public Accountant in a state, territory, or the District of Columbia will substitute for three years of general experience.
- *Specialized Experience:* One year of specialized experience may be substituted by completing all requirements for a bachelor's degree with any one of the following: a 2.9 grade point average (overall or in the last two years); a standing in the upper third of the class (overall or major subdivision); a 3.5 grade point average in law enforcement or related fields (overall or in the last two years); membership in a national honorary scholastic society; one academic year of graduate study.
- Three years of general experience and two years of specialized experience or completion of all requirements for a master's degree in law enforcement, police administration, or directly related fields will qualify an applicant for appointment consideration at grade GS-9.

There is *no written examination* for this position. In lieu of a written examination, applicants meeting minimum experience and/or educational substitution requirements will be evaluated on the quality of their job-related experience, education, and special skills. Competition will be on a nationwide basis. Applicants determined to be the most highly qualified will be scheduled for a panel interview. Candidates recommended for further consideration will be referred for selection consideration. Those selected from this list by the Drug Enforcement Administration are given a qualifying medical examination to determine physical and mental fitness. They must be free of any impairment that would interfere with normal work performance. Vision requirements for Special Agents are 20/40 in both eyes without glasses for distance vision and 20/20 in one eye and 20/30 in the other with glasses permitted. Candidates are further evaluated through personal interviews. They are rated for such factors as appearance, poise, and communication skills. *The physical examination and all travel for interviews are at the applicant's own expense.*

Finally, a thorough background investigation is made to determine general character, honesty, and suitability for this position. Previous infractions of the law may result in nonselection, and drug abuse in any form is disqualifying. Candidates must have a valid driver's license and be between the ages of 21 and 37.

Shortly after appointment, Special Agent trainees attend a formal 12- to 15-week training program at the Federal Law Enforcement Training Center in Glynco, Georgia. The subjects dealt with during this training period include agency rules, regulations, and procedures; use of firearms; methods of self-defense; arrest and surveillance techniques; criminal law; undercover operations; court procedures; investigation techniques; rules of evidence; criminology; drug and narcotics identification; and the use of legal warrants. After successfully concluding this program, new agents are assigned to DEA field offices where they work with experienced personnel until they can function independently. Special Agents continue to receive periodic training throughout their careers to keep them current with developments in their field of work.

FBI SPECIAL AGENT

Candidates for this position are carefully screened by the Federal Bureau of Investigation. They must be U.S. citizens between the ages of 23 and 37 and be *willing to accept assignment anywhere within the United States and Puerto Rico.* There are five entrance programs under which applicants can qualify for possible appointment to the position of Special Agent: Law, Accounting, Language, Modified, and Science. An applicant applying under the Law Program must be a graduate of a state-accredited resident law school with at least two years of resident, undergraduate college work. Those applying as Accountants must possess a four-year resident college degree with a major in accounting. Linguists must have a four-year resident college degree and fluency in a foreign language. Candidates for consideration under the Modified Program need three years of full-time work experience in addition to a four-year resident college degree, or two years of such work experience if they possess an advanced degree. Many options are available under the Science Program, and qualification is possible based on a background in such areas as electrical engineering, metallurgy, physics, chemistry, biological science, pharmacology, toxicology, and mathematics. These are not all inclusive, however, as backgrounds in business or public administration, computer science, or management information sciences or systems can also be qualifying, as can expertise as a firearms examiner, explosives examiner, or document or fingerprint examiner. As in the other programs, candidates under the Science Program must possess a resident college degree with advanced degrees or professional experience necessary in many instances. College transcripts and detailed resumés showing experience must be submitted by candidates seeking to qualify under the Science Program.

All candidates must qualify on batteries of *written and oral examinations* designed to measure emotional stability, resourcefulness, interpersonal and communication skills, and the ability to apply analytical methods to work assignments. Since Agents have to be able to use firearms and defensive tactics to participate in dangerous assignments and raids, each individual must pass a rigid physical examination; be capable of strenuous physical exertion; and have excellent hearing, eyesight, and normal color vision. In addition, before hiring, the FBI conducts an extensive background and character investigation.

Applicants who receive appointments as Special Agents undergo training at the FBI Academy located on the U.S. Marine Corps Base at Quantico, Virginia. For a period of about 15 weeks, they receive intensive training in defensive tactics, judo, and the use of various types of firearms. Thorough instruction is also given in federal criminal laws and procedures, investigative methods, fingerprinting techniques, and FBI rules and regulations. After successfully completing training, new Agents are appointed on a probationary basis. They are assigned to FBI field offices and initially team with experienced Agents under actual field conditions. After one year of satisfactory performance, they receive permanent employment status as Special Agent, FBI.

FEDERAL PROTECTIVE OFFICER

A candidate for this job must be a U.S. citizen and be at least 21 years of age at the time of appointment to duty. Exceptions may be made for veterans who are not yet 21 years old. In most cases, possession of a high school diploma or a recognized equivalent is necessary. A passing grade on a written examination developed and administered by the U.S. Office of Personnel Management for the General Services Administration, a qualifying rating on a personal interview, and a qualifying medical examination to determine physical and mental fitness are required of all candidates. In addition, a comprehensive background investigation is conducted to determine general character, honesty, and loyalty to the U.S. government. Added job requirements include availability for *weekend work and rotating shifts* as well as possession of a valid driver's license. In addition, the candidate must have two years of experience demonstrating the ability to meet and deal with the general public, the ability to understand and apply various rules and regulations, and the ability to maintain poise and self-control under stress (any type of military service may be credited toward meeting this requirement); or two years of education at a resident school above high school; or any combination of education and experience totalling two years.

Newly hired officers are given an eight-week basic training course at the Federal Law Enforcement Training Center located in Glynco, Georgia. Among the subjects taught during this course are GSA policies, procedures, and responsibilities; principles of physical security; protective-alarm systems; operation of the criminal justice systems; understanding human behavior; principles of communication; laws of arrest, evidence, search, and seizure; arrest and search procedures; patrol methods; safety procedures; traffic control; bomb searches; riot control; criminal investigation techniques; firearms training; first aid; and self-defense tactics. After successfully completing this basic training course, new Federal Protective Officers receive their work assignments and are placed on probation for a one-year period. After demonstrating satisfactory work performance throughout the probationary period, they are given permanent employment status. All Federal Protective Service personnel are continually trained in the latest innovations in the law enforcement and protection areas in order to keep them current.

BORDER PATROL AGENT

Each candidate for the position of Border Patrol Agent must be a U.S. citizen between the ages of 21 and 37 at the time of appointment. The age limitation may be waived for applicants with current or prior federal law enforcement work experience. The candidate must have a substantial background of experience (paid or voluntary, full- or part-time) of which at least one year must have been comparable in level of difficulty and responsibility to grade GS-4 in the Federal Service. (*Fully* describe all work experience in the application for employment to gain proper consideration.) The applicant may substitute a full four-year course of college undergraduate study for experience, provided that the college work indicates the ability to learn the activities of a Border Patrol Agent. A passing grade on the written Border Patrol Agent exam and a qualifying rating from a panel of interviewers are also required. Applicants who are able to read, write, and speak Spanish may have their language skills evaluated during the oral interview instead of taking the written language-aptitude exam. A good working knowledge of Spanish gives a real competitive edge to the Border Patrol Agent applicant. Knowledge of Spanish will also make the training period a little less arduous. Spanish proficiency is mandatory for appointment to a duty station.

The applicant must submit to a complete medical examination to determine physical and mental fitness for this work. The *physical examination is performed by a government physician at government expense, but travel to the physical examination is the responsibility of the applicant.* Vision requirements for this job are binocular vision of 20/40 in each eye without corrective lenses, uncorrected vision of at least 20/70 in each eye, vision in each eye corrected to 20/20, and the ability to distinguish basic colors. A thorough background investigation is conducted to determine character, honesty, and general suitability for this work. All candidates must possess a valid driver's license.

Newly hired Border Patrol Agents undergo 18 weeks of training at the Border Patrol Academy located in Glynco, Georgia. The course consists of training in such subject areas as Immigration and Naturalization Service regulations and procedures; immigration and nationality law; criminal law; laws of evidence and court procedures; Border Patrol methods and operations; methods of tracking and surveillance; methods of arrest, search, and seizure; care and use of firearms; marksmanship; judo and physical training; techniques of fingerprinting; patrol-vehicle operation and pursuit driving; first aid and lifesaving techniques; preparation of reports; and Spanish language instruction. Trainees must attend all classes and official functions in full uniform. Purchase of these uniforms is at the trainee's own expense. Initial outlay for the training academy is approximately $300 and for the first year's uniforms is in excess of $1,200. Upon entry to duty, the Border Patrol Agent receives $480 toward the cost of uniforms and then receives $480 annually toward maintenance and replacement of uniforms. After graduation from the Border Patrol Academy, trainees report to their duty stations and begin work under the guidance of experienced personnel.

During the first year of service, the trainee must meet academic and physical training requirements. This includes successfully completing the course of study at the Border Patrol Academy and demonstrating proficiency in law and Spanish. A trainee who cannot pass the Spanish examination will be separated at the end of the Academy period. After the Academy, training continues at the duty stations. During the one-year probationary period, progress is carefully evaluated and examinations are given to the trainee upon completion of six-and-a-half and ten months of service. The trainee's progress and work performance are reviewed by a panel of two top-level sector supervisors. The decision as to retention or separation is based on recommendations of these probationary examining boards. Suitability is also determined by the results of the personal background investigation. Initially, new Border Patrol Agents receive a *career conditional appointment that leads to a permanent career appointment after three years* of continuous and satisfactory service. The career appointment provides the Agents with tenure as well as other desirable rights and privileges.

IMMIGRATION INSPECTOR

Candidates for the position of Immigration Inspector must be U.S. citizens. There is no maximum age for entry to this position and no mandatory retirement age. The candidate must also have a bachelor's degree, three years of responsible experience, or an equivalent combination of education and experience. Qualifying experience is experience in clerical, administrative, or other work that shows the ability to deal with others in person-to-person relationships, to learn and interpret facts, and to seek the cooperation of others in following procedures and regulations.

To secure a place on the register, the applicant must establish an eligible rating on an examination administered by the Immigration and Naturalization Service. A physical and mental examination is required because an Immigration Inspector must be in excellent physical condition. All candidates must meet minimum physical requirements. Since the duties of the position are exacting and involve activities under trying conditions, candidates must also possess emotional and mental stability.

During the required 14-week training period at the Federal Law Enforcement Training Center (FLETC) in Glynco, Georgia, appointees must satisfactorily complete the prescribed training in immigration law. Training may also include courses in the Spanish language (depending on the location of the position being filled), human relations, and physical education.

CRIMINAL INVESTIGATOR, IMMIGRATION AND NATURALIZATION SERVICE (SPECIAL AGENT)

Candidates for the position of Criminal Investigator must be U.S. citizens between the ages of 21 and 37 at the time of appointment. This age limitation, however, is waived for applicants who are at present in federal civilian law enforcement positions or have prior experience in this field. Other requirements include a bachelor's degree from an accredited college or university, an equivalent combination of education and work experience, or three years of work experience. Qualifying experience may be administrative, professional, or investigative, indicating that the applicant is able to perform the basic duties of a Criminal Investigator. One academic year of full-time undergraduate study may be substituted for nine months of work experience. Applicants must also earn a competitive grade above 70 on the INS Criminal Investigator examination. When chosen from this list by the Immigration and Naturalization Service (INS), applicants undergo a comprehensive medical examination to determine physical and mental fitness as well as freedom from any impairment that would prevent the normal performance of duties. No exceptions to these standards are made. Since the duties are exacting, there are specific requirements for this position: *Manual dexterity*—comparatively free motion of fingers, wrists, elbows, shoulders, hips, and knee joints is required. *Vision*—you must possess sufficiently good vision in each eye with or without glasses. *Hearing*—the ability to hear the conversational voice and *whispered speech without the use of a hearing aid* is required. Applicants must possess emotional and mental stability. Any physical condition that would cause the applicant to be a hazard to himself/herself or to others would disqualify the applicant for appointment. The standards are considered minimum and will not be waived in any case. Candidates are interviewed by INS personnel and are evaluated for such factors as appearance, poise, and the ability to communicate effectively. Lastly, a personal background investigation is conducted to determine general character, honesty, and overall suitability for this job. At the time of appointment, each candidate must possess a valid driver's license.

Newly hired Criminal Investigators are initially given 14 weeks of training at the Federal Law Enforcement Training Center (FLETC) in Glynco, Georgia. The subjects taught during this training program include INS rules, regulations, and procedures; immigration and nationality law; laws of evidence; court procedures; investigation techniques; methods of arrest, search, and seizure; surveillance and undercover operations; use of legal warrants; care and use of firearms; physical training and methods of self-defense; fingerprinting; preparation of reports; and Spanish language training. Upon successful completion of this program, new investigators are assigned to INS field offices across the country where they work with experienced investigators and are guided by supervisory personnel until they are able to function on an independent basis. Periodically, Criminal Investigators receive additional training that is designed to keep them abreast of new developments affecting their work activities.

DEPORTATION OFFICER

The Deportation Officer candidate must be a U.S. citizen under the age of 37. The age limitation may be waived if the applicant is currently in a federal civilian law enforcement position or has served in such a position in the past. The applicant must have a bachelor's degree, three years of responsible experience, or an equivalent combination of education and experience. Qualifying experience is administrative, professional, investigative, or other responsible work that has prepared the applicant to enter the position. One academic year of full-time undergraduate study is equivalent to nine months of responsible experience. The candidate must also establish an eligible rating by achieving a score of 70 or better on an Immigration and Naturalization Service examination.

While the work of the Deportation Officer may be strenuous and exhausting, it does not tend to require the speed, agility, nor dexterity of many other positions within the Immigration and Naturalization Service. Much of the work is indoors and sedentary and may be performed by some handicapped persons. Still, a physical examination is required, and a Deportation Officer must be in excellent physical shape within his or her limitations. Since the duties of the position are exacting and responsible and may involve strenuous activities, applicants must possess emotional, mental, and physical stability. The duties of this position require good distant vision in one eye and the ability to read without strain printed material the size of typewritten characters, glasses permitted. The ability to hear the conversational voice, with or without a hearing aid, is required. In most instances, amputation of an arm, hand, leg, or foot will not disqualify an applicant for appointment, although it may be necessary that this condition be compensated by use of satisfactory prosthesis. Applicants are subject to a personal background investigation to determine suitability for employment.

Deportation Officers receive their training at the Federal Law Enforcement Training Center (FLETC) in Glynco, Georgia.

INTERNAL SECURITY INSPECTOR, INTERNAL REVENUE SERVICE

Candidates for the position of Internal Security Inspector must be U.S. citizens between the ages of 21 and 37 at the time of appointment *and be willing to relocate to any locality in the United States.* They are required to have a minimum of at least three years of work experience, consisting of at least one year of general experience and two years of specialized experience. General experience is that which shows an ability to work effectively with individuals or groups and to collect facts and prepare concisely written reports. Specialized experience includes any of the following: investigative work in the Armed Forces or for government agencies; investigations of criminal cases for reputable attorneys or of complex insurance claims, particularly those involving fraud; criminal investigations as a uniformed law officer or detective; or experience in the practice of criminal law. Education can be substituted for experience at the rate of one academic year (30 semester hours) for nine months of experience. A bachelor's degree from an accredited college or university or credentials as a Certified Public Accountant fully meet the minimum requirements for one year of general experience and two years of specialized work experience. All candidates must demonstrate the ability to speak and write clearly; have poise, initiative, and a good appearance; be capable of exercising tact and sound judgment in dealing with others; and have a valid driver's license. In addition to meeting these basic standards, each applicant must qualify on the Treasury Enforcement Agent Examination. Each candidate is given a thorough medical examination to determine physical and mental fitness to engage in normal work and training activities. Candidates are interviewed and a comprehensive background investigation is made to evaluate factors like honesty, character, stability, and overall suitability for the job.

Newly hired Internal Security Inspectors participate in an extensive training program that combines classroom instruction with on-the-job training. During their first year, they attend Internal Security Basic Schools, Phase I and Phase II, as well as Criminal Investigator School, which is conducted at the consolidated Federal Law Enforcement Training Center near Brunswick, Georgia. Phase I and Phase II training are each two weeks in length and, when possible, are scheduled nine to 11 months apart and are interspersed with on-the-job training. In Phase I, new inspectors are trained in techniques of planning, conducting, and reporting background investigations with emphasis on developing interviewing and interpersonal skills. Phase II provides instruction on criminal and complaint investigation methods and techniques; methods of collecting, recording, and documenting facts; automated data processing and computer operations; management/program analysis; financial investigative techniques; and techniques of photography. At the Criminal Investigator School, new inspectors take part in a seven-week course in which they receive instruction in such subjects as fundamentals of criminal law, rules of evidence and court procedures, rights of individuals, use of search warrants, IRS practices and procedures, use of firearms, investigative techniques and surveillance, and undercover and arrest techniques. After the successful completion of training, new inspectors begin working on a regular basis with experienced inspection service staff. They are on probation for a period of one year and are permanently appointed after demonstrating satisfactory work performance. To add to their skills and to keep them current on new developments in their field, Internal Security Inspectors receive continuous training throughout their careers. As they move upward in their careers, they take part in journey-level and advanced training classes including various types of computer training with continuing opportunities to participate in various inservice, outservice, and self-developmental training programs.

INTERNAL REVENUE SERVICE SPECIAL AGENT

Candidates for the position of Special Agent must be U.S. citizens up to age 37 at the time of appointment and must meet the following requirements: a bachelor's degree that includes at least 15 semester hours in accounting plus at least nine semester hours in related business subjects, or three years of professional work experience in accounting. Applicants with accounting credentials plus a law degree may enter this position at a higher grade level. In addition to meeting these basic requirements, it is necessary to receive a qualifying grade on the Treasury Enforcement Agent Examination.

A comprehensive medical examination is also required to determine physical and mental fitness and freedom from conditions that would interfere with normal work and training. Further evaluations through personal interviews and a comprehensive background investigation determine such factors as honesty, general character, stability, and suitability for this work.

Newly appointed Special Agents participate in an intensive training program that lasts approximately 20 weeks. The program is conducted at the consolidated Federal Law Enforcement Training Center in Glynco, Georgia, where Agents attend three separate schools. First, they attend Special Agent Basic School for instruction in such subjects as fundamentals of criminal law; rights of individuals; rules of evidence and court procedures; use of search warrants; IRS practices and procedures; interviewing techniques; use of firearms; criminal investigation techniques; surveillance, undercover, and arrest techniques; and techniques of photography. Next comes Criminal Investigation School, where training is received in basic income-tax law and simpler types of criminal tax investigations. Finally, they return to home offices for an extended period of on-the-job training and closely supervised conduct of simple investigations. If they progress satisfactorily, they are sent to Special Agent Intermediate School. After successfully concluding this program, new Agents report to their work stations where they work with experienced IRS staff. They remain on probation for a period of one year and are permanently appointed after demonstrating satisfactory work performance. Special Agents receive continuous training throughout their careers to sharpen skills and to keep them abreast of new developments in the field.

CUSTOMS AID

To qualify as a Customs Aid, the applicant must be a U.S. citizen and a high school graduate. The applicant must be in good physical condition and must possess emotional and mental stability. There is no age restriction. The candidate may establish his or her name on the list of eligibles by scoring high on the Federal Clerical Examination and by presenting at least two years of progressively responsible experience in government, business, or the Armed Forces demonstrating the ability to interpret and apply laws, rules, and regulations. Study successfully completed in a resident school above high school level may be substituted for experience at the rate of one academic year of study for nine months of experience.

CUSTOMS INSPECTOR

A candidate for this job must be a U.S. citizen at least 21 years of age and must have a high school education. There is no maximum age for appointment as a Customs Inspector. Other requirements include three years of paid experience in government, business, or the Armed Forces in positions that involved dealing with the public, applying regulations, or using instructional materials. One scholastic year of education above the high school level may be substituted for nine months of work experience. There is no written examination, but the applicant's education and experience are evaluated and are assigned numerical values that combine to yield a rating score. The applicant must achieve a score above 70 and must successfully complete an oral interview. Each candidate must pass a qualifying physical examination and must possess emotional and mental stability. There should be no disability that would interfere with normal work performance. Minimum standards include distant vision of at least 20/40 in one eye and 20/100 in the other, good color vision, and accurate hearing of the conversational voice without a hearing aid. Amputation or loss of function of an arm, leg, foot, or hand is disqualifying.

All candidates must also pass a thorough background investigation. Once hired, new Customs Inspectors receive extensive on-the-job as well as formal classroom training at the Federal Law Enforcement Training Center near Glynco, Georgia, in subjects such as U.S. Customs Service regulations and procedures, search and questioning techniques, duty assessment, self-defense, and the use of firearms. After successful completion of a probationary period, usually one year, the trainee receives permanent employment status.

IMPORT SPECIALIST

Candidates for this job must be U.S. citizens and have a high school education. They must also have three years of work experience in government, business, or the Armed Forces in positions that involved dealing with the public and correctly applying regulations or instructional materials. One scholastic year of education above the high school level may be substituted for nine months of work experience. All candidates must establish eligibility with a passing score based on evaluation of education and experience. The applicant must successfully complete an oral interview and must convince the examiners of his or her skill in dealing satisfactorily with others and in correctly applying regulations or instructional material. The candidate must also submit to a personal background investigation. While there are no age restrictions, the applicant must be able to pass a qualifying physical examination, must be able to distinguish basic colors, and must be emotionally and mentally stable. Although much of the work can be performed by persons with some physical handicaps, candidates must be free of any disability that would interfere with normal work performance.

Newly hired Import Specialists are given extensive on-the-job training as well as classroom instruction. The areas of instruction include U.S. Customs Service regulations and procedures, duty and tax assessment, document procedures, questioning techniques, and court procedures. After successful completion of a probationary period, usually one year, the trainee receives permanent employment status.

SPECIAL AGENT, CUSTOMS

Applicants for this position must be U.S. citizens under the age of 37 and must be *willing to accept assignment anywhere within the Customs territory of the United States.* An applicant should be a college graduate, preferably with a degree in police science, law, or business administration specialties such as accounting, economics, or finance. In addition, each candidate must have at least two years of specialized criminal investigative or related work experience. This work background must demonstrate the individual's ability to exercise tact, judgment, and resourcefulness; interpersonal skills; and proficiency in analyzing and evaluating data and evidence. Relevant work experience may be substituted for college training at the rate of one scholastic year for nine months of experience. All candidates must also attain a qualifying grade on the Treasury Enforcement Agent Examination, which is designed to measure investigative skills.

All applicants must pass a rigid physical examination, must be capable of strenuous physical activity, must have excellent hearing and eyesight and normal color vision, and must be free of any disabilities that would interfere with training and work performance. In short, the applicant must be in excellent physical condition with good muscular development. Minimum standards include distant vision of at least 20/40 in one eye and 20/100 in the other without glasses, correctable to at least 20/20 in one eye and 20/30 in the other with glasses, and good near vision and color and depth perception. Persons with a hearing aid or with noticeable deformities or disfiguring conditions should not apply. Finally, each candidate must pass a thorough personal background investigation. Those who meet all the various requirements receive about 11 weeks of basic law enforcement training at the Treasury Agents' School in Glynco, Georgia. This consists of extensive training in the use of firearms, undercover operations, surveillance techniques, rules of evidence and courtroom procedures, Customs laws and regulations, and current law enforcement and investigative techniques. After successful completion of training, appointments are made on a probationary basis. New Agents work with experienced Agents and are guided by supervisory personnel who assist in the development of work skills. After satisfactory completion of probation, usually one year, new Agents receive permanent employment status as Special Agent, U.S. Customs.

U.S. PARK POLICE OFFICER

A candidate for this position must be a U.S. citizen at least 21 years of age but not yet 31 (though this may be raised to 35 in the near future). He or she must be a high school graduate with at least two years of relevant work experience, military service, or college study.

To qualify, the candidate must earn a competitive score on a two-hour written exam that tests mathematics, reading and grammar skills, and incident-report writing ability. The candidate must have at least 20/100 vision correctable to 20/20 and must undergo and pass physical fitness and medical testing, drug screening, and a background check.

Final appointment is contingent upon passing an 18-week training course in standard law enforcement, proper use of firearms, and so on, at the Federal Law Enforcement Training Center near Glynco, Georgia.

DEPUTY U.S. MARSHAL

Applicants for the job of Deputy U.S. Marshal must be U.S. citizens between the ages of 21 and 37 at the time of appointment. All candidates must have a minimum of three years of general work experience in one of the following areas: law enforcement; supervision of criminal offenders in a correctional institution; sales or instructional activities other than order taking or counter sales; interviewing clients in public or private agencies and explaining, interpreting, and applying regulations and procedures; public contact work concerned with information gathering; active participation in community action programs in teaching and counseling roles; or civilian or military supervisory work involving leadership and decisionmaking.

Qualifying work experience should demonstrate that the candidate can communicate effectively, both orally and in writing, and is able to exercise tact in dealing with others. It should also show that the applicant has poise and self-confidence and is able to make decisions quickly while exercising sound judgment. The length of this work experience is of less importance than demonstrated success in positions of responsibility, and possession of the required length of experience does not automatically qualify an applicant. One academic year of study in an accredited college or university may be substituted for nine months of general work experience up to a maximum of three years of experience. Individuals with four-year college degrees meet the full work-experience requirement and qualify for the entry-level position.

In addition to meeting these experience and/or educational requirements, candidates must qualify on the Treasury Enforcement Agent (TEA) Exam. Along with the verbal reasoning, arithmetic reasoning, and problems for investigation sections of the TEA exam, the Deputy U.S. Marshal candidate must answer self-rating questions on a personal achievement inventory. Answers to these questions will help the Justice Department examiners to determine whether the candidate has the pattern of interests and achievements of successful Deputy U.S. Marshals currently in service. Similarity of pattern of interests and achievements in a well-qualified candidate tends to predict success on the job.

After the applicant has passed the written test, agency personnel conduct interviews to evaluate such qualities as appearance, poise, and other traits required for successful work performance. The interview also serves as an oral examination. At the interview, the candidate is presented with a number of hypothetical scenarios and is asked how he or she would react if faced with these situations. This is basically a test of judgment. Persons selected from the list of eligibles are given an extensive medical examination to determine physical and mental fitness and freedom from conditions that would hamper normal work performance. These standards are the minimums and are not waived in any case. Finally, a personal background investigation is conducted to determine loyalty, honesty, character, and general suitability for the job. Each candidate must have a valid driver's license when hired and must be able to operate motor vehicles in accordance with appropriate government regulations.

Newly hired Deputies initially enter a 12-week basic training program given at the Federal Law Enforcement Training Center (FLETC) in Glynco, Georgia. Basic training consists of an eight-week course at the Criminal Investigator School, conducted by FLETC personnel, followed by a four-week program at the U.S. Marshals Service Basic Training School. The subject matter dealt with during this training period includes U.S. Marshals Service policies, rules, and regulations; methods of arrest, search, and seizure; investigation techniques; court procedures; use of legal warrants; protection of witnesses; riot control; care and use of firearms; physical training; methods of self-defense; and preparation of reports. After the successful completion of this program, new Deputies work along with experienced personnel of the U.S. Marshals Service until they gain sufficient expertise to work independently. At varying intervals, Deputy U.S. Marshals are offered specialized and refresher-type training to keep their skills current and to aid in career development.

POSTAL POLICE OFFICER

An applicant for the position of Postal Police Officer must be at least 20 years of age and, unless a veteran, cannot be appointed until reaching the age of 21 years. The Postal Police Officer must be physically able to perform the duties of the job, must have weight in proportion to height, must have good color vision and good distant vision (no weaker than 20/40 in one eye and 20/50 in the other eye correctable to 20/20), and must have keen hearing. Emotional and mental stability are essential for the armed officer, and a psychological interview is part of the qualification process. Drug testing is required as well. The candidate must demonstrate the ability to deal with the public in a courteous and tactful manner; to work in stressful situations; to collect, assemble, and act on pertinent facts; to prepare clear and accurate records; to deal effectively with individuals and groups; and to express him- or herself in both oral and written communications. A background investigation will be made on all otherwise qualified candidates. To be considered, each applicant must pass a written qualifying exam with a score of 70 or better out of a possible 100. The examination tests accuracy in comparing names and numbers, reading comprehension, and arithmetic reasoning ability. It also includes a self-rating inventory.

Male applicants born after 12/31/59, unless for some reason exempt, must be registered with the Selective Service System.

The Immigration Reform and Control Act of 1986 applies to postal workers. All postal workers must be citizens of the U.S. or must be able to prove identity and the right to work in the United States (permanent resident alien status—Green Card).

New employees are trained in an eight-week program at the Federal Law Enforcement Training Center (FLETC) in Glynco, Georgia.

POSTAL INSPECTOR

Candidates for this position are carefully screened by the U.S. Postal Service. They must be U.S. citizens between the ages of 21 and 37 and must be *willing to relocate* to any part of the United States or Puerto Rico. Each applicant must have a bachelor's degree from an accredited institution and must have at least one year's experience. Applicants must have a minimum of four years of general or three years of specialized work experience. General work experience is that which shows an ability to work effectively with individuals or groups and to collect facts and prepare clear and concisely written reports. Or the experience might have required a knowledge of mail handling and distribution operations or postal personnel or finance systems. Specialized work experience can involve one of any number of specific work backgrounds. These include experience in investigations of complex insurance claims, particularly those involving frauds; investigations of criminal cases for reputable attorneys; investigations for government agencies; or investigations for the Armed Forces conducted as a uniformed law officer or detective. Experience may be in work as a practicing attorney, work involving application of financial or operations-management techniques, Postal Service positions such as supervisor or postmaster, or technical work dealing with finances or operations. A law degree; a master's degree in accounting, police science, or public or business administration; or credentials as a CPA may be substituted for three years of specialized experience. In all cases, candidates must demonstrate the ability to speak and write clearly; have poise, initiative, and a good appearance; be capable of exercising tact and sound judgment in dealing with others; and have a valid driver's license.

All candidates are given a qualifying oral interview and a general aptitude test as well as thorough physical and psychological evaluations to be sure they are free of any disability that would interfere with normal work performance. A thorough background investigation is made of each applicant including arrest records and interviews with neighbors, work associates, and supervisors who provide personal references. Candidates who meet all the preceding requirements are given a numerical rating based on their written examination, education, experience, and veteran's preference, if any, and are placed on an eligibility roster for possible future openings.

Newly hired trainees receive 16 weeks of intensive training. This consists of eight weeks of basic instruction at the Inspection Service Management Academy located in Potomac, Maryland; four weeks of field training in the postal division to which the trainee is assigned; and an additional four weeks of specialized instruction that includes use of firearms, defensive tactics, search and seizure techniques, court and legal procedures, postal operations, auditing techniques, and federal laws that apply to Inspection Service activities. After the completion of training, new Postal Inspectors begin work at their assigned locations. They are given on-the-job training until they can function independently and successfully complete their probationary period. Throughout their postal careers, they continue to receive training to keep them current with new laws, procedures, and court decisions involving their work.

U.S. SECRET SERVICE UNIFORMED DIVISION OFFICER

Applicants for this position are carefully selected according to the high standards of the U.S. Secret Service. Each applicant must be a U.S. citizen, must be at least 21 years of age at the time of appointment to duty, and must have a high school diploma, a recognized equivalent, or one year of work experience as a Police Officer in a city with a population over a half million persons. Other requirements include a passing grade on the written Secret Service Entrance Examination, a qualifying rating on a personal interview conducted by agency personnel, and successful passing of a qualifying medical examination to determine physical and mental fitness. The physical examination either is taken at the candidate's own expense or is obtained free of charge at the Washington, D.C., Police and Fire Clinic. Vision requirements are at least 20/40 in each eye, correctable to 20/20, and weight must be in proportion to height. A comprehensive background investigation is made to determine the individual's general character, honesty, and loyalty to the U.S. government and to ensure suitability for top security-clearance rating. In addition, applicants must be able to work *rotating shifts, including weekends,* and must possess a valid automobile driver's license.

Newly hired officers are given intensive training at the Federal Law Enforcement Training Center in Glynco, Georgia. This program provides instruction in areas such as criminal law; police procedures; police-community relations; rules of arrest, search, and seizure; self-defense techniques; the use of various firearms; first aid and lifesaving techniques; physical fitness; psychology; and rules of diplomatic immunity and protocol.

Classroom instruction is supplemented by on-the-job training. Periodic inservice training is received as new techniques are developed. After successfully completing this program of training, new officers are assigned on a probationary basis and work alongside experienced personnel. After demonstrating satisfactory work performance during the probationary period, new officers receive permanent appointments.

SECRET SERVICE SPECIAL AGENT

Candidates for the position of Special Agent are carefully selected according to the rigid standards of this agency. They must be U.S. citizens between the ages of 21 and 37 at the time of appointment to duty. They must meet one of the following requirements: a bachelor's degree in a major field of study; three years of work experience, two of these years involving criminal investigations; or a suitable combination of investigative experience and education. Each candidate is required to make a qualifying grade on the Treasury Enforcement Agent Examination. Those who qualify on this test are further evaluated by oral and written examinations that assess such areas as communication skills both verbal and written; analytical ability; emotional stability; and appearance, poise, and adaptability to changing situations. Each candidate is given a qualifying medical examination to determine physical and mental fitness and freedom from any disabilities that would interfere with normal work or training activities. Among the rigorous physical requirements is a requirement of 20/40 vision correctable to 20/20. A comprehensive background investigation of each applicant is conducted to determine general character, honesty, and loyalty to the U.S. government. This is extremely important as Agents receive a top-secret security clearance.

Candidates who meet all these requirements undergo intensive training at the Federal Law Enforcement Training Center in Glynco, Georgia, and specialized instruction at the U.S. Secret Service training facilities in Washington, D.C. Subject matter covered during this training period includes criminal law, investigation techniques, agency rules and regulations, scientific investigative devices, document and handwriting examination and analysis, first aid, lifesaving techniques, self-defense, use of various firearms, arrest and surveillance techniques, undercover operations, court procedures, and rules of evidence. New Agents also receive on-the-job training to supplement classroom courses and continue to receive inservice training throughout their careers. After successful completion of training, new Agents are assigned to Secret Service field offices on a probationary basis. They work with experienced Special Agents and, after satisfactory performance during the probationary period, receive permanent appointments.

PART

FOUR

The Exams

CONTENTS

THE EXAMS

Every law enforcement agency has health standards, physical ability standards, and mental ability standards. Every recruit must undergo a comprehensive medical examination. All agencies require overall good health because law enforcement work is always demanding. In addition, many agencies have specific requirements with respect to size, vision, hearing, or some other dimension. The requirements of some federal agencies are enumerated in the chapter called How to Qualify. If you have any doubts about your own medical qualifications for the position you seek, ask questions before you go through the time and trouble of applying.

Physical fitness is another prerequisite for nearly all law enforcement positions. Some agencies have pre-entry requirements, a physical power exam that applicants must pass to be admitted to training. Others have a physical exam that must be passed at the end of training and conditioning. Each agency devises its own exam; each exam differs in details. Each exam seeks to measure stamina for the job at hand.

The following sample physical fitness test for Police Officers is a typical one. This particular test is given to candidates who have passed the written exam and the medical examination. Admission to the police academy is contingent upon passing this physical fitness test.

Sample Physical Fitness Test

To become a Police Officer, candidates must pass a qualifying physical fitness test. Only candidates who have passed the written test for Police Officers will be called for the physical test.

Medical evidence to allow participation in the physical fitness test may be required, and the Department of Personnel reserves the right to exclude from the physical test any eligibles who, upon examination of such evidence, are apparently medically unfit. Eligibles will take the physical fitness test at their own risk of injury, although efforts will be made to safeguard them. Candidates must complete the entire course consisting of 10 events in not more than 2 minutes and 15 seconds. Candidates who do not successfully complete events 4, 5, 7, or 9 will be considered to have taken the maximum amount of time indicated for each event not successfully completed. Candidates who do not successfully complete events 3, 6, or 8 will be penalized the amount of time indicated. Candidates who do not successfully complete an event should immediately proceed to the next event. Penalty times for events 3, 6, or 8 and additional time for not successfully completing events 4, 5, 7, or 9 will be added to the total time of candidates after they have completed the test.

DESCRIPTION OF EVENTS

1. Run up 3 flights of stairs, down 1 flight, and then 9 yards to a track.
2. Run 90 yards around the track.
3. Run approximately 5 yards to a maze of 6 cones set 3 feet apart and follow a prescribed course through the maze. Penalty time is *5 seconds* for missing a turn in the maze.
4. Run 10 yards and go over a 5-foot wall. Maximum time *30 seconds.*
5. Run approximately 5 feet to a wooden box weighing approximately 100 pounds. Push the box a distance of 10 feet. Maximum time *30 seconds.*
6. Run approximately 4 yards and jump across a 3-foot space. Penalty time *15 seconds.*
7. Run 7 yards and go over a 3-foot-high barrier. Maximum time *15 seconds.*

8. Run 5 yards to a maze of 6 cones set 3 feet apart and follow a prescribed course through the maze. Penalty time is *5 seconds* for missing a turn in the maze.
9. Run 5 yards and lift or drag a 70-pound dummy 25 feet. Maximum time *30 seconds.*
10. Run 90 yards to the end of the course.

Although continuous running through all events is not mandatory, candidates must remember that they have only *2 minutes and 15 seconds* to complete the entire course. The maximum time permitted for an individual event, where a maximum time is given, will begin when a candidate touches the apparatus used for the event.

As a condition of continued employment, persons appointed from the list resulting from this examination will be required to maintain physical fitness standards prescribed by the police department and will be subject to periodic reexamination.

There is also a great deal of variation among the written exams that are designed to measure the applicant's ability to learn and perform the duties of the job. Some written exams seem to dwell on the applicant's judgment, some on memory, and others on general scholastic ability and aptitude. Still others combine elements from all types of exams.

The exam samples that follow are meant to introduce you to the varieties of questions utilized on law enforcement exams. The federal sample questions are the official questions distributed by the Treasury Department, the Office of Personnel Management, the Immigration and Naturalization Service, and the Postal Service. The city police and state trooper questions have been culled from old exams or have been written expressly for this book based on actual recent exams.

Federal testing is in a state of flux at this time. Many changes have recently been made both in format and in types of questions asked on a number of federal law enforcement application exams. The sample questions for the named federal exams in this book reflect the latest versions available at the time of publication. If you are taking one of the named federal exams, your exam will probably conform closely to the official sample questions. However, it is possible that a still newer version will have appeared by the time you apply for a federal law enforcement position. Give careful attention to any sample questions you receive with application materials. Any other exam—federal, state, or local—will probably draw on a number of question types from many different exams. Practice with all sample questions we have provided almost guarantees you familiarity with the types of test questions you will have to answer. One fact is certain: Your exam will not presuppose any familiarity with law enforcement rules, practices, or procedures. Applicants for entry-level jobs are not expected to know anything about the work itself or about agency rules. A well-rounded scholastic background, a clear head, common sense, and the confidence created by previous introduction to the question styles are all you need.

Answer Sheet for Sample Questions: Police Officer Exam I

1. Ⓐ Ⓑ Ⓒ Ⓓ	11. Ⓐ Ⓑ Ⓒ Ⓓ	21. Ⓐ Ⓑ Ⓒ Ⓓ	31. Ⓐ Ⓑ Ⓒ Ⓓ	41. Ⓐ Ⓑ Ⓒ Ⓓ
2. Ⓐ Ⓑ Ⓒ Ⓓ	12. Ⓐ Ⓑ Ⓒ Ⓓ	22. Ⓐ Ⓑ Ⓒ Ⓓ	32. Ⓐ Ⓑ Ⓒ Ⓓ	42. Ⓐ Ⓑ Ⓒ Ⓓ
3. Ⓐ Ⓑ Ⓒ Ⓓ	13. Ⓐ Ⓑ Ⓒ Ⓓ	23. Ⓐ Ⓑ Ⓒ Ⓓ	33. Ⓐ Ⓑ Ⓒ Ⓓ	43. Ⓐ Ⓑ Ⓒ Ⓓ
4. Ⓐ Ⓑ Ⓒ Ⓓ	14. Ⓐ Ⓑ Ⓒ Ⓓ	24. Ⓐ Ⓑ Ⓒ Ⓓ	34. Ⓐ Ⓑ Ⓒ Ⓓ	44. Ⓐ Ⓑ Ⓒ Ⓓ
5. Ⓐ Ⓑ Ⓒ Ⓓ	15. Ⓐ Ⓑ Ⓒ Ⓓ	25. Ⓐ Ⓑ Ⓒ Ⓓ	35. Ⓐ Ⓑ Ⓒ Ⓓ	45. Ⓐ Ⓑ Ⓒ Ⓓ
6. Ⓐ Ⓑ Ⓒ Ⓓ	16. Ⓐ Ⓑ Ⓒ Ⓓ	26. Ⓐ Ⓑ Ⓒ Ⓓ	36. Ⓐ Ⓑ Ⓒ Ⓓ	46. Ⓐ Ⓑ Ⓒ Ⓓ
7. Ⓐ Ⓑ Ⓒ Ⓓ	17. Ⓐ Ⓑ Ⓒ Ⓓ	27. Ⓐ Ⓑ Ⓒ Ⓓ	37. Ⓐ Ⓑ Ⓒ Ⓓ	47. Ⓐ Ⓑ Ⓒ Ⓓ
8. Ⓐ Ⓑ Ⓒ Ⓓ	18. Ⓐ Ⓑ Ⓒ Ⓓ	28. Ⓐ Ⓑ Ⓒ Ⓓ	38. Ⓐ Ⓑ Ⓒ Ⓓ	48. Ⓐ Ⓑ Ⓒ Ⓓ
9. Ⓐ Ⓑ Ⓒ Ⓓ	19. Ⓐ Ⓑ Ⓒ Ⓓ	29. Ⓐ Ⓑ Ⓒ Ⓓ	39. Ⓐ Ⓑ Ⓒ Ⓓ	49. Ⓐ Ⓑ Ⓒ Ⓓ
10. Ⓐ Ⓑ Ⓒ Ⓓ	20. Ⓐ Ⓑ Ⓒ Ⓓ	30. Ⓐ Ⓑ Ⓒ Ⓓ	40. Ⓐ Ⓑ Ⓒ Ⓓ	50. Ⓐ Ⓑ Ⓒ Ⓓ

Sample Questions: Police Officer Exam I

Directions: *For each question, read all the choices carefully. Select the choice that you consider to be the most correct or the best of all choices. Then mark your answer on the answer sheet.*

Questions 1 through 15 are to be answered on the basis of the police action described in the following passage. You will have 10 minutes to read and study the description of the incident. Then you will have to answer 15 questions about the incident without referring back to the description of the incident.

Police Officers Brown and Reid are on patrol in a radio car on a Saturday afternoon in the fall. They receive a radio message that a burglary is in progress on the fifth floor of a seven-floor building on the corner of 7th Street and Main. They immediately proceed to that location to investigate and take appropriate action.

The police officers are familiar with the location, and they know that the Fine Jewelry Company occupies the entire fifth floor of the building. They are also aware that the owner, who is not in the office on weekends, often leaves large amounts of gold in his office safe. The officers, upon arrival at the scene, lock their radio car and proceed to look for the building superintendent to get into the building. The superintendent states that he has not seen or heard anything unusual, although he admits that he did leave the premises for approximately one hour to have lunch. The officers start for the fifth floor using the main elevator. As they reach that floor and open the door, they hear noises followed by the sound of the freight elevator door in the rear of the building closing and the elevator descending. They quickly run through the open door of the Fine Jewelry Company and observe that the office safe is open and empty. The officers then proceed to the rear of the building and use the rear staircase to reach the ground floor. They open the rear door and go out onto the street, where they observe four individuals running up the street, crossing at the corner. At that point, the police officers get a clear view of the suspects. There are three males and one female. One of the males appears to be white, one is obviously Hispanic, and the other male is black. The female is white.

The white male is bearded. He is dressed in blue jeans, white sneakers, and a red and blue jacket. He is carrying a white duffel bag on his shoulder. The Hispanic male limps slightly and has a large dark moustache. He is wearing brown pants, a green shirt, and brown shoes. He is carrying a blue duffel bag on his shoulder. The black male is clean-shaven and is wearing black pants, a white shirt, a green cap, and black shoes. He is carrying what appears to be a toolbox. The white female is carrying a sawed-off shotgun, has long brown hair, and is wearing white jeans, a blue blouse, and blue sneakers. She has a red kerchief around her neck.

The officers chase the suspects for two blocks without being able to catch them. At that point, the suspects separate. The white and black males quickly get into a black 1983 Chevrolet station wagon with Connecticut license plates containing the letters AWK on them and drive away. The Hispanic male and the white female get away in an old light blue Dodge van. The van has a prominent CB antenna on top and large yellow streaks running along the doors on both sides. There is a large dent on the right rear fender, and the van bears New Jersey license plates that the officers are unable to read.

The station wagon turns left and enters the expressway headed toward Connecticut. The van makes a right turn and proceeds in the direction of the tunnel headed for New Jersey.

The officers quickly return to their radio car to report what has happened.

Do NOT refer back to the passage while answering questions 1 through 15.

1. The officers were able to read the following letters from the license plates on the station wagon:
   (A) WAX
   (B) EWK
   (C) AUK
   (D) AWK

2. The van used by the suspects had a dented
   (A) left front fender.
   (B) right front fender.
   (C) right rear fender.
   (D) left rear fender.

3. The officers observed that the van was headed in the direction of
   (A) Long Island.
   (B) Pennsylvania.
   (C) New Jersey.
   (D) Connecticut.

4. The best description of the female suspect's hair is
   (A) short and light in color.
   (B) long and light in color.
   (C) short and dark in color.
   (D) long and dark in color.

5. The suspect who was wearing a white shirt was the
   (A) white male.
   (B) Hispanic male.
   (C) black male.
   (D) white female.

6. The suspect who wore white jeans was the
   (A) white male.
   (B) Hispanic male.
   (C) black male.
   (D) white female.

7. The Hispanic male suspect carried a duffel bag of what color?
   (A) Yellow
   (B) Red
   (C) Blue
   (D) Brown

8. Of the following, the best description of the shoes worn by the Hispanic suspect is
   (A) white sneakers.
   (B) black shoes.
   (C) black boots.
   (D) brown shoes.

9. The suspect who was carrying the white duffel bag was the
   (A) white female.
   (B) black male.
   (C) Hispanic male.
   (D) white male.

10. The suspect who was carrying the shotgun was the
    (A) white female.
    (B) black male.
    (C) Hispanic male.
    (D) white male.

11. The green cap was worn by the
    (A) white female.
    (B) black male.
    (C) Hispanic male.
    (D) white male.

12. The suspect who limped when he or she ran was the
    (A) white female.
    (B) black male.
    (C) Hispanic male.
    (D) white male.

13. Of the following, the best description of the station wagon used by the suspects is
    (A) a 1983 black Chevrolet.
    (B) a 1981 blue Ford.
    (C) a 1981 green Dodge.
    (D) a 1986 red Ford.

14. The best description of the suspects who used the station wagon to depart is
    (A) a black male and a white female.
    (B) a black male and a white male.
    (C) a white female and a Hispanic male.
    (D) a black male and a Hispanic male.

15. The van's license plates were from which of the following states?
   (A) New York
   (B) Delaware
   (C) New Jersey
   (D) Connecticut

16. The characteristics that should be emphasized in a wanted-person report are those that most easily set an individual apart from the general public. Which one of the following descriptions would be of greatest help to a police officer trying to locate a wanted person in a large crowd of people on a cold winter day?
   (A) The person is wearing a blue coat and has short cropped hair.
   (B) The person has a patch on his right eye and a long thin scar on his left cheek.
   (C) The person talks with a lisp and has two upper front teeth missing.
   (D) The person has a scar on his right knee and has blue eyes.

Answer questions 17 and 18 on the basis of the following information.

Police Officer DiSisto has observed that there is a pattern to criminal activity in her sector. She has noticed that burglaries tend to occur on High Street, and auto thefts occur on York Street. Most rapes take place on Chapel Street and most assaults on Whitney. The rapes occur between 10 P.M. and 4 A.M., auto thefts between midnight and 6 A.M., burglaries between 10 A.M. and 4 P.M., and assaults between 6 P.M. and 10 P.M. Auto thefts seem most common on Monday, Tuesday, and Thursday. Assaults occur most often on Friday, Saturday, and Sunday. Most rapes happen over the weekend and most burglaries on Monday, Wednesday, and Saturday.

17. Police Officer DiSisto would most likely be able to reduce the incidence of rape by concentrating her patrol on
   (A) York Street between midnight and 8 A.M.
   (B) Chapel Street between 7 P.M. and 3 A.M.
   (C) High Street between 2 A.M. and 10 P.M.
   (D) Chapel Street between 4 P.M. and midnight.

18. Auto theft has been a special problem in the precinct, and Police Officer DiSisto's supervisor has requested that she make a special effort to eliminate auto theft on her patrol. Officer DiSisto should request assignment to patrol on
   (A) Sunday through Thursday from 10 P.M. to 6 A.M.
   (B) Friday through Wednesday from 3 A.M. to 11 A.M.
   (C) Monday through Friday from 8 A.M. to 4 P.M.
   (D) Wednesday through Sunday from 2 P.M. to 10 P.M.

Answer question 19 on the basis of the following definitions.

> **Harassment** occurs when a person annoys or alarms another person but does not intend or cause physical injury.
>
> **Menacing** occurs when a person threatens to cause serious physical injury to another person but does not cause a serious physical injury.
>
> **Assault** occurs when a person causes physical injury to another person.

19. On a foggy Friday night after work, a group of men met at the Jolly-O Tavern for a few beers. The conversation centered on the merits of the two local hockey teams, and Warren Wu stoutly defended his favorite team against that of Tomas Ramos. Ramos could stand just so much taunting. As he became more angry, Ramos told Wu that he had better "shut up" before he, Tomas Ramos, knocked Wu's block off. Wu continued to praise his team, whereupon Ramos gave him such a punch to the jaw that Wu's lip was split and a tooth was knocked out. Based on the definitions above, Ramos should be charged with

(A) harassment, menacing, and assault.
(B) menacing and assault.
(C) assault.
(D) no crime.

Questions 20 through 24 are to be answered solely on the basis of the following passage.

> Police officers responding to complaints of loud or violent disagreements between members of a family are directed to follow this procedure:

1. When knocking on the door of the apartment in which the dispute is taking place, do not stand directly in front of it.
2. Separate the people taking part in the dispute by taking them into different rooms.
3. Attempt to calm the people involved while interviewing them.
4. Stay out of the dispute; do not take sides.
5. If an insult is directed at you, ignore it.
6. Advise the parties in the argument where they may go for counseling.
7. Do not say anything that will direct the people's anger at you.
8. Make no arrests unless one of the participants is hurt.

20. Two officers, arriving at the scene of a family dispute, separate a screaming couple into different rooms. The wife shouts that her husband is having an affair with his secretary and that she is going to file for divorce. The wife picks up the ringing telephone, listens briefly, and then slams it down. She shouts to her husband, "Your secretary just called, but she didn't leave a message." At this point, it would be proper for the police officer to advise that the

(A) husband end this affair at once.
(B) wife go ahead with her divorce plans.
(C) wife trust her husband.
(D) couple seek the help of local marriage counselors.

21. Two officers respond to a complaint of gunshots and loud arguing taking place in an apartment. They approach the apartment and hear a television set playing. They stand in front of the door, knock on it, and are told to enter. A man and a woman are sitting on a couch watching a murder mystery on television. The couple states that they have been watching the program for almost two hours. The officers evaluate the situation and decide that a mistake has been made. They apologize and leave. One of the actions taken by the officers does not conform to the procedure for dealing with this type of situation. This occurred when they

(A) determined that a mistake had been made, and they apologized and left the premises.
(B) interviewed the people involved in the complaint.
(C) investigated the complaint even though they could hear no argument.
(D) stood in front of the door while knocking on it.

22. Two police officers are assigned to respond to a family dispute taking place in an apartment. The officers approach the door leading to the apartment and hear loud arguing. They knock and the husband opens the door. He tells the officer that an argument is taking place because of his wife's excessive drinking habits. The wife is sitting on the couch with what appears to be a glass of whiskey in her hand. The officers advise the husband that, if the problem should occur again, he should call the police. The actions of the officers in this situation were

(A) improper; the officers should have interviewed both parties, the husband and the wife.

(B) proper; no one was hurt, so the officers left.

(C) improper; the officers should have ordered the wife to stop drinking.

(D) proper; the officers advised the husband to call the police if they were needed.

23. Officers Cohn and Blue respond to a family dispute that involves a young couple and the mother of the wife. They enter the apartment and notice that it is very dusty and untidy. The couple is dressed in soiled clothing, and the husband has not shaved in days. The wife's mother tells the officers that the couple is a pair of "good-for-nothings" and that she is always arguing with her daughter. Officer Blue then tells the couple to clean themselves and the apartment. In response to this remark, the couple angrily states that they can live in whatever manner they please. Of the following, Officer Blue's statement to the couple can be evaluated as

(A) inappropriate; he should have told the mother not to interfere.

(B) appropriate; he did give good advice to the couple.

(C) inappropriate; he should not have angered the couple.

(D) appropriate; people should not be permitted to live in a dirty apartment.

24. Two officers are responding to a complaint of a family dispute taking place in an apartment. As they approach the door to the apartment, they are able to hear loud arguing and the sound of things being thrown about. After knocking on the door, they are admitted by the wife who tells them that her husband has been throwing dishes at the wall and she wants him locked up. The husband states that the wife is constantly nagging him to make more money and that he is being driven out of his mind. At this point, both parties resume shouting. The officers arrest the husband and take him to the police station. The procedure followed by the officers was

(A) improper; they should not have arrested the husband.

(B) proper; they prevented the husband from hurting his wife.

(C) improper; both husband and wife should have been arrested.

(D) proper; the husband in all probability started the fight.

25. Police officers are required to remove potentially dangerous objects from a prisoner prior to placing that prisoner in a jail cell. Which one of the following items should be removed from a prisoner?

(A) A card case

(B) A digital wristwatch

(C) Two sticks of chewing gum

(D) A leather belt

26. Police Officer Barton has finished investigating a report of grand larceny and has obtained the following information:

Time of Occurrence:	Between 3 P.M. and 5 P.M.
Place of Occurrence:	In front of victim's home, 37 Deere Drive
Victim:	Mrs. Tromwell, owner of the vehicle
Crime:	Automobile broken into
Property Taken:	Radio and tape player valued at $1,000

Officer Barton is preparing a report on the incident. Which one of the following expresses the preceding information most clearly and accurately?

(A) While parked in front of her home, Mrs. Tromwell states that between 3 P.M. and 5 P.M. an unknown person broke into her vehicle. Mrs. Tromwell, who lives at 37 Deere Drive, lost her $1,000 radio and tape player.
(B) Mrs. Tromwell, who lives at 37 Deere Drive, states that between 3 P.M. and 5 P.M. her vehicle was parked in front of her home when an unknown person broke into her car and took her radio and tape player, worth $1,000.
(C) Mrs. Tromwell was parked in front of 37 Deere Drive, which is her home, when it was robbed of a $1,000 radio and tape player. When she came out, she observed between 3 P.M. and 5 P.M. that her car had been broken into by an unknown person.
(D) Mrs. Tromwell states between 3 P.M. and 5 P.M. that an unknown person broke into her car in front of her home. Mrs. Tromwell further states that she was robbed of a $1,000 radio and tape player at 37 Deere Drive.

Answer questions 27 through 30 on the basis of the information given in the following passage.

Automobile tire tracks found at the scene of a crime constitute an important link in the chain of physical evidence. In many cases, these are the only clues available. In some areas, unpaved ground adjoins the highway or paved streets. A suspect will often park his or her car off the paved portion of the street when committing a crime, sometimes leaving excellent tire tracks. Comparison of the tire-track impressions with the tires is possible only when the vehicle has been found. However, the initial problem facing the police is the task of determining what kind of car probably made the impressions found at the scene of the crime. If the make, model, and year of the car that made the impressions can be determined, it is obvious that the task of elimination is greatly lessened.

27. The one of the following that is the most appropriate title for this passage is
(A) The Use of Automobiles in the Commission of Crimes.
(B) The Use of Tire Tracks in Police Work.
(C) The Capture of Criminals by Scientific Police Work.
(D) The Positive Identification of Criminals Through Their Cars.

28. When searching for clear signs left by the car used in the commission of a crime, the most likely place for the police to look would be on the
(A) highway adjoining unpaved streets.
(B) highway adjacent to paved streets.
(C) paved streets adjacent to a highway.
(D) unpaved ground adjacent to a highway.

29. Automobile tire tracks found at the scene of a crime are of value as evidence in that they are
(A) generally sufficient to trap and convict a suspect.
(B) the most important link in the chain of physical evidence.
(C) often the only evidence at hand.
(D) circumstantial rather than direct.

30. The primary reason that the police try to determine the make, model, and year of the car involved in the commission of a crime is to
    (A) compare the tire tracks left at the scene of the crime with the type of tires used on cars of that make.
    (B) determine whether the mud on the tires of the suspected car matches the mud in the unpaved road near the scene of the crime.
    (C) reduce, to a large extent, the amount of work involved in determining the particular car used in the commission of a crime.
    (D) alert the police forces to question the occupants of all automobiles of this type.

Questions 31 through 33 are to be answered solely on the basis of the following information.

While questioning people taken into custody, it is essential that police officers give them as much information as possible concerning the crime for which they have been arrested. To accomplish this and at the same time gain the cooperation of the people taken into custody, the following procedure should be used:

1. Be sympathetic.
2. Lighten the person's fear of the punishment he or she faces.
3. Convince the person that his or her family will understand if he or she confesses to the crime.
4. Attempt to convince the person that, if he or she wishes to confess, he or she is not squealing on partners in the crime; if they were caught, they would squeal.
5. If the person in custody seems reluctant to admit guilt, point out the fact that the police possess enough evidence for a conviction without a confession.

31. Two police officers, responding to a call that a liquor store is being robbed, are able to capture and arrest a suspect. Two other men who participated in the robbery get away. The arrested man indicates that he would be willing to give the officers the names of the other two men, but if he did, he would be considered an informer. It would be appropriate at this point for the officers to tell the man they have in custody that
    (A) his partners would have told on him if they had been caught.
    (B) the facts point to the guilt of his partners.
    (C) he will receive a longer jail term if he does not tell them the names of his partners.
    (D) his partners will not hold it against him if he reveals their names.

32. Police Officer Jane Paxton has just taken a man into custody for the commission of a minor crime. During questioning, the man remains silent, finally telling Officer Paxton that he is very much ashamed and he fears what his family will think when they discover his predicament. He states that, if he confesses to the crime, his family will never forgive him. Officer Paxton should tell the man that
    (A) he should immediately confess before everyone finds out how stupid he is for committing the crime.
    (B) his family is likely to forgive him if he confesses to the crime.
    (C) his family will not forgive him anyway, so he should confess to the crime.
    (D) if he does not confess at once, she will personally tell his family.

33. A police officer on foot patrol observes a woman running out of a department store with a small television set in her arms. She is followed by a security guard who shouts, "Stop that woman! She has just stolen a television set!" The police officer chases the woman, who runs to a station wagon and places the set in the back of it. The driver of the station wagon, seeing the approaching officer, drives away before the woman can get into the car. At this point, the officer arrests the woman. She claims that she has not committed any crime and that she is willing to fully cooperate with the police. It would be most appropriate for the police officer to tell the woman that

(A) she is a thief and she should admit to it.
(B) she will have her day in court.
(C) she is only hurting herself by not admitting to her guilt.
(D) he and the security guard can both testify against her since they both saw her running from the store with the television set in her arms.

34. Police Officer Crane obtained the following details relating to a suspicious package:

Place of Occurrence:	Wales Bank, 6 Main Street
Time of Occurrence:	6:20 A.M.
Date of Occurrence:	March 30
Complaint:	Suspicious package in doorway
Found by:	Night watchman

Officer Crane is preparing a report for department records. Which one of the following expresses the preceding information most clearly and accurately?

(A) At 6:20 A.M., the night watchman reported that he found a package on March 30 that appeared suspicious. This occurred in a doorway at 6 Main Street, Wales Bank.
(B) A package that appeared suspicious was in the doorway of Wales Bank. The night watchman reported this at 6 Main Street at 6:20 A.M. on March 30 when found.
(C) On March 30 at 6:20 A.M., a suspicious package was found by the night watchman in the doorway of Wales Bank at 6 Main Street.
(D) The night watchman found a package at the Wales Bank. It appeared suspicious at 6:20 A.M. in the doorway of 6 Main Street on March 30.

35. Police Officer Carmina received the following information regarding a case of child abuse:

Victim:	Martha James
Victim's Age:	Eight years old
Victim's Address:	Resides with her family at 10–15 Lombard Street, Apartment 4A
Complainant:	Victim's uncle, John James
Suspects:	Victim's parents

Police Officer Carmina is preparing a report to send to the Department of Social Services. Which one of the following expresses the preceding information most clearly and accurately?

(A) John James reported a case of child abuse to his eight-year-old niece, Martha James, by her parents. She resides with her family at 10–15 Lombard Street, Apartment 4A.
(B) John James reported that his eight-year-old niece, Martha James, has been abused by the child's parents. Martha James resides with her family at 10–15 Lombard Street, Apartment 4A.
(C) Martha James has been abused by her parents. John James reported that his niece resides with her family at 10–15 Lombard Street, Apartment 4A. She is eight years old.
(D) John James reported that his niece is eight years old. Martha James has been abused by her parents. She resides with her family at 10–15 Lombard Street, Apartment 4A.

Study the following definitions but do not try to memorize them. You will be asked questions based on these definitions. You may refer back to the definitions as needed while answering the questions.

Definitions of Crimes Listed Alphabetically

Arson is committed when an individual intentionally starts a fire that causes damage to a building or that ignites an explosion.

Assault is committed when a person intentionally causes physical injury to another person or when a person acting recklessly causes physical injury to another person.

Burglary is committed when an individual, without authorization, enters or remains in a building with the intent of committing a crime.

Criminal Mischief is committed when a person intentionally damages the property of another person, having no right to do so nor any reasonable ground to believe that he or she has the right to do so.

Criminal Trespass is committed when a person enters or remains in a building that he or she has no right to be in and, while there, possesses, or has knowledge of another person accompanying him or her possessing, a weapon.

Criminally Negligent Homicide is committed when the behavior of an individual creates a substantial risk for others and results in the unintentional death of a person.

Felony Murder is committed when a person, acting alone or with others, commits or attempts to commit the crimes of robbery, burglary, kidnapping, arson, or rape, and in the course and furtherance of such a crime or immediate flight therefrom, that person, or another participant if there is one, causes the death of a person other than one of the participants.

Harassment is committed when an individual, with intent to annoy or frighten another individual, strikes, shoves, kicks, or subjects that individual to physical contact, attempts or threatens to do the same, uses abusive or obscene language, makes an obscene gesture in a public place, follows a person in a public place, or repeatedly engages in conduct that serves no legitimate purpose but results in alarming or seriously annoying another person.

Jostling is committed when a person, with intent, unnecessarily places a hand near a person's pocket or handbag or pushes or crowds another person at the same time that another participant's hand is in the proximity of such person's pocket or handbag.

Larceny is committed when a person intentionally deprives another person of property or wrongfully takes, obtains, or withholds property from the owner of that property without the use of force, violence, or threat of injury. Larceny is committed, for example, when property is obtained under false pretenses, when lost property is found and not returned, or when a bad check is intentionally issued.

Manslaughter is committed when one person recklessly causes the death of another person, when a person causes the death of another person while in the act of intentionally causing serious physical harm to that person, or when a person, intending to cause the death of another person, causes that death while acting under the influence of an extreme emotional disturbance.

Menace is committed when a person, by physical threat, intentionally places or attempts to place another person in a state of fear of imminent and serious physical injury.

Murder is committed when a person intentionally causes the death of another person after a period of lengthy planning.

Reckless Endangerment is committed when a person, failing to exercise caution, engages in conduct that creates a substantial risk of serious injury to another person.

Reckless Endangerment of Property is committed when a person, in the act of failing to exercise proper caution, engages in conduct that creates a risk of damage to the property of another person.

Robbery is committed when a person, against another person's will, takes property from that person.

Questions 36 through 41 are to be answered on the basis of the preceding legal definitions of crimes. Although these definitions may vary slightly from state to state, you are to answer the questions solely on the basis of the definitions stated here.

36. As the result of a dispute over a parking space, Anne Blount and Bea Wallace engage in an argument during which Blount pushes Wallace in an attempt to scare her. Wallace is not hurt, but she makes an obscene gesture in the direction of Blount. Referring to the definitions given, which one of the following best describes the incident?
(A) Blount committed assault, and Wallace committed harassment.
(B) Blount and Wallace both committed harassment.
(C) Neither Blount nor Wallace committed harassment.
(D) Wallace committed assault, and Blount committed harassment.

37. William Hammer, fully intending to scare James Bates, drives his car at a high speed in the direction of Bates, who quickly jumps out of the path of the vehicle. In turning in the direction of Bates, Hammer narrowly misses Fred Collins, a bystander. Neither Bates nor Collins is injured. According to the definitions, Hammer
(A) did not commit an assault against Bates or Collins.
(B) did not commit a crime.
(C) committed an assault against Bates and Collins.
(D) committed an assault against Collins only.

38. Jon Ochtes picks the pocket of Will Ronge and takes his wallet. Ronge is unaware that his wallet has been taken. According to the definitions, Ochtes committed the crime of
(A) robbery.
(B) burglary.
(C) larceny.
(D) criminal trespass.

39. James Calvin is driving his car and has as his passenger his four-year-old daughter, Pamela. Calvin's car is suddenly struck by another car, and as a result of the accident, Pamela is instantly killed. Calvin, upon learning of his daughter's death, approaches the driver of the other vehicle, takes out a gun and shoots him dead. The definitions indicate that Calvin had committed the crime of
(A) felony murder.
(B) criminally negligent homicide.
(C) murder.
(D) manslaughter.

40. James Floyd has an argument with John Rudd. Floyd then sets fire to Rudd's car, totally destroying it. According to the definitions given, James Floyd has committed the crime of
(A) arson.
(B) criminal mischief.
(C) reckless endangerment of property.
(D) harassment.

41. Roger Brown enjoys and engages in the practice of making obscene gestures towards passengers on subway trains. According to the definitions given, when Brown is in the act of making obscene gestures, he is committing the crime of

(A) menace.
(B) jostling.
(C) reckless endangerment.
(D) harassment.

42. Police Officer Summer responds to a call regarding a report of a missing person. The following information is obtained by the officer:

Time of Occurrence:	11 A.M.
Place of Occurrence:	Forest Park
Reported by:	Diane Marcus (daughter)
Description of Missing Person:	Janet Marcus (mother), 72 years old, 5'4", blue eyes, brown hair

Officer Sumner is completing a report on the incident. Which of the following expresses the above information most clearly and accurately?

(A) Mrs. Janet Marcus, reported missing by her daughter Diane, was seen in Forest Park. The last time she saw her was at 11 A.M. She is 72 years old with brown hair, blue eyes, and is 5'4".
(B) Diane Marcus reported that her mother, Janet Marcus, is missing. Janet Marcus is 72 years old, has brown hair, blue eyes, and is 5'4". She was last seen at 11 A.M. in Forest Park.
(C) Diane Marcus reported Janet, her 72-year-old mother at 11 A.M. to be missing after being seen last at Forest Park. Described as being 5'4", she has brown hair and blue eyes.
(D) At 11 A.M. Diane Marcus's mother was last seen by her daughter in Forest Park. She has brown hair and blue eyes. Diane reported Janet is 5'4" and 72 years old.

43. Under certain circumstances, Police Officers may be required to use their handguns. In which one of the following situations would it be justified for an Officer to draw a gun from its holster?

(A) A teenager pushes his way onto a bus without paying a fare and knocks an elderly woman into the farebox.
(B) A chain-snatcher yanks a chain from a woman's neck and runs with it.
(C) A hit-and-run driver is speeding from the scene.
(D) A half-clad man is swinging an axe on a crowded sidewalk and is threatening to kill anyone who comes near him.

44. Police Officers must sometimes rely on eyewitness accounts of incidents, even though eyewitnesses often make mistakes with regard to certain details. Warren Chen was the victim of a hit-and-run accident. When Police Officer Potocki arrived at the scene, he interviewed a number of bystanders who claimed to have witnessed a blue, two-door, compact car hit the victim and leave the scene. The following are the license numbers reported by four witnesses. Which one of these numbers should Officer Potocki consider to be most likely to be correct?

(A) C-82324
(B) C-82342
(C) G-83424
(D) G-62323

Questions 45 through 47 are to be answered solely on the basis of the following procedure.

1. When a prisoner requests medical attention or is in apparent need of it, the police officer should arrange for the prisoner to be promptly examined by a doctor.
2. In the event that a prisoner is in need of medical treatment, the police officer should notify a supervisor immediately so that an ambulance can be summoned. Prisoners who are drug addicts and are in need of treatment for their addiction should be taken to a hospital by a radio car.
3. Under no circumstances should a police officer prescribe any medication for a prisoner.
4. A police officer should not attempt to diagnose a prisoner's illness or injury and should not attempt to treat the prisoner except in a situation in which first aid is required. First aid should be administered promptly.
5. A doctor is the only person authorized to administer medicine to a prisoner. When a doctor is not available, the police officer in charge of the prisoner should then give him or her the medicine and watch him or her take it.

45. Alan Fox, a prisoner well known to police because of his long record, is in custody when he claims that he has a severe headache as a result of being badly beaten. There are no apparent signs of a physical injury, but the prisoner demands medical attention. The police officer in charge of Alan Fox should

(A) consider the prisoner's long record before deciding to call a doctor.
(B) give the prisoner aspirin tablets.
(C) ignore the prisoner's request for medical attention since there are no apparent physical injuries.
(D) see that Alan Fox is promptly examined by a doctor.

46. It is a hot summer day, and Officer David Stone has in his custody a prisoner who is a drug addict. The prisoner opens his shirt to reveal a large unhealed wound that is obviously infected. Officer Stone suggests to the prisoner that he call a doctor in to examine him, but the prisoner refuses, saying the wound is of no consequence. In this instance, Officer Stone should

(A) request that his supervisor call an ambulance.
(B) closely examine the wound to evaluate its severity.
(C) adhere to the prisoner's wishes and do nothing about the matter.
(D) take the prisoner at once to a hospital in a radio car.

47. Melanie Feeney, a prisoner, is in court waiting to make an appearance. She informs Officer Dorkin, who is guarding her, that she is terrified and is about to faint. She states that a tranquilizer would relieve her anxiety. Police Officer Dorkin takes tranquilizers on occasion and happens to have some with him. These tranquilizers are prescribed by Officer Dorkin's physician. Officer Dorkin offers Feeney a tranquilizer and she takes it. Police Officer Dorkin acted

(A) properly; his action relieved the situation.
(B) improperly; all medicines given to a prisoner must be prescribed by a doctor.
(C) properly; he watched her take the medicine.
(D) improperly; he should have summoned an ambulance.

Answer questions 48 through 50 on the basis of the information given in the following passage.

In addition to making the preliminary investigation of crimes, police patrol officers should serve as eyes, ears, and legs for the detective division. The patrol division may be used for surveillance, to serve warrants and bring in suspects and witnesses, and to perform a number of routine tasks for the detectives that will increase the time available for tasks that require their special skills and facilities. It is to the advantage of individual detectives, as well as the detective division, to have patrol officers working in this manner. More cases are cleared by arrest, and a greater proportion of stolen property is recovered when, in addition to the detective regularly assigned, a number of patrol officers also work on the case. Detectives may stimulate the interest and participation of patrol officers by keeping them informed of the presence, identity or description, hangouts, associates, vehicles, and method of operation of each criminal known to be in the community.

48. According to this passage, a patrol officer should

(A) assist the detective in certain routine functions.

(B) be considered for assignment as a detective on the basis of patrol performance.

(C) leave the scene once a detective arrives.

(D) perform as much of the detective's duties as time permits.

49. According to this passage, patrol officers should aid detectives by

(A) accepting from detectives assignments that give promise of recovering stolen property.

(B) making arrests of witnesses for the detective's interrogation.

(C) performing all special investigative work for detectives.

(D) producing for questioning individuals who may aid the detective in investigation.

50. According to this passage, detectives can keep patrol officers interested by

(A) ascertaining that patrol officers are doing investigative work properly.

(B) having patrol officers directly under their supervision during an investigation.

(C) informing patrol officers of the value of their efforts in crime prevention.

(D) supplying the patrol officers with information regarding known criminals in the community.

ANSWER KEY

1. **D**	11. **B**	21. **D**	31. **A**	41. **D**
2. **C**	12. **C**	22. **A**	32. **B**	42. **B**
3. **C**	13. **A**	23. **C**	33. **D**	43. **D**
4. **D**	14. **B**	24. **A**	34. **C**	44. **A**
5. **C**	15. **C**	25. **D**	35. **B**	45. **D**
6. **D**	16. **B**	26. **B**	36. **B**	46. **A**
7. **C**	17. **B**	27. **B**	37. **A**	47. **B**
8. **D**	18. **A**	28. **D**	38. **C**	48. **A**
9. **D**	19. **C**	29. **C**	39. **D**	49. **D**
10. **A**	20. **D**	30. **C**	40. **B**	50. **D**

EXPLANATORY ANSWERS

Questions 1 to 15: If you made any errors, read back through the passage to confirm the correct answers.

16. **(B)** The long, thin scar on the cheek would be highly visible. The eye patch also makes for good identification because very few people wear them. Points of identification must be distinctive or unusual, visible, and not easily subject to change.

17. **(B)** You must read for details and then use these details to reason. This type of question highlights the value of reading the questions before you read the paragraph. Question 17 deals with rape, question 18 with auto theft. In your initial reading of the paragraph, you will underscore details concerning rape and auto theft, ignoring information relating to burglary and assault. With your information thus narrowed, note that the rape area is Chapel Street. Eliminate choices (A) and (C). The rapes occur in the six-hour span from 10 P.M. to 4 A.M. Choice (B) covers five hours of this six-hour span; (D) covers only the two hours from 10 P.M. to midnight.

18. **(A)** Approach this question in the same way. Auto theft appears to be a midweek event. Only choices (A) and (C) include the three target days of Monday, Tuesday, and Thursday. Auto thefts occur under cover of darkness, making (C) a poor choice.

19. **(C)** The fact of assault seems clear. Ramos caused physical injury to Wu. According to the definitions, assault is the only charge. Harassment requires that no injury be intended, but Ramos stated intent to harm Wu. Menacing requires that no injury be caused. These definitions are mutually exclusive. Only one can apply. Definitions of other crimes may allow for one definition to be included within another. Careful reading is the number one requirement.

20. **(D)** Refer to Rule 6 of the procedure and select choice (D).

21. **(D)** Refer to Rule 1 of the procedure and select choice (D). The reason for not standing in front of the door is that, if the inhabitants of the apartment had a gun, the officer would be vulnerable if the weapon were fired at the door.

22. **(A)** The actions of the officers should be evaluated as improper. They should have interviewed the husband and the wife to get both sides of the story.

23. **(C)** Officer Blue's statement was inappropriate. Refer to Rules 4 and 7 and then select (C) as the correct answer. A police officer does

not have the authority to direct an individual to change his or her mode of living if it is not unlawful.

24. **(A)** The officers acted improperly. No arrest should have been made since no one was hurt (see Rule 8).

25. **(D)** Prisoners have been known to hang themselves with their belts. The other three choices offer no conceivable danger.

26. **(B)** This choice identifies the victim, tells where she lives, and tells when and where the crime took place, what happened, and the nature and value of the stolen property.

27. **(B)** The passage talks exclusively about tire tracks. No mention is made of autos being used in the commission of crimes, scientific police work, or positive identification through cars.

28. **(D)** Refer to the third and fourth sentences of the passage.

29. **(C)** Refer to the second sentence of the passage.

30. **(C)** Refer to the last sentence of the passage.

31. **(A)** The objective of the officers is to get the prisoner to supply the names of the other parties involved. Refer to Rule 4 of the procedure.

32. **(B)** Refer to Rule 3 of the procedure. If the officer is sufficiently convincing, the man is likely to confess.

33. **(D)** This approach is the most direct, and it will probably convince the woman to cooperate with the police in the upcoming proceedings.

34. **(C)** When date and time are indicated in a report, the most coherent summary usually begins with this information. Focus first on the choice that begins with date and time but do not take it for granted. Be sure to read it through to be certain it includes all other pertinent information in a logical arrangement.

35. **(B)** The report must make it clear just who was abused, who is accused of the abusing, who has made the report, and where the abused and abusers may be found. You can be certain only from choice (B).

36. **(B)** Blount and Wallace both committed harassment: Blount because she pushed Wallace in an attempt to scare her and Wallace because she made an obscene gesture at Blount.

37. **(A)** William Hammer did not injure either Bates or Collins, so he is not guilty of assault. He was, however, intentionally reckless.

38. **(C)** Larceny is the wrongful taking of property from its owner without use of force, violence, or threat of injury.

39. **(D)** Since Calvin may be considered "under the influence of an extreme emotional disturbance" over the death of his daughter, the crime Calvin committed was manslaughter.

40. **(B)** The definition of the crime of criminal mischief involves the intentional destruction of another person's property. This was not arson because a car is not a building and there was no explosion.

41. **(D)** Making obscene gestures in public places is considered harassment.

42. **(B)** This is a well-written report. It states the nature of the problem (a missing person), describes the missing person, and tells when and where that person was last seen.

43. **(D)** A police officer must always hesitate to use a gun in a crowd because of the danger to innocent bystanders. In this case, however, the man with the axe is already presenting a clear and present danger to the people who surround him. A well-aimed shot to the man with the axe may preserve the safety of a far greater number. The officer must take this calculated risk.

44. **(A)** Reconstruct the number as best as you can based on the principle of frequently occurring elements. The digits 8-2-3-2 all appear in three of the four eyewitness accounts in these respective positions. Of the final digits, only 4 appears more than once. Your choice is far from certain, but in balance (A) is the best bet.

45. **(D)** Refer to Rule 1. An officer should never assume the responsibility of deciding whether a prisoner requires the services of a doctor.

46. **(A)** Refer to Rule 2. It is apparent that the prisoner requires medical attention even though there is no emergency. Medical attention is required for the prisoner's wound, not his drug addiction; therefore, an ambulance should be called.

47. **(B)** Officer Dorkin acted improperly. Rule 3 states that *under no circumstances* should a police officer prescribe medication for a prisoner. Medicine prescribed for Officer Dorkin might have been harmful to the prisoner.

48. **(A)** The first sentence of the passage states that the patrol officer "should serve as eyes, ears, and legs for the detective division." No statement in the passage makes any mention of police officers being considered for assignment to the detective division, leaving the scene when detectives arrive, or performing detectives' duties.

49. **(D)** Refer to the second sentence of the passage.

50. **(D)** Refer to the last sentence of the passage.

Answer Sheet for Sample Questions: Police Officer Exam II

1. Ⓐ Ⓑ Ⓒ Ⓓ	11. Ⓐ Ⓑ Ⓒ Ⓓ	21. Ⓐ Ⓑ Ⓒ Ⓓ	31. Ⓐ Ⓑ Ⓒ Ⓓ	41. Ⓐ Ⓑ Ⓒ Ⓓ
2. Ⓐ Ⓑ Ⓒ Ⓓ	12. Ⓐ Ⓑ Ⓒ Ⓓ	22. Ⓐ Ⓑ Ⓒ Ⓓ	32. Ⓐ Ⓑ Ⓒ Ⓓ	42. Ⓐ Ⓑ Ⓒ Ⓓ
3. Ⓐ Ⓑ Ⓒ Ⓓ	13. Ⓐ Ⓑ Ⓒ Ⓓ	23. Ⓐ Ⓑ Ⓒ Ⓓ	33. Ⓐ Ⓑ Ⓒ Ⓓ	43. Ⓐ Ⓑ Ⓒ Ⓓ
4. Ⓐ Ⓑ Ⓒ Ⓓ	14. Ⓐ Ⓑ Ⓒ Ⓓ	24. Ⓐ Ⓑ Ⓒ Ⓓ	34. Ⓐ Ⓑ Ⓒ Ⓓ	44. Ⓐ Ⓑ Ⓒ Ⓓ
5. Ⓐ Ⓑ Ⓒ Ⓓ	15. Ⓐ Ⓑ Ⓒ Ⓓ	25. Ⓐ Ⓑ Ⓒ Ⓓ	35. Ⓐ Ⓑ Ⓒ Ⓓ	45. Ⓐ Ⓑ Ⓒ Ⓓ
6. Ⓐ Ⓑ Ⓒ Ⓓ	16. Ⓐ Ⓑ Ⓒ Ⓓ	26. Ⓐ Ⓑ Ⓒ Ⓓ	36. Ⓐ Ⓑ Ⓒ Ⓓ	46. Ⓐ Ⓑ Ⓒ Ⓓ
7. Ⓐ Ⓑ Ⓒ Ⓓ	17. Ⓐ Ⓑ Ⓒ Ⓓ	27. Ⓐ Ⓑ Ⓒ Ⓓ	37. Ⓐ Ⓑ Ⓒ Ⓓ	47. Ⓐ Ⓑ Ⓒ Ⓓ
8. Ⓐ Ⓑ Ⓒ Ⓓ	18. Ⓐ Ⓑ Ⓒ Ⓓ	28. Ⓐ Ⓑ Ⓒ Ⓓ	38. Ⓐ Ⓑ Ⓒ Ⓓ	48. Ⓐ Ⓑ Ⓒ Ⓓ
9. Ⓐ Ⓑ Ⓒ Ⓓ	19. Ⓐ Ⓑ Ⓒ Ⓓ	29. Ⓐ Ⓑ Ⓒ Ⓓ	39. Ⓐ Ⓑ Ⓒ Ⓓ	49. Ⓐ Ⓑ Ⓒ Ⓓ
10. Ⓐ Ⓑ Ⓒ Ⓓ	20. Ⓐ Ⓑ Ⓒ Ⓓ	30. Ⓐ Ⓑ Ⓒ Ⓓ	40. Ⓐ Ⓑ Ⓒ Ⓓ	50. Ⓐ Ⓑ Ⓒ Ⓓ

Sample Questions: Police Officer Exam II

MEMORY BOOKLET

Directions: *You will be given 10 minutes to study the following six "Wanted Posters" and to try to remember as many details as you can. You may not take any notes during this time.*

WANTED FOR ASSAULT

Name: John Markham
Age: 27
Height: 5'11"
Weight: 215 lbs.
Race: Black
Hair color: black
Eye color: brown
Complexion: dark
Identifying marks: eagle tattoo on back of right hand; very hard of hearing
Suspect is a former boxer.
He favors brass knuckles as his weapon.

WANTED FOR RAPE

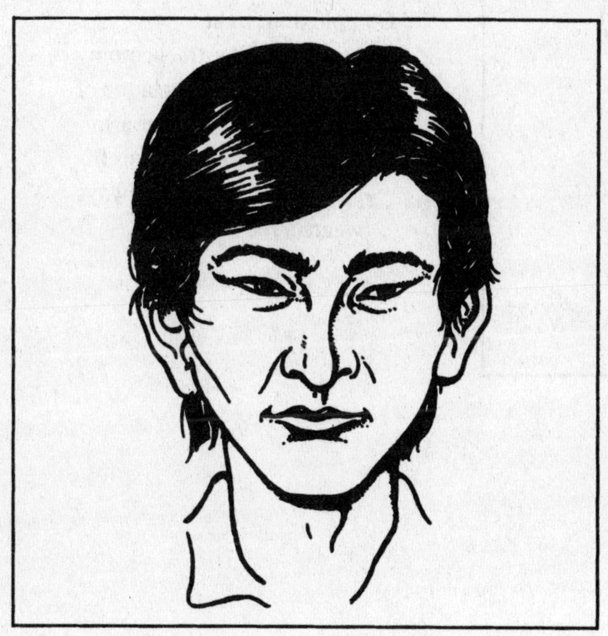

Name: Arthur Lee
Age: 19
Height: 5'7"
Weight: 180 lbs.
Race: Asian
Hair color: black
Eye color: brown
Complexion: medium
Identifying marks: none
Suspect carries a pearl-handled knife with an eight-inch curved blade. He tends to attack victims in subway passageways.

WANTED FOR ARMED ROBBERY

Name: Antonio Gomez
Age: 31
Height: 5'6"
Weight: 160 lbs.
Race: Hispanic
Hair color: brown
Eye color: brown
Complexion: medium
Identifying marks: missing last finger of right hand; tattoo on back says "Mother"; tattoo on left biceps says "Linda"; tattoo on right biceps says "Carmen"
Suspect was seen leaving the scene in a stolen yellow 1987 Corvette. He carries a gun and must be considered dangerous.

WANTED FOR CAR THEFT

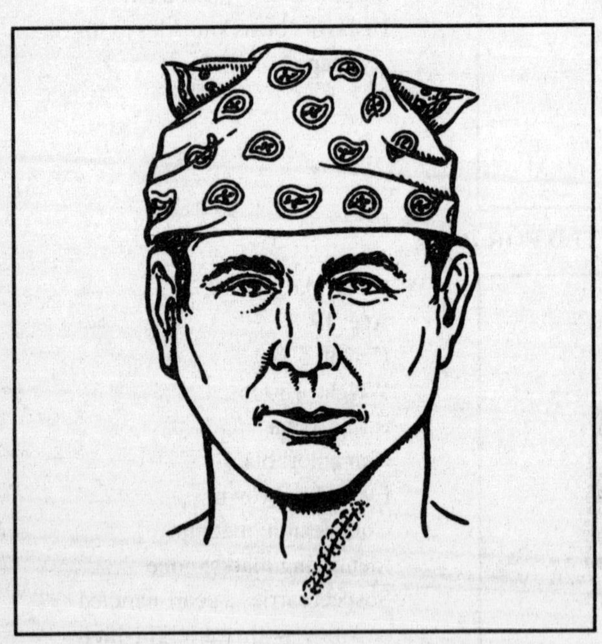

Name: Robert Miller
Age: 24
Height: 6'3"
Weight: 230 lbs.
Race: White
Hair color: brown
Eye color: blue
Complexion: light
Identifying marks: tracheotomy scar at base of neck; tattoo of dragon on right upper arm
Suspect chain-smokes unfiltered cigarettes. He always wears a red head scarf.

WANTED FOR MURDER

Name: Janet Walker
Age: 39
Height: 5'10"
Weight: 148 lbs.
Race: Black
Hair color: black
Eye color: black
Complexion: dark
Identifying marks: large hairy mole on upper left thigh; stutters badly
Suspect has frequently been arrested for prostitution. She often wears multiple ear and nose rings.

WANTED FOR ARSON

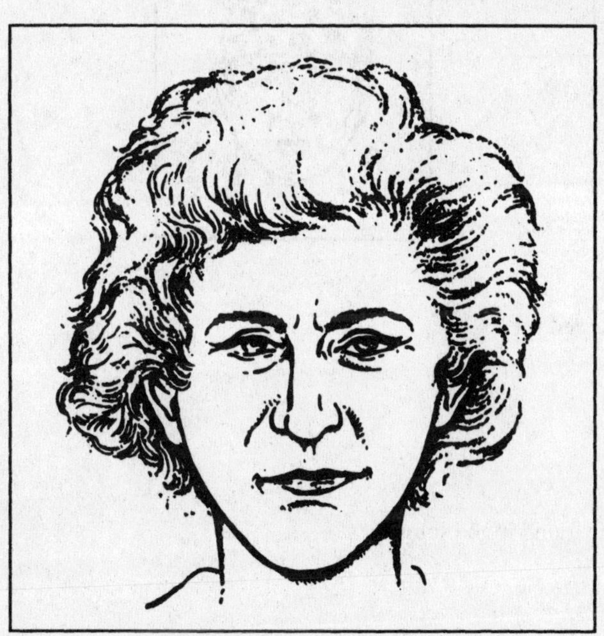

Name: Margaret Pickford
Age: 42
Height 5'2"
Weight: 103 lbs.
Race: White
Hair color: red
Eye color: green
Complexion: light
Identifying marks: known heroin addict with track marks on forearms; walks with decided limp because left leg is shorter than right
Suspect has a child in foster care in Astoria. She usually carries two large shopping bags.

TEST QUESTION BOOKLET

Directions: *The first 10 questions are based on the information given on the "Wanted Posters." Answer these questions first. Then proceed directly to the remaining questions. Choose the best answer to each question and mark its letter on your answer sheet.*

1. Which of the following suspects may have committed a crime to support a drug habit?

(A)

(C)

(B)

(D)

2. The suspect that is missing a finger is wanted for
(A) rape
(B) assault
(C) murder
(D) armed robbery

3. Which of the suspects is most likely to be found in the subway?
(A) John Markham
(B) Margaret Pickford
(C) Arthur Lee
(D) Robert Miller

4. Which of these suspects has a dragon tattoo?

(A)

(C)

(B)

(D)

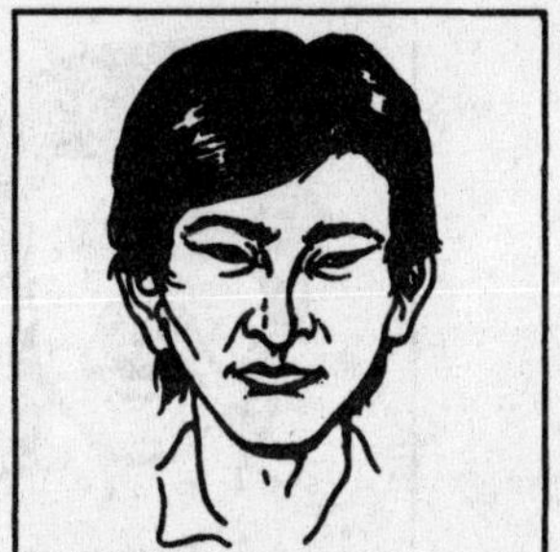

5. Which is an identifying mark of this suspect?
   (A) Deafness
   (B) A large mole
   (C) A tattoo that reads "Mother"
   (D) Needle tracts

6. Which one of the following is considered to be the most dangerous?

(A)

(C)

(B)

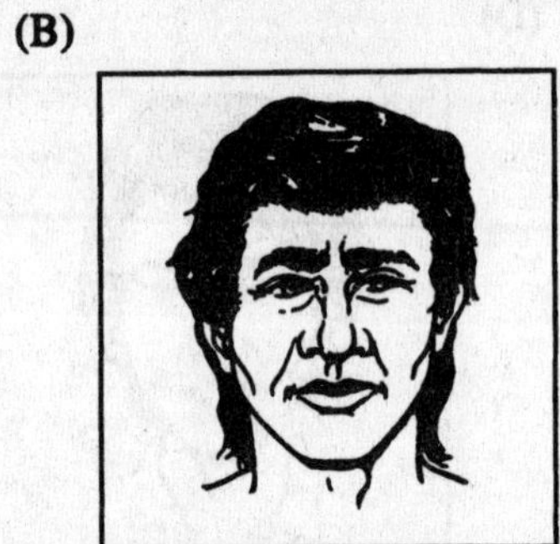

(D)

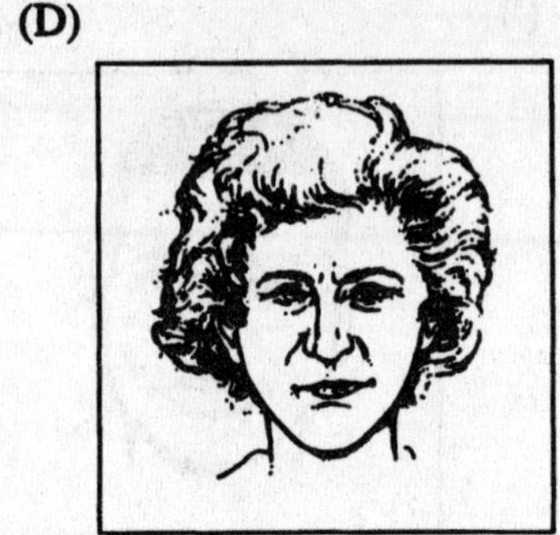

7. Which of these suspects is known to be a parent?
   (A) The suspect who stutters
   (B) The former boxer
   (C) The smoker
   (D) The suspect who limps

8. Which of these suspects escaped the scene of his or her crime in a stolen car?

(A)

(C)

(B)

(D)

9. Which of these suspects would have the hardest time running from the police?
   (A) The heroin addict
   (B) The suspect who is nearly deaf
   (C) The suspect who wears lots of jewelry
   (D) The suspect with brass knuckles in his pocket

10. Which of these suspects is wanted for rape?

(A)

(C)

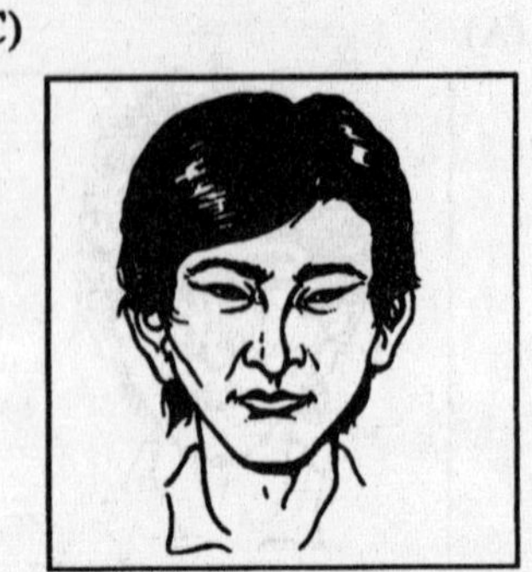

(B)

(D)

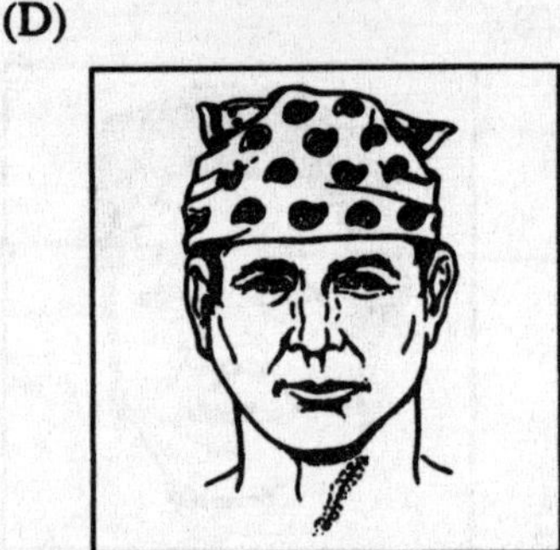

11. Police Officer Barros has received a report of a chain snatching and has obtained the following information:

Date of Occurrence:	August 12, 1993
Place of Occurrence:	In front of 4312 Third Avenue
Time of Occurrence:	5:10 P.M.
Incident:	Chain snatching
Victim:	Marina Marzycki, age 35, of 887 West Houston Street
Witness:	Bonita Bonds, age 56, of 4309 Third Avenue
Suspect:	White male about 18 years of age, 5'9", 165 lbs., dark brown hair, clean-shaven

Officer Barros is preparing a report on the incident. Which one of the following expresses the preceding information most clearly and accurately?

(A) Marina Marzycki of 887 West Houston Street had her chain snatched in front of 4309 Third Avenue by a white male. Bonita Bonds saw it at 5:10 P.M.

(B) A 5'9", 165 lbs. white male of 4312 Third Avenue snatched the chain of Marina Marzycki, age 35, at 5:10 P.M.

(C) On August 12 at 5:10 P.M., Bonita Bonds of 4309 Third Avenue witnessed a chain snatching in front of 4312 Third Avenue. It was committed by an 18-year-old clean-shaven white male with brown hair.

(D) Bonita Bonds says that Marina Marzycki's chain was snatched at 887 West Houston Street by a medium-sized teenager.

12. Officer Hollis has just issued a summons to a driver and has obtained the following information:

Time of Occurrence:	4:08 A.M.
Place of Occurrence:	Baylor Boulevard between 16th Street and Highland Road
Offense:	Illegal U-turn
Driver:	Robert Richards Jr., age 29
Address of Driver:	92 Carolina Street

Officer Hollis is making an entry in his memo book regarding the incident. Which one of the following expresses the preceding information most clearly and accurately?

(A) Robert Richards Jr., age 29, made a U-turn at 92 Carolina Street. I arrested him.
(B) At 4:08 A.M. I stopped Robert Richards of 92 Carolina Street for making an illegal U-turn on Baylor Boulevard.
(C) 29-year-old Robert Richards Jr. made an illegal U-turn on Baylor Boulevard at 92 Carolina Street. It was early this morning.
(D) When Robert Richards Jr., age 29, made an illegal U-turn on Baylor Boulevard between 16th Street and Highland Road, I gave him a summons at 92 Carolina Street at 4:08.

13. Police officers are sometimes required to respond to the scene of a traffic accident involving two vehicles. In situations in which one of the drivers involved in the accident has left the scene before the arrival of a police officer, the responding officer must use the following procedures in the order given:

1. Question the driver of the remaining vehicle as to the license plate number of the vehicle that fled.
   a. If the complete license plate number is known, call the Vehicle Inquiry Section to determine the name and address of owner.
   b. Write down the name and address of the owner of the vehicle that fled.
   c. Give the name and address of the owner of the vehicle that fled to the driver remaining at scene of accident.
2. Obtain from the driver remaining at the scene all details of the accident including a description of the vehicle that fled.
3. Call the Stolen Vehicle Desk.
4. Prepare a Complaint Form in duplicate.

Police Officer Yoshida has arrived at the scene of a traffic accident involving two cars. One of the drivers fled the scene immediately after the impact, but the driver of the remaining vehicle, Louis Santangelo, noticed that the last three digits of the license plate were 7-9-7, and he has given this information to Officer Yoshida. Which one of the following actions should Officer Yoshida take next?

(A) Call the Vehicle Inquiry Section to determine the name and address of the owner.
(B) Call the Stolen Vehicle Desk.
(C) Write down the name and address of Louis Santangelo.
(D) Ask Santangelo for a description of the other car and for details of the accident.

14. Transit Police Officer Padula has responded to a complaint of drug sales in a subway entrance stairwell. Officer Padula obtains the following information at the scene:

Time of Occurrence:	6:15 A.M.
Place of Occurrence:	Stairwell of northbound entrance, 50th Street Station, Broadway line
Witnesses:	Mary Jones, age 58, homeless Tom Harriman, age 25, 1189 Ninth Ave.
Suspect:	Hispanic male about age 20 wearing torn blue jeans and a long-sleeved plaid shirt; known as "Tony"
Crime:	Drug sales
Action taken:	Suspect ran onto northbound #1 train

Officer Padula must file a report of this incident. Which one of the following expresses the preceding information most clearly and accurately?

(A) Tony was selling drugs in the Broadway subway station, but he got away on the #1. Mary Jones and Tom Harriman saw him.

(B) At 6:15 this morning a homeless man named Tony sold drugs to Mary Jones who lives on Ninth Avenue and Tom Harriman in a plaid shirt. This happened in the 50th Sweet subway station. He got away.

(C) At 6:15 A.M. Tom Harriman sold drugs to a homeless man called Tony in the northbound 50th Street subway station. Mary Jones said that he escaped to 1189 Ninth Avenue.

(D) Tom Harriman of 1189 Ninth Avenue and Mary Jones, homeless, report that a man called Tony wearing torn blue jeans and a plaid shirt was selling drugs in the northbound 50th Street Broadway stairwell at 6:15 A.M. The suspect escaped on a northbound #1 train.

15. Foreign diplomats cannot be arrested or personally served with a summons. When a police officer arrives at the scene of an incident involving a diplomat, the officer must:

1. Take necessary action to protect life and property.
2. Obtain the name and title of the diplomat and his government.
   a. Ask to see the diplomat's identification.
   b. If the diplomat cannot produce identification, telephone the Operations Unit for verification.
3. If a vehicle bearing DPL license plates is unoccupied, illegally parked, and creating a safety hazard, place a summons on the windshield. As Police Officer Schuman is patrolling her assigned area, she is approached by an agitated citizen carrying a black bag. The gentleman identifies himself as Dr. Forster. Dr. Forster has been called by the hospital to attend to a patient, but a double-parked car with DPL license plates is blocking his car. Officer Schuman notices that there is a person sitting in the back seat of the car with DPL plates. The passenger identifies himself as a diplomat and produces identification. He does not move the car. Officer Schuman suggests to Dr. Forster that he had better take a cab to the hospital. Schuman writes a parking summons and places it on the windshield of the vehicle. Police Officer Schuman's action in giving the car a parking summons is

(A) appropriate; the car created a safety hazard in blocking a doctor's car.

(B) inappropriate; Schuman should have checked first with the Operations Unit.

(C) appropriate; a summons cannot be handed to a diplomat but may be placed on a diplomat's car.

(D) inappropriate; the car was unoccupied.

16. A small art gallery on Police Officer Bannai's regular patrol has been burglarized. The owner of the gallery, Karel White, has prepared this inventory of missing objects:

2 small bronze sculptures, each valued at	$4,500
5 oil paintings, each valued at	$930
3 porcelain urns, each valued at	$2,220
7 framed prints, each valued at	$90
contents of cash register	$436

By what formula should Officer Bannai calculate the value of the missing property?

(A) 2 + 4500 + 5 + 930 + 3 + 2220 + 7 + 90 + 436
(B) 2 (4500) + 5 (930) + 3 (2220) + 7 (90) + 436
(C) (2 + 5 + 3 + 7)(4500 + 930 + 2220 + 90 + 436)
(D) (2 + 5 + 3 + 7)(4500 + 930 + 2220 + 90) + 436

17. Police officers are required to respond to areas where people have become ill or been injured and to render necessary aid, take corrective action, and prepare prescribed forms. Upon arrival at a scene at which aid is required, a police officer should:

1. Render reasonable aid to the sick or injured person.
2. Request an ambulance or doctor if necessary.
3. Wait in view to direct the ambulance or assign a responsible person to do so.
4. If the ambulance does not arrive in 20 minutes, make another call.
5. Accompany the unconscious or unidentified aided person to the hospital in the body of ambulance.

Off-duty Police Officer McGonnigle is in the vicinity of a construction site where a heavy steel beam has fallen from the roof and struck a woman passing by on the sidewalk. Officer McGonnigle runs to the scene and finds that the woman is unconscious and is bleeding profusely from a wound to the groin. The first thing Officer McGonnigle should do is

(A) identify himself as a police officer.
(B) send for an ambulance.
(C) attempt to stop the bleeding by applying pressure.
(D) reassure the woman that he will go to the hospital with her.

Answer questions 18–20 on the basis of the following map.

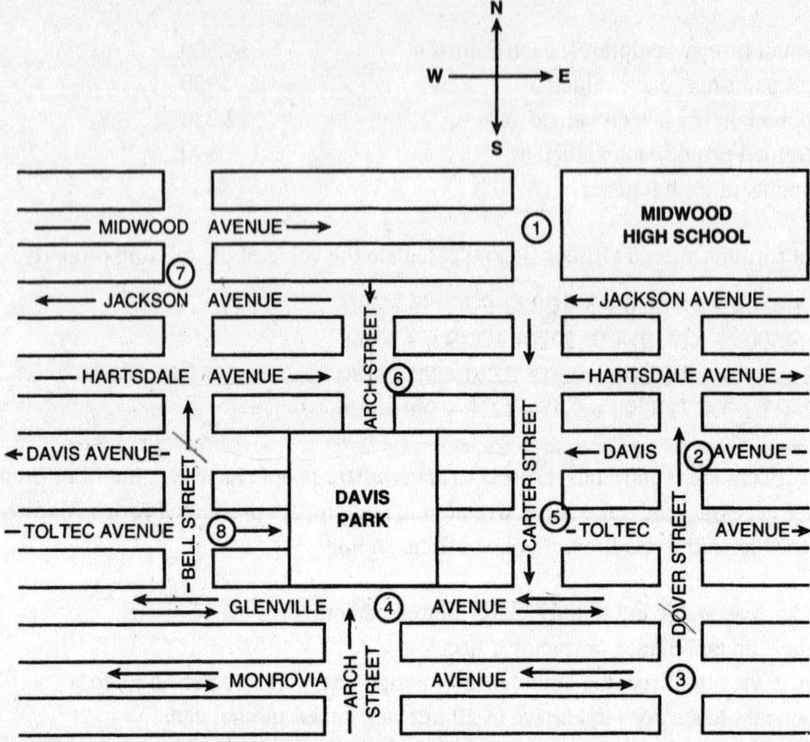

18. You are located at Carter Street and Davis Avenue. You receive a call to respond to a traffic accident at the intersection of Midwood Avenue and Carter Street. Which one of the following is the most direct route for you to take in your patrol car, making sure to obey all traffic regulations?

(A) Travel south on Carter Street for one block, then one block east on Toltec Avenue, then three blocks north on Dover Street, then one block west on Jackson Avenue, then one block north on Carter Street.

(B) Travel two blocks south on Carter Street, then west for two blocks on Glenville Avenue, then north for five blocks on Bell Street, then one block east on Midwood Avenue.

(C) Travel one block east on Davis Avenue, then two blocks north on Dover Street, then three blocks west on Jackson Avenue, then north for one block on Bell Street, then one block east on Midwood Avenue.

(D) Travel two blocks south on Carter Street, then east for one block on Glenville Avenue, then north for four blocks on Dover Street, then west for three blocks on Jackson Avenue, then north for one block on Bell Street, then east for one block on Midwood Avenue.

19. If you are located at point (4) and travel west for one block, then turn north and travel three blocks, then turn east and travel one block, then turn north and travel one block, and then turn west for one block, you will be closest to point

(A) 7
(B) 6
(C) 1
(D) 8

20. You are located at Davis Avenue and Bell Street. You receive a call of a burglary in progress at Glenville Avenue and Dover Street. Which of the following is the most direct route for you to take in your patrol car, making sure to obey all traffic regulations?

(A) Travel south for two blocks on Bell Street, then east for three blocks on Glenville Avenue.

(B) Travel north three blocks on Bell Street, then east for one block on Midwood Avenue, then south for five blocks on Carter Street, then one block east on Glenville Avenue.

(C) Travel north one block on Bell Street, then east for two blocks on Hartsdale Avenue, then south for three blocks on Carter Street, then one block east on Glenville Avenue.

(D) Travel north one block on Bell Street, then east for three blocks on Hartsdale Avenue, then south for three blocks on Dover Street.

21. Police Officer Jaime Veldez, riding alone in his patrol car in the early morning of November 12, spots an active fire. Officer Veldez quickly notes the following information:

Location of Fire:	112 Lorelei Lane, just north of Industrial Highway
Time of Report:	3:12 A.M.
Type of Structure:	Plastics warehouse
Origin of Fire:	Unknown
Extent of Involvement:	Active and total; heavy, foul-smelling smoke

Officer Veldez must radio an alarm right away. Which of the following conveys all the information most clearly and accurately?

(A) A plastics warehouse caught fire all by itself at 3:12 A.M. today at 112 Lorelei Lane. It is north of Industrial Highway and smoking.

(B) There is a big fire at the plastics warehouse at Industrial Highway, North and 112 Lorelei Lane right now. It is November 12 and it is 3:12 A.M. so no one is at work, but it smells awful.

(C) A fire at 112 Lorelei Lane, a plastics warehouse, is burning out of control for unknown reasons north of Industrial Highway. Someone should put it out.

(D) It is 3:12 A.M., and I am approaching a major fire at the plastics warehouse at 112 Lorelei Lane just north of Industrial Highway. The smoke is heavy and may well be toxic.

22. ROUTINE SICK AT HOME—The New York City police department classifies a routine sick at home call as a call for service in which a sick person is aided at his or her residence and:

a. He or she is conscious and properly identified.
b. No other police service or notification is required.
c. No dependent adults or uncared for children are in the household.
d. No other investigation is needed.

According to the preceding definition, which of the following should be entered in a police officer's log as a routine sick at home call?

(A) Myrtle Cubbage, age 97, became dizzy in her apartment and fell to the living room floor. Her full-time live-in aide, Millie Mohan, was unable to lift her and called emergency services. Police Officer Ataturk responded to the call, helped Ms. Mohan in lifting Ms. Cubbage to her bed, and found Ms. Cubbage's vital signs to be normal. Ms. Mohan thanked Officer Ataturk for his assistance and assured him that she had the situation well under control.

(B) Police Officer Barbini responded to the call of Hattie Cool who had cut herself very badly while splitting a three-day-old bagel. Officer Barbini noted that the baby appeared to be safely sleeping in his crib and called for an ambulance to transport Ms. Cool to the emergency room to have her hand sutured.

(C) Officer Kaliopolis was called to an apartment house airshaft where she found an unidentified man lying unconscious on the ground. Officer Kaliopolis summoned an ambulance and accompanied the victim to the hospital.

(D) Jimmy Jordan, age 9 and home alone, felt very nauseated and began vomiting. Police Officer Llewellyn, responding to Jimmy's call, found him feeling much better but frightened at having been sick all by himself.

23. Police Officer Phansonboom, while on foot patrol, has surprised a suspect in the process of breaking into a car. He has taken the suspect into custody and has obtained the following information:

Suspect:	Nick Harrison, age 17
Address of Suspect:	8768 East 99th Street
Crime:	Attempted auto theft
Location of Crime:	In front of Kimberly Hotel
Date of Occurrence:	March 19
Time of Occurrence:	6:12 A.M.

Officer Phansonboom must write up his arrest for the booking officer. Which of the following expresses this information most clearly and accurately?

(A) Nick Harrison, age 17, who lives at the Kimberly Hotel, 8768 East 99th Street, tried to steal a car on March 19 at 6:12 A.M.

(B) 17-year-old Nick Harrison tried to steal a car in front of the Kimberley Hotel, 8768 East 99th Street, at 6:12 A.M. on March 19th.

(C) On March 19th at 6:12 A.M., Nick Harrison, 17, of 8768 East 99th Street, attempted to steal a car from the front of the Kimberley Hotel.

(D) The 17-year-old suspect, Nick Harrison of 8678 East 99th Street, attempted to steal a car parked in front of the Kimberly Hotel at 6:12 on the morning of March 19.

24. A police officer who stops a person under suspicion for driving under the influence of alcohol should follow this procedure:

1. Ask the driver to step out of the vehicle.
2. Pat down the driver for weapons.
3. Ask to see his or her license and registration.
4. Ask the driver to walk a straight line.
5. Smell his or her breath.
6. Bring the driver to the police station for chemical testing.

Police Officer Gambino has been following a driver who has been weaving back and forth across the center line of the highway. Officer Gambino pulls the driver to the shoulder and asks to see her driver's license and registration. Officer Gambino has acted:

(A) correctly because the driver was weaving as if intoxicated.

(B) incorrectly because the driver might have been armed.

(C) correctly because there was alcohol on the driver's breath.

(D) incorrectly because Officer Gambino should first have asked the driver to get out of the car.

25. Police Officer Jorgenson is dispatched to investigate an allegation of child abuse in progress. Officer Jorgenson collects the following information:

Complaint:	Child abuse
Location:	1530 East 18th St., Apt. 7A
Complaint by:	Martje vanDam, 79, Apt. 7E
Alleged Victim:	Jonathan Grant, age 9
Alleged Abusers:	Mary Grant, mother, and Jack Frost, her boyfriend
Finding:	Allegation unfounded

Officer Jorgenson is preparing a report of this incident. Which of the following expresses the information most clearly and accurately?

(A) Martje vanDam said that Mary Grant and Jack Frost were beating Jonathan Grant. They weren't.
(B) Mary Grant and Jack Frost, Apt. 7A, 1530 East 18th Street, were accused by Martje vanDam, age 79, Apt. 7E, of abusing Mary Grant's 9-year-old son Jonathan Grant. I found no signs of child abuse.
(C) Mary Grant and Jack Frost, who is her boyfriend, said that they did not abuse Jonathan Grant at Apt. 7E. Martje vanDam of 1530 East 18th Street said they did. She is 79.
(D) Jonathan Grant, 9, of Apt. 7A, 1530 East 18th St., was not abused by his mother or her boyfriend even though Martje vanDam of Apt. 7E said he was.

26. Jared Kevy parked his BMW in a municipal parking garage overnight. The next morning, he discovered that the car had been broken into. He told police officers that the missing items were:

1 radio valued at	$900
1 tape player valued at	$655
9 tapes, each valued at	$12
15 bridge tokens, each valued at	$6
1 winter coat valued at	$237

By what formula should police calculate the value of the missing items?

(A) $900 + $655 + (9 + 15)($12 + $6) + $237
(B) $900 + $655 + (9)($12) + (15)($6) + $237
(C) $900 + $655 + $9 + $12 + $15 + $6 + $237
(D) $900 + $655 + (9)(15) + ($12)($6) + $237

27. If a police officer discovers a vehicle that appears to have been abandoned, the officer should do the following:

1. Make a memo book entry describing the vehicle and the location at which the vehicle was found.
2. Notify the desk officer and request a registration check.
3. Check the registration and vehicle identification number against stolen automobile files.
4. Arrange for removal of the vehicle.
5. Notify the owner.

Police Officer Fulco, covering a regular beat in a patrol car, has noticed a badly battered red Camaro that has not been moved from a spot too close to a crosswalk for a full week. Officer Fulco makes a memo book entry, notifies the desk officer, and requests a registration check. Next, Officer Fulco should

(A) arrange for removal of the vehicle.
(B) notify the owner.
(C) check the stolen automobile files.
(D) write a complete report.

28. Police Officer Ruiz, on patrol in a residential area, arrives at the scene of a fire and, after speaking with a bystander on the street, makes the following notes:

Place of Occurrence:	1520 Clarendon Road, Brooklyn
Time of Occurrence:	6:32 A.M.
Type of Building:	Two-family frame dwelling
Event:	Fire; suspected arson
Suspect:	Male, white, approx. 6-foot, wearing jeans
Witness:	Mary Smith of 1523 Clarendon Road, Brooklyn

Officer Ruiz must now write up a report of the incident. Which of the following expresses the information most clearly, accurately, and completely?

(A) At 6:32 A.M., Mary Smith of 1523 Clarendon Road, Brooklyn, saw a white male wearing approximately 6-foot blue jeans running from the building across the street.
(B) A white male wearing blue jeans ran from the house at 1520 Clarendon Road at 6:32 A.M. Mary Smith saw him.
(C) At 6:32 A.M., a 6-foot white male wearing blue jeans ran from a burning two-family frame structure at 1520 Clarendon Road, Brooklyn. He was observed by a neighbor, Mary Smith.
(D) A two-family frame house is on fire at 1520 Clarendon Road in Brooklyn. A white male in blue jeans probably did it. Mary Smith saw him run.

29. As a student at the police academy, you are handed the following scenario: Police Officer Wu, assigned to the transit division, reports to a token booth and obtains this information from a sobbing woman.

Time of Occurrence:	1:22 A.M.
Place of Occurrence:	Uptown-bound platform, 59th Street Station, 7th Avenue line
Victim:	Juana Martinez
Crime:	Purse snatching
Description of suspect:	Unknown, fled down steps to lower platform

Officer Wu must now call in an alert to the police dispatcher. Which of the following expresses the information most clearly, accurately, and completely?

(A) Juana Martinez had her purse snatched on the subway platform at 59th Street Station. She didn't see him.
(B) A purse was just snatched by a man who ran down the steps from the 7th Avenue token booth at 59th Street Station. Her name is Juana Martinez.
(C) It is 1:22 A.M. The person who snatched Juana Martinez' purse is downstairs at 59th Street Station.
(D) I am at 59th Street Station, uptown-bound 7th Avenue token booth. A Juana Martinez reports that her purse was just snatched by a man who fled down the steps to a lower platform.

30. Police officers assigned to patrol in a radio car are instructed to adhere to the following rules concerning the use of the police radios in patrol cars:

1. The use of the radio is to be restricted to performance of duty only.
2. All conversations should be to the point and as short as possible.
3. Names of people are not to be used.
4. All conversations should begin by identifying the vehicle by number.
5. A message received should be acknowledged by "ten-four."

Police Officers Abel and Flynn apprehend two men in the act of robbing a jewelry store. They place the men in Patrol Car 14 and radio in a report of the activity. Which one of the following messages would be in conformance with the procedure specified?

(A) "Officers Abel and Flynn, car one-four, proceeding to station house with two prisoners."
(B) "Car one-four, proceeding to station house with two prisoners."
(C) "Car one-four, Officers Abel and Flynn, proceeding to station house with two prisoners."
(D) "Car one-four, proceeding to station house with prisoners Bossey and Warren."

31. Quite often, a police officer is required to give assistance to an injured person. Upon responding to a call to assist an injured person, a police officer should be guided by the following procedure:

1. Administer first aid.
2. Call for medical assistance.
3. Call again if the ambulance does not respond within 20 minutes.
4. Accompany the injured person to the hospital if he or she is unconscious or unidentified.
5. Witness the search of an unconscious or unidentified person.
6. Attempt to identify the person who is unconscious or unidentified by a search of his or her property.

Officer Alcorn, while on patrol, observes a man lying in the front yard of a four-family house. Upon questioning, the man reveals that he fell while repairing the roof of his house. He says he is in a great deal of pain and is unable to move. Officer Alcorn summons an ambulance and gives the man first aid. He then requests that the man give his name, but the man refuses. The ambulance arrives in 15 minutes, and Officer Alcorn resumes patrol. Officer Alcorn failed to fulfill his obligations in this incident because he

(A) did not make a second call for the ambulance when the man was in great pain.
(B) failed to accompany the man to the hospital.
(C) did not attempt to locate a physician while waiting for the ambulance.
(D) failed to relieve the injured man's pain through the administration of proper first aid.

Question 32 is based on the following situation:

On a hot summer afternoon, three prisoners are missing from the state penitentiary located on the wooded outskirts of a small upstate city. Their means of escape has not yet been established, so search parties are dispatched near and far.

32. Police car 43 leaves the city traveling west on highway 9. After three miles, the car makes a right turn onto route 21. Two miles up route 21, a dirt road forks off in a diagonal right. Car 43 turns onto the dirt road and continues until it reaches a farmhouse on the right-hand side of the road. The car turns into the driveway, and both officers get out. When the driver gets out, in which direction is she facing?

(A) Northeast
(B) Southwest
(C) East
(D) South

33. Taxes are deducted each pay period from the amount of salaries or wages, including payments for overtime, paid to law enforcement personnel in excess of the withholding exemptions allowed under the Internal Revenue Act. The amount of tax to be withheld from each payment of wages to any employee will be determined from the current official table of pay and withholding exemptions to be found on page 32 of the employee manual.

The paragraph best supports the statement that salaries of law enforcement personnel
(A) do not include overtime.
(B) are determined by provisions of the Internal Revenue Act.
(C) are paid from tax revenues.
(D) are subject to tax deductions.

34. A police officer on foot patrol is stopped by a man who shouts that a neighbor's child has just been raped. The officer goes to the scene of the alleged crime and is told by the hysterical mother that her eight-year-old daughter was raped in the apartment while she was in the basement with the laundry. The child is crying and bleeding on the bed. The mother screams that she believes the man is on the roof. The police officer should first
(A) call for medical assistance.
(B) attempt to calm the hysterical mother.
(C) go to the roof to search for the accused man.
(D) question the child as to what actually took place.

35. In taking a report of a missing person, a police officer must request the following information in the following order:

1. The sex of the missing person
2. The age of the missing person
3. The name of the missing person
4. The name and relationship of the person making the report
5. The place and time the missing person was last seen
6. A physical description of the person and his or her clothing
7. Other special identifying features

Police Officer Manning is practically bowled over by a hysterical, tearful woman who is wailing, "My baby, she missing." Officer Manning's first question should be:

(A) Where did you lose the baby?
(B) How old is the baby?
(C) Is the baby a boy or a girl?
(D) Are you the baby's mother?

36. Police Officer Klein leaves the police garage by the western gate, makes a left turn, and begins to cover her assigned area. After four blocks, Officer Klein turns west. When Officer Klein has driven five more blocks, she is passed by a speeding car going in the opposite direction. She makes a quick U-turn and follows the speeding car. After eight blocks, the speeding car turns left, loses control, and crashes into a telephone pole. The location of the crash is
(A) in front of the police garage.
(B) due south of the police garage.
(C) southeast of the police garage.
(D) northeast of the police garage.

37. Police Officer Ling reports to her precinct from a corner police call box six blocks north of the precinct house along her assigned patrol route. She turns left at that corner, walks one block, and turns left again. After walking three more blocks, Officer Ling turns right, walks two full blocks, and checks in from another comer call box. The call box from which Officer Ling is now calling is located

(A) four blocks north and two blocks east of the precinct house.
(B) three blocks north and three blocks east of the precinct house.
(C) three blocks north and three blocks west of the precinct house.
(D) two blocks north and four blocks west of the precinct house.

38. As Officer Ling stands at the call box, she witnesses a car sideswiping a parked car almost directly in front of her and continuing on its way at a high speed. This is the information that Officer Ling rapidly takes note of:

Location:	In front of 158 Broome Street, just south of Potter Avenue
Incident:	Sideswipe of a parked car by a speeding car; hit and run
Damage:	Removed right side mirror and badly smashed right front fender
Description of Speeding Car:	Red two-door Honda Accord, approximately 1994; no occupants besides male driver; New Jersey license plate beginning 7T4, traveling west
Description of Damaged Car:	Black four-door Saturn SL-1, 1993, license plate Connecticut XYZ-123

Officer Ling is on foot and cannot pursue the speeding car, but she can transmit the information directly to the sergeant with whom she is checking in. Which of the following expresses the needed information *most clearly, accurately and completely*?

(A) A speeding red car and driver from New Jersey going west just hit a black four-door 1993 Saturn, Connecticut license plate XYZ-123 on Broome Street.
(B) A red two-door Honda Accord, New Jersey license plate beginning 7T4, with only male driver, last seen traveling west on Broome Street near Potter at high speed after hitting black Saturn on right side.
(C) A black 1993 four-door Saturn SL-1 parked in front of 158 Broome Street just south of Potter Avenue was just hit and damaged by a red two-door Honda Accord from New Jersey that was speeding and didn't stop. It is speeding west.
(D) A speeding car, a red two-door Honda Accord from Connecticut, license plate beginning 7T4, just sideswiped a black Saturn in front of 158 Broome Street. Its only occupant is the male driver, and the car is speeding west.

Answer questions 39 and 40 on the basis of the following drawing. This drawing shows some vital interior parts of a police revolver and the order in which they fit together.

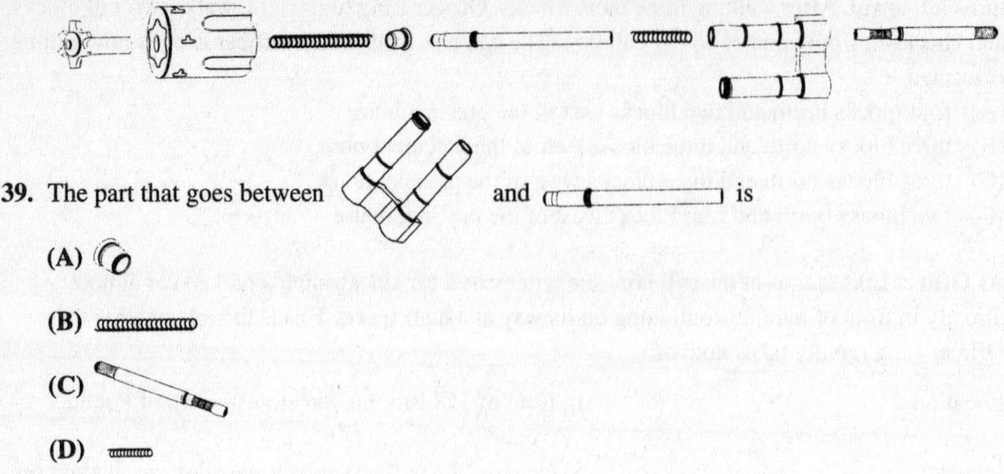

39. The part that goes between and is

(A)

(B)

(C)

(D)

40. The part that does NOT belong to this portion of the revolver is

(A)

(B)

(C)

(D)

Answer questions 41 and 42 on the basis of the following paragraph:

> Proper firearms training is one phase of law enforcement that cannot be ignored. No part of the training of a law officer is more important or more valuable. The officer's life, and often the lives of his or her fellow officers, depends directly upon skill with the weapon he or she is carrying. Proficiency with the revolver is not attained exclusively by the volume of ammunition used and the number of hours spent on the firing line. Supervised practice and the use of training aids and techniques help make the shooter. It is essential to have a good firing range where new officers are trained and older personnel can practice in scheduled firearms sessions. The fundamental points to be stressed are grip, stance, breathing, sight alignment, and trigger squeeze. Coordination of thought, vision, and motion must be achieved before the officer gains confidence in his or her shooting ability. Attaining this ability will make the student a better officer and will enhance his or her value to the force.

41. The paragraph best supports the statement that

(A) skill with weapons is a phase of law enforcement training that is too often ignored.

(B) the most useful and essential single factor in the training of a law officer is proper firearms training.

(C) the value of an officer to the force is enhanced by the officer's self-confidence and coordination.
(D) the lives of law enforcement officers always depend directly upon the skill with weapons displayed by fellow officers.

42. The word stance as used in this paragraph means
(A) attitude.
(B) opinion.
(C) angle of head.
(D) placement of feet.

43. As a student at the police academy, you are handed the following scenario: Police Officer Hakim, on routine nighttime patrol in a commercial area, discovers that the front door of a dark liquor store is not locked. She carefully opens the door a crack and hears sounds inside. Prudently, she steps away from the door and radios for backup. Three fellow officers promptly arrive to reinforce her. They open the door and surprise the burglars into surrender without firing a shot. Here are the details:

Location:	Sam's Spirits, 250 Main Street
Date:	Tuesday, May 9
Time:	1:20 A.M.
Event:	Break-in; attempted theft
Officers Involved:	Peter Nwazota, Amy Zadrozny, and Frank O'Kun
Suspects:	Seth Dowling and Tim Farr

Officer Hakim must file a report about this incident. Which of the following expresses the information most clearly, accurately, and completely?

(A) Seth Dowling and Tim Farr broke into the liquor store at 1:20 on Tuesday, May 9. Peter Nwazota, Amy Zadrozny, Frank O'Kun, and I captured them.
(B) At 1:20 A.M. on Tuesday, May 9, a break-in was discovered at Sam's Spirits, 250 Main Street. With backup assistance of Peter Nwazota, Amy Zadrozny, and Frank O'Kun, the suspects Seth Dowling and Tim Farr were peacefully arrested.
(C) Peter Nwazota, Amy Zadrozny, and Frank O'Kun helped me take Seth Dowling and Tim Farr into custody when they broke in to Sam's Spirits on Tuesday night at 1:20 A.M.
(D) Theft of the liquor store at 250 Main Street was averted on May 9 at 1:20 A.M. when the suspects were surprised and didn't shoot at Peter Nwazota, Amy Zadrozny, Tim Farr, and me.

44. An assumption commonly made in regard to the reliability of testimony is that, when a number of persons report the same matter, the details upon which there is an agreement may generally be considered substantiated. Experiments have shown, however, that there is a tendency for the same errors to appear in the testimony of different individuals and that, apart from any collusion, agreement of testimony is no proof of dependability. This paragraph suggests that
(A) if the testimony of a group of people is in substantial agreement, it cannot be ruled out that those witnesses have not all made the same mistake.
(B) if details of the testimony are true, all witnesses will agree to it.
(C) if most witnesses do not independently attest to the same facts, the facts cannot be true.
(D) unless there is collusion, it is impossible for a number of persons to give the same report.

45. Police officers must be trained in the safe and efficient operation of motor vehicles. Principles and techniques are thoroughly explained in the classroom before students are allowed to participate in the actual performance of practical exercises. Under close supervision and guidance, the students train until they recognize their personal limitations as well as the limitations of the vehicle. The training curriculum should include courses in highway response, defensive driving, skid control, transportation of prisoners, pursuit driving, evasive-maneuver driving techniques, and accident investigation.

The paragraph best supports the statement that

(A) it is important for police officers to understand the principles of motor vehicle operation.
(B) the training curriculum is specific to the special requirements of police driving.
(C) police officers have personal limitations and must be closely supervised.
(D) vehicle maintenance is an important part of police driver training.

Answer questions 46 through 50 on the basis of the following sketches. The first face on top is a sketch of an alleged criminal based on witnesses' descriptions at the crime scene. One of the four sketches below that face is the way the suspect might look after changing his or her appearance. Assume that NO surgery has been done on the suspect's face.

46.

(A)

(C)

(B)

(D)

47.

(A)

(C)

(B)

(D)

48.

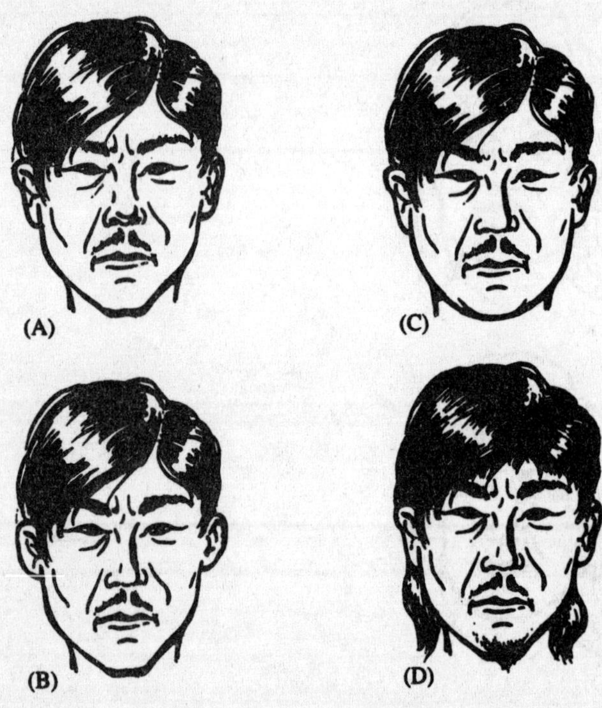

49.

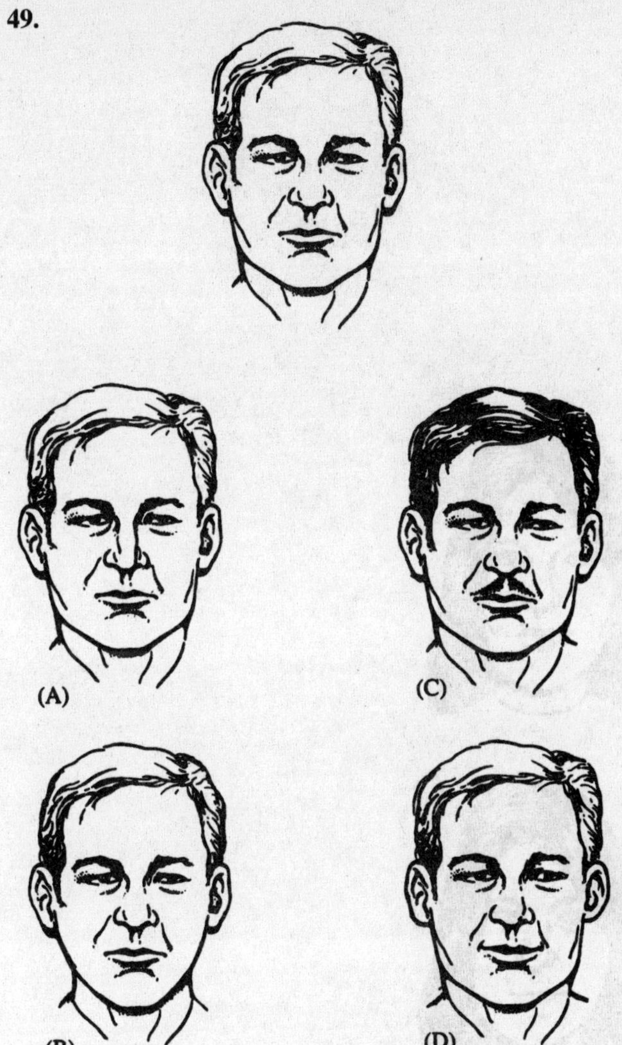

50.

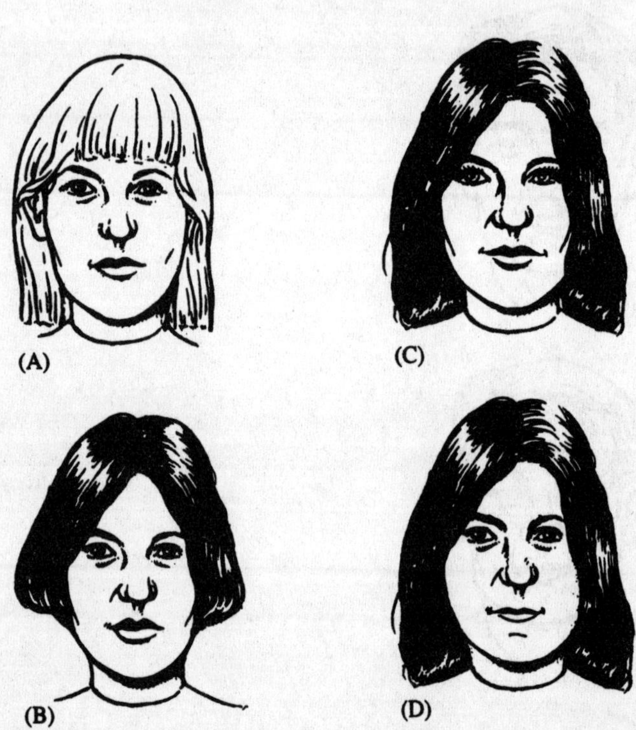

(A) (C)

(B) (D)

ANSWER KEY

1. **B**	11. **C**	21. **D**	31. **B**	41. **B**
2. **D**	12. **B**	22. **A**	32. **A**	42. **D**
3. **C**	13. **D**	23. **C**	33. **D**	43. **B**
4. **A**	14. **D**	24. **D**	34. **A**	44. **A**
5. **B**	15. **D**	25. **B**	35. **C**	45. **B**
6. **B**	16. **B**	26. **B**	36. **C**	46. **B**
7. **D**	17. **C**	27. **C**	37. **C**	47. **B**
8. **C**	18. **B**	28. **C**	38. **B**	48. **D**
9. **A**	19. **A**	29. **D**	39. **D**	49. **C**
10. **C**	20. **C**	30. **B**	40. **B**	50. **B**

EXPLANATORY ANSWERS

1. **(B)** Margaret Pickford is a known heroin addict.

2. **(D)** Antonio Gomez is wanted for armed robbery. He is missing the last finger of his right hand.

3. **(C)** Arthur Lee often attacks his victims in subway passageways.

4. **(A)** Robert Miller has a tattoo of a dragon on his right upper arm.

5. **(B)** Janet Walker has a large hairy mole on her upper left thigh.

6. **(B)** Antonio Gomez carries a gun. Arthur Lee carries a wicked-looking knife, but Lee is not offered among the choices.

7. **(D)** Margaret Pickford, who walks with a limp because her left leg is shorter than her right, has a child in foster care so she obviously is a parent.

8. **(C)** Antonio Gomez escaped from the scene of a recent armed robbery in a stolen yellow 1987 Corvette.

9. **(A)** Margaret Pickford, who is a drug addict, has a severe limp caused by one leg being shorter than the other, so she would have a hard time running from police.

10. **(C)** Arthur Lee is wanted for rape.

11. **(C)** All other choices confuse addresses, thereby giving misinformation.

12. **(B)** All other choices confuse locations.

13. **(D)** The complete license number of the vehicle that fled is not known, so the name and address of its owner cannot be immediately determined. Officer Yoshida must get as much information as possible from the remaining driver.

14. **(D)** None of the other choices covers the facts.

15. **(D)** The car was not unoccupied.

16. **(B)** In words, this formula reads: two times $4,500 for the bronze sculptures plus five times $930 for the oil paintings plus three times $2,220 for the porcelain urns plus seven times $90 for the framed prints plus $436.

17. **(C)** First aid comes first.

18. **(B)** Choice (A) is wrong because Carter Street is one-way southbound; (C) is wrong because Davis Avenue is one-way westbound; (D) is legal but is unnecessarily long and roundabout.

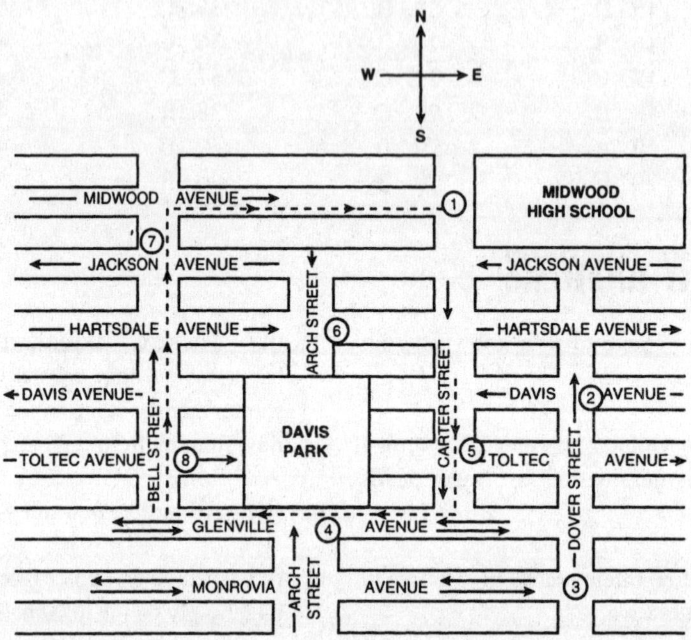

19. **(A)**

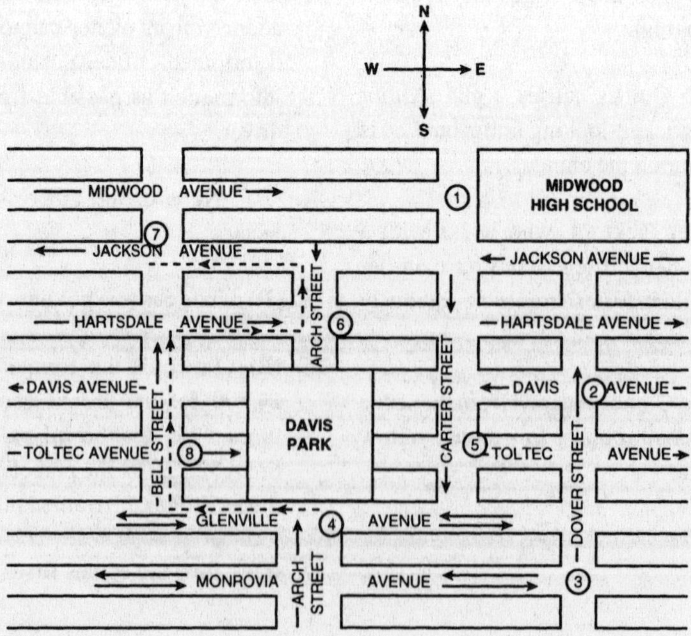

20. **(C)** Choice (A) is wrong because Bell Street is one-way northbound; (B) is legal but is longer than necessary; (D) is wrong because Dover Street is one-way northbound.

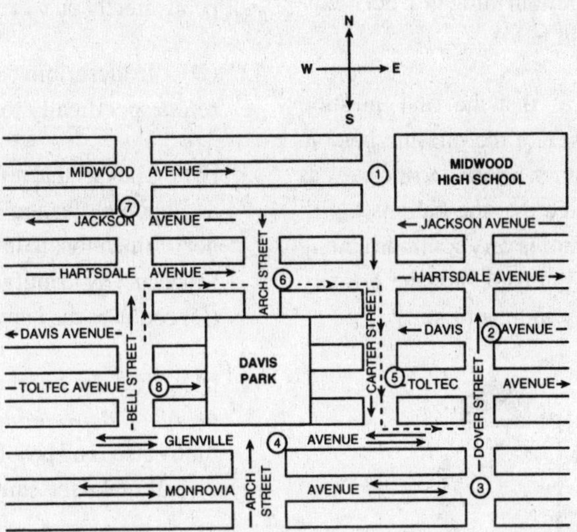

21. **(D)** All the choices place the fire correctly and give the most vital information, but (D) is clearest and most easily followed.

22. **(A)** In choice (B), action was required and there was an infant in the household; in (C), further action was taken; in (D), there was a child needing care.

23. **(C)** Choices (A) and (B) confuse locations of crime and residence; (D) reverses digits in the suspect's address.

24. **(D)** These rules are for the officer's protection. The suspect should be removed from the vehicle and checked for weapons before license and registration are requested.

25. **(B)** Choice (A) is very incomplete; (C) and (D) are stated very childishly.

26. **(B)** In words, this formula reads: $900 for the radio plus $655 for the tape player plus nine times $12 for the tapes plus 15 times $6 for the bridge tokens plus $237 for the coat.

27. **(C)** The next step is to determine if the car has been stolen.

28. **(C)** Choices (A) and (B) neglect to mention the fire. (D) leaves out the time and expresses an opinion. A report should be factual, not conjectural.

29. **(D)** Only this statement gives all relevant information in logical order. Choice (A) does not give adequate location information; the other choices are garbled.

30. **(B)** Rule 3 prohibits use of names over the radio.

31. **(B)** Rule 4 of the procedure indicates that Officer Alcorn should have accompanied the man to the hospital since the man refused to identify himself.

32. **(A)**

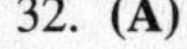

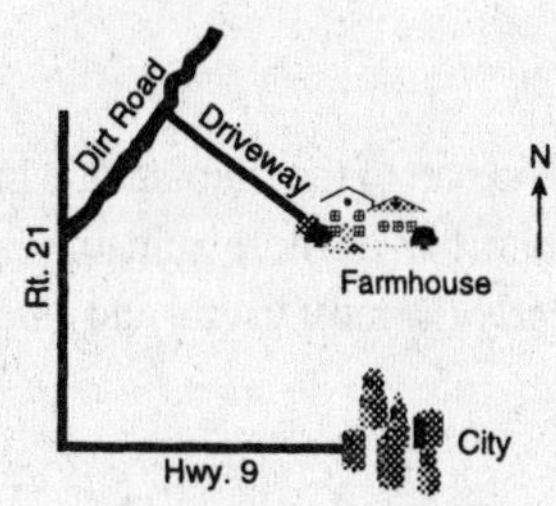

33. **(D)** The paragraph tells us that the payroll department complies with IRS regulations in withholding taxes from salaries and wages. The IRS determines the tax, not the salaries.

34. **(A)** The most important thing is to get medical help for the child.

35. **(C)** The rule states that the first question must relate to the sex of the missing person. The fact that the woman referred to the baby as "she" is no guarantee that the baby is a girl. Confusion of pronouns is very common among people for whom English is not the primary language, especially in time of stress.

36. **(C)**

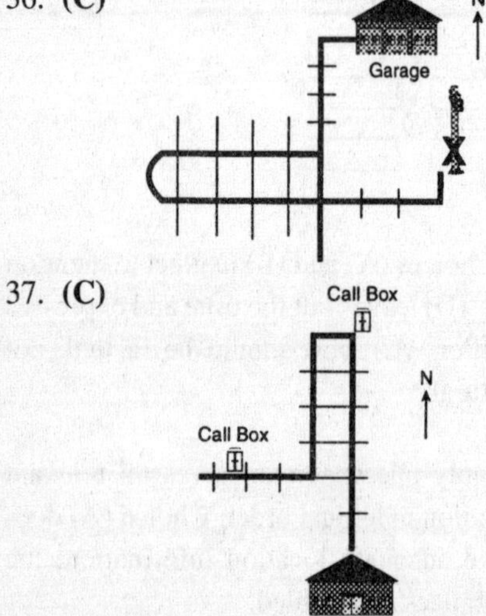

37. **(C)**

38. **(B)** At this moment, police cars in the area would need as much information as possible about the offending car. Details about the car that was hit, aside from color, are not relevant to pursuit. Choices (A) and (C) give incomplete descriptions; choice (D) has the state of registration wrong.

39. **(D)**

40. **(B)**

41. **(B)** If no part of the training of a law officer is more important or more valuable (sentence 2), then clearly the most useful and essential single factor in the training of a law officer is proper firearms training. Choice (A) is incorrect because the first sentence says only that firearms training *cannot* be ignored not that it *is* ignored. Choice (D) is an overstatement; lives often depend directly on weapons skills, but not always.

42. **(D)** In describing standing posture, *stance* refers specifically to placement of feet.

43. **(B)** The fact that no shots were fired should be an important feature of this report. Neither (A) nor (C) mentions it. In addition, these choices fail to adequately identify and locate the liquor store. (D) confuses the names of the participants.

44. **(A)** Just as *agreement of testimony is no proof of dependability,* agreement of testimony also is no proof of undependability; they can all make the same mistake either way.

45. **(B)** The paragraph lists some of the specialized courses in the police driving curriculum.

46. **(B)** The suspect in choice (A) has larger eyes; the suspect in choice (C) has different ears; the suspect in choice (D) has a fuller face.

47. **(B)** The suspect in choice (A) has a smaller nose; the suspect in choice (C) has a fuller face and fuller lips; the suspect in choice (D) has lighter eyes and thinner lips.

48. **(D)** The suspect in choice (A) has a different nose; the suspect in choice (B) has different ears; the suspect in choice (C) has an entirely different head and face shape.

49. **(C)** The suspect in choice (A) has a much finer nose; the suspect in choice (B) has a narrower jaw structure; the suspect in choice (D) has different ears.

50. **(B)** The suspect in choice (A) has a smaller nose; the suspect in choice (C) has lighter eyes and a wider mouth; the suspect in choice (D) has a fuller face and thinner lips.

Answer Sheet for Sample Questions: State Trooper Exam

1. Ⓐ Ⓑ Ⓒ Ⓓ	11. Ⓐ Ⓑ Ⓒ Ⓓ	21. Ⓐ Ⓑ Ⓒ Ⓓ	31. Ⓐ Ⓑ Ⓒ Ⓓ	41. Ⓐ Ⓑ Ⓒ Ⓓ
2. Ⓐ Ⓑ Ⓒ Ⓓ	12. Ⓐ Ⓑ Ⓒ Ⓓ	22. Ⓐ Ⓑ Ⓒ Ⓓ	32. Ⓐ Ⓑ Ⓒ Ⓓ	42. Ⓐ Ⓑ Ⓒ Ⓓ
3. Ⓐ Ⓑ Ⓒ Ⓓ	13. Ⓐ Ⓑ Ⓒ Ⓓ	23. Ⓐ Ⓑ Ⓒ Ⓓ	33. Ⓐ Ⓑ Ⓒ Ⓓ	43. Ⓐ Ⓑ Ⓒ Ⓓ
4. Ⓐ Ⓑ Ⓒ Ⓓ	14. Ⓐ Ⓑ Ⓒ Ⓓ	24. Ⓐ Ⓑ Ⓒ Ⓓ	34. Ⓐ Ⓑ Ⓒ Ⓓ	44. Ⓐ Ⓑ Ⓒ Ⓓ
5. Ⓐ Ⓑ Ⓒ Ⓓ	15. Ⓐ Ⓑ Ⓒ Ⓓ	25. Ⓐ Ⓑ Ⓒ Ⓓ	35. Ⓐ Ⓑ Ⓒ Ⓓ	45. Ⓐ Ⓑ Ⓒ Ⓓ
6. Ⓐ Ⓑ Ⓒ Ⓓ	16. Ⓐ Ⓑ Ⓒ Ⓓ	26. Ⓐ Ⓑ Ⓒ Ⓓ	36. Ⓐ Ⓑ Ⓒ Ⓓ	46. Ⓐ Ⓑ Ⓒ Ⓓ
7. Ⓐ Ⓑ Ⓒ Ⓓ	17. Ⓐ Ⓑ Ⓒ Ⓓ	27. Ⓐ Ⓑ Ⓒ Ⓓ	37. Ⓐ Ⓑ Ⓒ Ⓓ	47. Ⓐ Ⓑ Ⓒ Ⓓ
8. Ⓐ Ⓑ Ⓒ Ⓓ	18. Ⓐ Ⓑ Ⓒ Ⓓ	28. Ⓐ Ⓑ Ⓒ Ⓓ	38. Ⓐ Ⓑ Ⓒ Ⓓ	48. Ⓐ Ⓑ Ⓒ Ⓓ
9. Ⓐ Ⓑ Ⓒ Ⓓ	19. Ⓐ Ⓑ Ⓒ Ⓓ	29. Ⓐ Ⓑ Ⓒ Ⓓ	39. Ⓐ Ⓑ Ⓒ Ⓓ	49. Ⓐ Ⓑ Ⓒ Ⓓ
10. Ⓐ Ⓑ Ⓒ Ⓓ	20. Ⓐ Ⓑ Ⓒ Ⓓ	30. Ⓐ Ⓑ Ⓒ Ⓓ	40. Ⓐ Ⓑ Ⓒ Ⓓ	50. Ⓐ Ⓑ Ⓒ Ⓓ

Sample Questions: State Trooper Exam

Directions: *Each question has four suggested answers. Decide which is the best answer and darken its letter next to the question number on your answer sheet.*

1. You are driving south on Railroad Avenue. You make a U-turn to pursue a suspect and then make a left turn. In which direction are you now heading?
(A) North
(B) South
(C) East
(D) West

2. You are driving north. You make a left turn to get to an accident scene and pass a tow truck traveling the opposite way. In what direction is the tow truck traveling?
(A) North
(B) South
(C) East
(D) West

3. You are traveling south on Highway 307. At the junction of Highway 307 and Route 41, you turn and proceed east on Route 41. At the next stop sign, you stop to yield the right of way to a car crossing Route 41 and entering the intersection from your right. The car is traveling
(A) north.
(B) south.
(C) east.
(D) west.

Answer questions 4 through 6 by choosing the most grammatical and precise sentence.

4. (A) There is several ways to organize a good report.
(B) Several ways exist in organizing a good report.
(C) To organize a good report, several ways exist.
(D) There are several ways to organize a good report.

5. (A) Most all these statements have been supported by persons who are reliable and can be depended upon.
(B) The persons which have guaranteed these statements are reliable.
(C) Reliable persons guarantee the facts with regards to the truth of these statements.
(D) These statements can be depended on, for their truth has been guaranteed by reliable persons.

6. (A) Because the report lacked the needed information, it was of no use to him.
(B) This report was useless to him because there were no needed information in it.
(C) Since the report did not contain the needed information, it was not real useful to him.
(D) Being that the report lacked the needed information, he could not use it.

7. The supply sergeant requests your ammunition needs for the next three months. Last month you used 260 rounds including those needed for target practice. Assuming you'll be using about the same amount per month, how many rounds should you request?
(A) 720 rounds
(B) 750 rounds
(C) 780 rounds
(D) 800 rounds

8. Twenty-four officers and their commanding officer arrive at the scene of a traffic pileup on the westbound thruway. The commanding officer sends four officers to set up roadblocks one mile back down the thruway to halt all traffic temporarily. The commanding officer then assigns five officers to redirect the traffic already within one mile of the accident onto the shoulder and around the area and out of the way. Five more officers are dispatched to keep the flow of traffic moving in the eastbound lanes. The commanding officer is busy radioing for ambulances and tow vehicles. How many officers remain on hand to assist accident victims?
   (A) 9
   (B) 10
   (C) 11
   (D) 12

9. In a 55 mph zone, Officer Mallon pursues and pulls over a speeding motorist. Officer Mallon tells the driver, "You were doing 28 percent over the speed limit." The driver was driving slightly more than
   (A) 69 mph.
   (B) 70 mph.
   (C) 71 mph.
   (D) 72 mph.

10. A patrol car with a gasoline tank capacity of 18 gallons gets an average of 35 miles per gallon. Troopers are instructed never to permit the tank to fall below one-fourth full. On a particular morning, Officer Berry takes out a patrol car with a full tank of gasoline and an odometer reading of 10,350. Officer Berry should fill up the tank before the odometer reads
   (A) 10,800.
   (B) 10,820.
   (C) 10,850.
   (D) 10,980.

Questions 11 through 13 are based on the following personnel chart.

PERSONNEL CHART

Name	Sex	SS Number	Date of Birth	Date Hired	Position	Supervisor
Gall, A.C.	M	123-26-2426	5/5/57	3/20/80	security	Fox, I.G.
Gall, G.T.	F	095-22-1243	6/10/63	9/5/87	gunsmith	Hunt, T.S.
Gala, B.D.	F	674-09-8343	7/21/61	10/2/90	clerk	Wolf, A.C.
Gale, P.S.	M	912-88-7652	11/29/50	3/15/86	reception	Wolf, A.C.
Gales, R.N.	M	343-56-0624	2/6/62	4/10/84	mechanic	Hunt, T.S.

11. Which person does A.C. Wolf supervise?
   (A) A.C. Gail
   (B) R.N. Gales
   (C) B.D. Gala
   (D) G.T. Gail

12. Which job does the youngest person hold?
   (A) Gunsmith
   (B) Reception
   (C) Security
   (D) Clerk

13. What is P.S. Gale's social security number?
   (A) 912-88-7562
   (B) 343-56-0624
   (C) 912-88-7652
   (D) 095-22-1243

Questions 14 through 16 are based on the following work schedule.

WORK SCHEDULE

	S	M	T	W	Th	F	S
Group 1	West Quad	off	South Quad	Training	North Quad	East Quad	off
Group 2	East Quad	North Quad	West Quad	off	Training	off	North Quad
Group 3	Training	West Quad	off	East Quad	off	South Quad	South Quad

Group 1 Supervisor: John Stone	Group 2 Supervisor: Bill Bey	Group 3 Supervisor: Tom Monk
Tim Green	Robert Roh	Kerry O'Keefe
Malcolm McGregor	Gino Valenti	Brian Briggs
Paula Leong	Sheldon Smith	Jose Gonzalez
Roman Polski	Patrick Conlon	Gordon Hassan

Training at: 942 Longview Road
Training supervisor: Captain Williams

AUGUST

S	M	T	W	Th	F	S
		1	2	3	4	5
6	7	8	9	10	11	12
13	14	15	16	17	18	19
20	21	22	23	24	25	26
27	28	29	30	31		

14. Where is Roman Polski working on August 17?
(A) East Quad
(B) 942 Longview Road
(C) North Quad
(D) Cannot be determined from the information given

15. Who is the supervisor of the group that works in the same quadrant two days in a row?
(A) Captain Williams
(B) Bill Bey
(C) John Stone
(D) Tom Monk

16. Who will be off on August 26?
(A) Sheldon Smith
(B) Tom Monk
(C) Captain Williams
(D) Cannot be determined from the information given

Questions 17 through 19 are based on the following daily arrest report.

DAILY ARREST REPORT

Area	Arresting Officer	Drunk Driving	Burglary	Murder	Total
Bay	Sgt. White		X		1
Park	Sgt. Gelb	X		X	2
Lane	Sgt. Wales	X	X		2
Heights	Sgt. Liu			X	1
	Total	2	2	2	6

* Those arrested today are P. Herman, G. Farwell, D. Dragoon, H. Hynes, B. Bailey, and C. Martens.

- G. Farwell lives in Heights.
- The person arrested by Liu does not live in the area in which the arrest took place.
- B. Bailey was arrested for murder.
- G. Farwell and P. Herman are roommates.
- C. Martens was arrested by Sgt. White.
- H. Hynes lives alone.
- Sgt. Wales did not arrest any residents of Heights.
- D. Dragoon does not have a driver's license.
- Sgt. Gelb did not arrest any residents of the area in which he made arrests.

17. What was C. Martens arrested for?
(A) Burglary
(B) Murder
(C) Drunk driving
(D) Cannot be determined from the information given

18. Whom did Sgt. Liu arrest?
(A) G. Farwell
(B) B. Bailey
(C) H. Hynes
(D) Cannot be determined from the information given

19. Who could NOT have been arrested for drunk driving?
(A) H. Hynes
(B) P. Herman
(C) D. Dragoon
(D) Cannot be determined from the information given

In the diagrams for questions 20 and 21, symbols are used to represent vehicles and pedestrians and their movements.

- Vehicles are shown by the symbol: front ⬡ rear
- Pedestrians are represented by a circle: O
- Solid lines show the path and direction of a vehicle or person *before* an accident happened: ⟶
- Dotted lines show the path and direction of a vehicle or person *after* an accident happened: - - - - ➔

20. Mrs. Wagner was walking across the intersection of Elm Street and Willow Avenue when she was struck by a car approaching from her right. After hitting Mrs. Wagner, the car swerved left and ran into a tree. Which of the following four diagrams best represents the accident described?

(A)

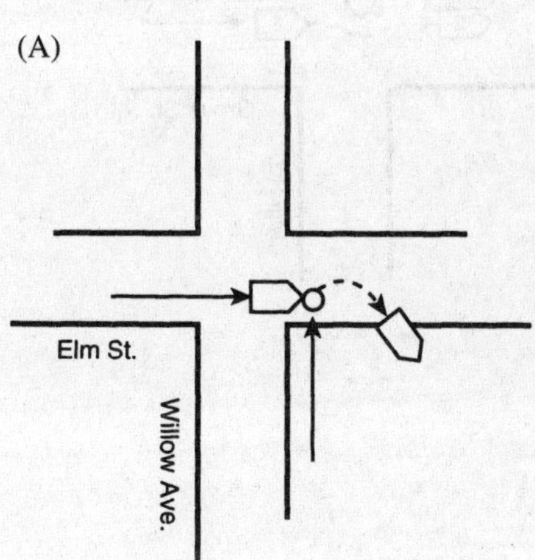

(B)

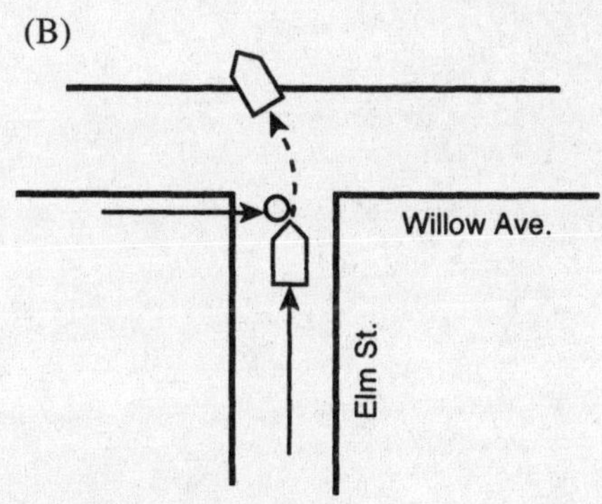

(C)

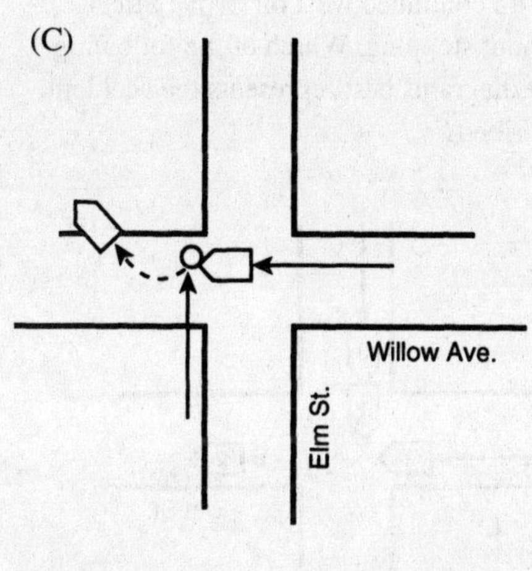

(D)

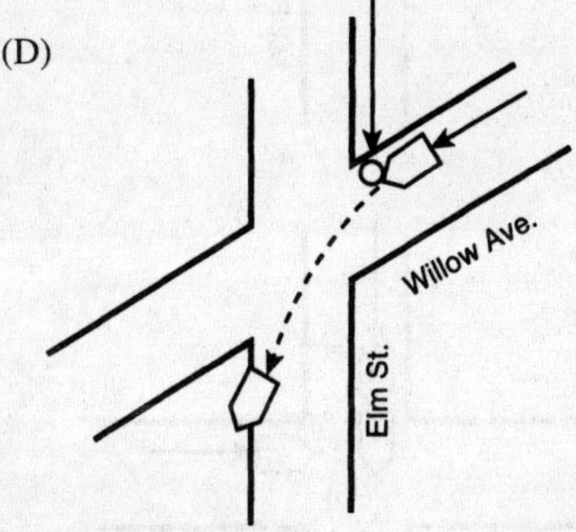

21. An automobile accident occurred at the intersection of Mill Road and Grove Street. Cars #1 and #3 were proceeding south on Mill Road, and Car #2 was proceeding west on Grove Street. When Car #1 stopped quickly to avoid hitting Car #2, it was immediately struck from behind by Car #3.

Car #2 continued west on Grove Street without stopping. Which of the following four diagrams best represents the accident described?

(A)

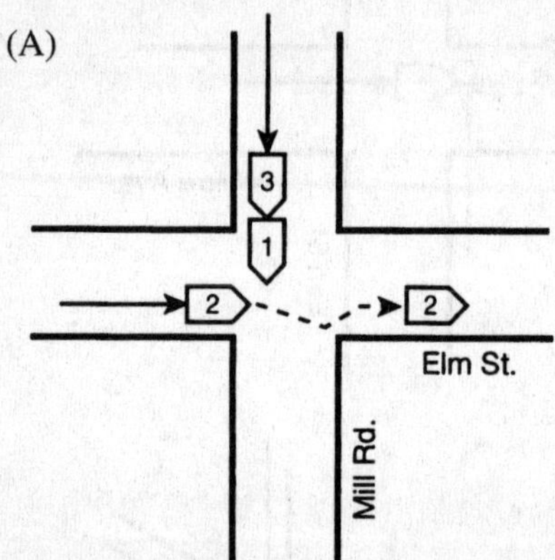

(B)

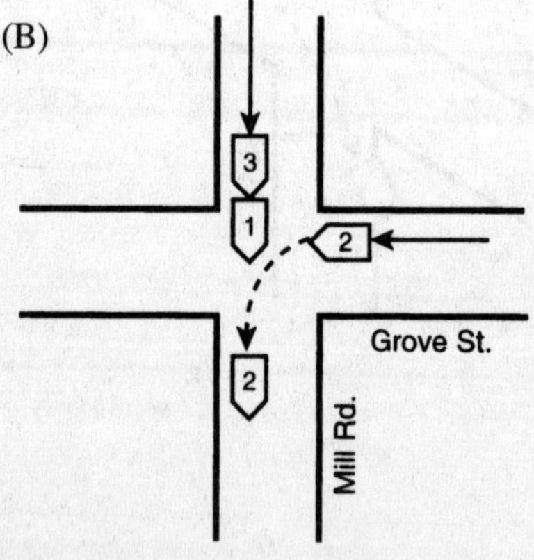

(C)

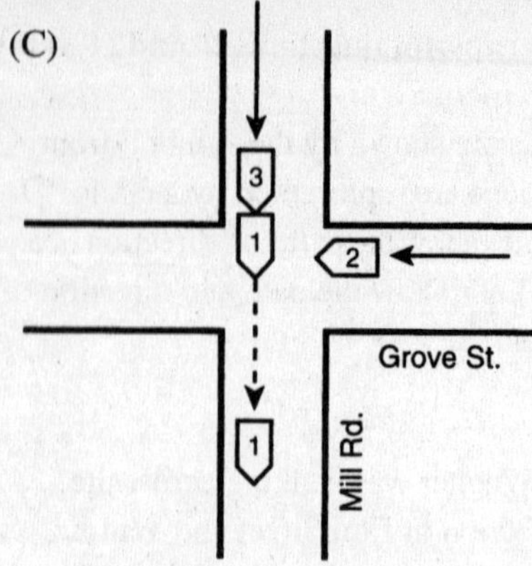

(D)

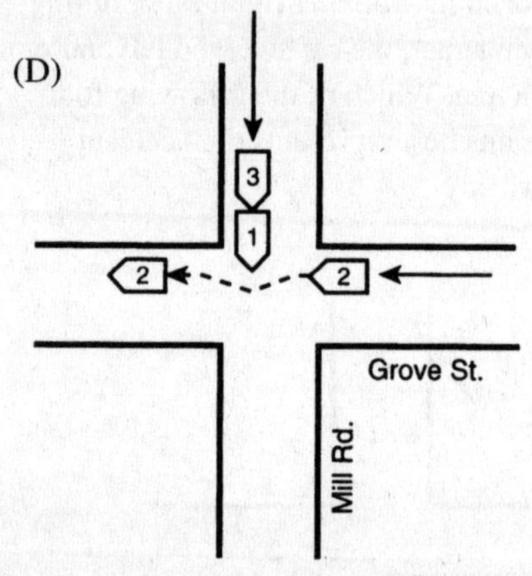

Use the following map to answer questions 22 and 23. The flow of traffic is indicated by the arrows. If only one arrow is shown, then traffic flows only in the direction indicated by the arrow. If two arrows are shown, then traffic flows in both directions. You must follow the flow of traffic.

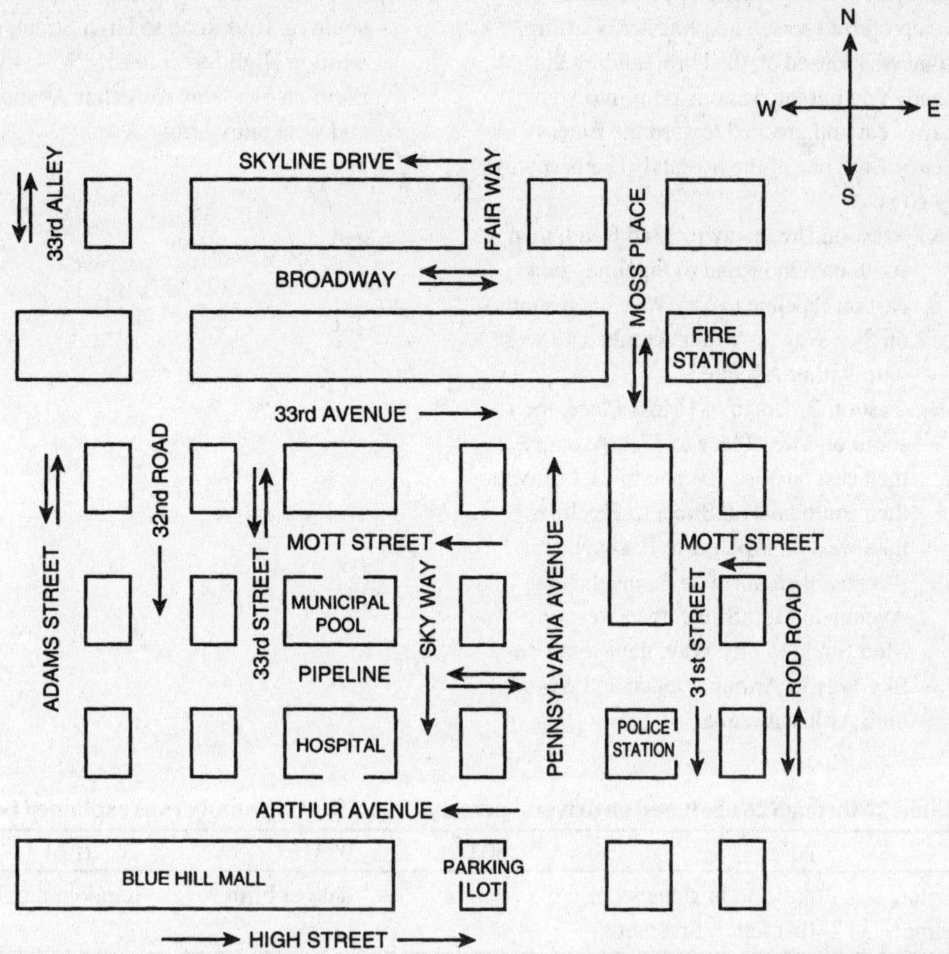

22. You are in the police station when you receive word of a labor demonstration in the middle of the street on Broadway. You pull a patrol car out of the police station onto 31st Street and proceed in the most direct, legal way to the scene of the demonstration. The way to go is

(A) north on 31st Street to 33rd Avenue, then west on 33rd Avenue to Moss Place, then north on Moss Place and west onto Broadway.

(B) north on 31st Street to Pipeline, then west on Pipeline to Pennsylvania Avenue, then north on Pennsylvania Avenue to 33rd Avenue, then east on 33rd Avenue to Moss Place, then north on Moss Place and west onto Broadway.

(C) south on 31st Street to High Street, then east on High Street to Rod Road, then north on Rod Road to Broadway and west onto Broadway.

(D) south on 31st Street to Arthur Avenue, then west on Arthur Avenue to 33rd Street, then north on 33rd Street to 33rd Avenue, then west on 33rd Avenue to 32nd Road, then north on 32nd Road to Broadway and east onto Broadway.

23. You and your fellow officers have dispersed the demonstration, but in the course of the demonstration, one protester was hit over the head by an irate bystander who was annoyed at being unable to cross Broadway at a preferred spot. The protester is sitting somewhat dazed on the curb, holding his head. You put the demonstrator into your patrol car and proceed toward the Emergency Entrance of the hospital. The best way to go is
(A) west on Broadway to 32nd Road, then south on 32nd Road to Pipeline, then east on Pipeline to Sky Way, then south on Sky Way to Arthur Avenue and west onto Arthur Avenue.
(B) east on Broadway to Moss Place, then south on Moss Place to 33rd Avenue, then east on 33rd Avenue to 31st Street, then south on 31st Street to Pipeline, then west on Pipeline to Pennsylvania Avenue, then north on Pennsylvania Avenue to Mott Street, then west on Mott Street to Sky Way, then south on Sky Way to Arthur Avenue and west onto Arthur Avenue.
(C) west on Broadway to 33rd Alley, south on 33rd Alley as it changes its name to Adams Street and onto Arthur Avenue, then east onto Arthur Avenue.
(D) east on Broadway to Rod Road, then south on Rod Road to High Street, then west on High Street to Sky Way, then north on Sky Way to Arthur Avenue and west onto Arthur Avenue.

Questions 24 through 26 are based on drivers' personal identification numbers as explained below.

C	20	503	03316	8 1234
first letter, last name	position in alphabet of first letter, first name	height	date of birth	random numbers

24. James Harcourt was in elementary school in 1950. Which of the following could be his number?
(A) H 10510 06144 31234
(B) H 10600 12064 95678
(C) J 08601 09306 04321
(D) J 08511 02292 49876

25. Which of the people with the following ID numbers would be easiest to pick out in a crowd?
(A) B 01507 03064 52468
(B) L 24611 11117 11357
(C) F 18510 09228 02579
(D) T 14505 05096 69643

26. Which of the following could NOT be a real ID number?
(A) K 01507 05056 11234
(B) U 13501 1212499076
(C) S 35505 09186 31423
(D) T 12411 10235 58567

Questions 27 through 29 are based on roadside mile markers as explained below.

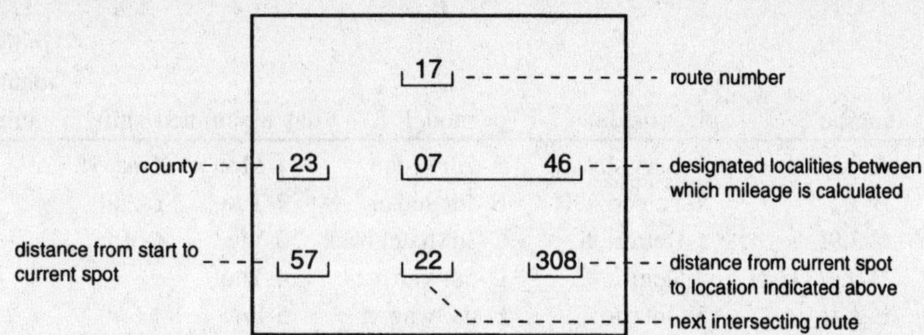

27. A driver traveling west on Route 46 passes a marker that looks like this:

	46	
21	73	04
140	23	36

He makes a left turn onto Route 23 and proceeds to drive three more miles. The next marker he passes could look like which of the following?

(A)

	46	
21	73	04
143	23	33

(B)

	23	
21	18	29
103	46	71

(C)

	23	
21	14	12
95	18	36

(D)

	23	
21	46	12
39	23	80

28. A highway traveler passes a road marker that looks like this:

	37	
14	10	42
80	06	110

The next highway marker that she notices looks like this:

	37	
24	10	2
85	06	105

This marker indicates that

(A) the traveler has turned onto another highway.

(B) the route number has changed.

(C) the traveler has gone 10 miles since the last marker.

(D) the traveler has crossed a county line.

29. A trooper patrolling an assigned sector passes a route marker that looks like this:

	95	
04	11	38
83	13	42

Fifteen minutes later, the marker that the trooper passes looks like this:

	95	
04	38	11
78	36	47

Indications are that the trooper

(A) has made a U-turn.

(B) has exceeded the speed limit in the line of duty.

(C) is now on a cloverleaf.

(D) has changed highways.

Questions 30 through 33 are based on vehicle identification numbers as explained below.

A	C	I	B	4	X	123456
year	engine	plant made	model	day assembled	shift	individual identifying numbers
A-1986	A-3.7*l*	1-Gary, IN	A-2dr sedan	1-Mon	X-lst	
B-1987	B-3.1*l*	2-Toledo, OH	B-4dr sedan	2-Tue	Y-2nd	
C-1988	C-3.9*l*	3-Detroit #1	C-3dr hatchback	3-Wed	Z-3rd	
D-1989	D-3.9*l* diesel	4-Detroit #2	D-5dr van	4-Thu		
E-1990	E-3.4*l*	5-Ontario	E-sta. wagon	5-Fri		
F-1991		6-Flint, MI	F-2dr convert.	6-Sat		
G-1992						
H-prototype						

- Racers and Royals come in 2dr or 4dr sedans.
- Vans are made only at the Gary plant.
- Convertibles do not have diesel engines.
- Diesel engines are assembled only at the Toledo plant.
- Prototypes use only diesel engines.
- Only sedans are assembled on the third shift.
- Vans are made only with 3.7*l* or 3.9*l* engines.
- Station wagons and hatchbacks are not assembled on Saturday.
- Ontario does not manufacture 3.1*l* engines.
- No convertibles were made in 1985 or 1986.
- Prototypes do not follow the preceding guidelines.

30. The vehicle with ID#DC4B 4Y78 4465 is a

(A) 1989 4dr sedan with a 3.9*l* diesel engine assembled at Detroit #2 during the second shift on a Thursday.

(B) 1989 4dr Royal with a 3.9*l* engine assembled at Detroit #2 during the second shift on a Thursday.

(C) 1989 4dr sedan with a 3.9*l* engine assembled at Detroit #2 during the second shift on a Wednesday.

(D) 1988 4dr Racer with a 3.4*l* engine assembled at Detroit #2 during the second shift on a Thursday.

31. A 1992 hatchback with a 3.7*l* engine could be identified by which of the following serial numbers?

(A) GA2C 6Y24 1189

(B) HA2C 3X42 6309

(C) GA2C 2Z84 0760

(D) GA2C 2X33 5764

32. The vehicle with ID#BB2F 6Y87 6543 is a

(A) 1987 4dr convertible with a 3.1*l* engine assembled at the Toledo plant during the second shift on a Saturday.

(B) 1987 convertible with a 3.9*l* diesel engine assembled at the Toledo plant during the second shift on a Saturday.

(C) 1987 convertible with a 3.1*l* engine assembled at the Toledo plant during the second shift on a Saturday.

(D) 1985 2dr convertible with a 3.1*l* engine assembled at the Toledo plant during the third shift on a Saturday.

33. A prototype van could be identified with which of the following serial numbers?

(A) HD2E 1X07 5528

(B) HD1D 5Y83 1234

(C) HC6D 6Z15 6821

(D) HB5E 3X82 5764

Questions 34 through 36 are based on the following rules for the use of a college gym.

Since budgetary constraints have halted construction of the gym and pool at our new state police barracks, the superintendent of the barracks has made special arrangements with the local community college for our use of college athletic facilities at specified times and subject to certain restrictions.

Locker room: The locker room and showers are available to troopers from our barracks at any time that the swimming pool is available for our use. For any other use of the college facilities—gym, weight room, outdoor track—troopers are required to use shower and changing facilities at our own barracks and to travel between campus and barracks in exercise clothing.

Swimming pool: The swimming pool is reserved for our exclusive use from 6 A.M. to 7:30 A.M. on Tuesday and Wednesday and from 8:30 P.M. to 10 P.M. on Friday. In addition, upon presentation of trooper identification, troopers may be admitted to the general public swim sessions from 7:30 A.M. to 9 A.M. on Monday, Wednesday, and Friday and from 8:30 P.M. to 10 P.M. on Tuesday and Thursday. Sundays from 4 P.M. to 6 P.M. there is a "women only" swim period to which women troopers are welcome. Likewise, the "men only" swim period on Sundays from 1 P.M. to 3 P.M. is open to men troopers.

Weight room: The weight room is "ours" every morning except Tuesday and Friday between 5:30 A.M. and 8 A.M.

Gym: We have use of the gym for individual purposes or for organized group activities (see Bulletin Board for a schedule of organized games) every morning at the same times that we have use of the weight room and on Saturday between 3 P.M. and 5:30 P.M.

Track: The track is available for use by the general public at any time that it is not specifically reserved for use by a college group. College use changes each semester: A schedule is posted on the bulletin board in each college locker room. As a general rule, the track is available every day before 8 A.M. and after 8 P.M. Lighting at the track makes this an attractive exercise option at these uncrowded hours.

34. The total number of hours per week that the state troopers have use of the college gym is

(A) $12\frac{1}{2}$ hours.

(B) 15 hours.

(C) $16\frac{1}{2}$ hours.

(D) 19 hours.

35. Women troopers may use the locker facilities from

(A) 6 A.M. to 9 A.M. on Wednesday and from 8:30 P.M. to 10 P.M. on Thursday.

(B) 7:30 A.M. to 9 A.M. on Monday and Friday and from 1 P.M. to 3 P.M. on Sunday.

(C) 6 A.M. to 7:30 A.M. on Tuesday and from 3 P.M. to 5:30 P.M. on Saturday.

(D) 6 A.M. to 9 A.M. on Thursday and from 4 P.M. to 6 P.M. on Sunday.

36. What athletic activity is occurring at the college on Tuesday evening?

(A) Organized games for troopers in the gym

(B) Women's swim

(C) Free swim for the general public

(D) Troopers' weight lifting

Answer questions 37 to 39 on the basis of the following paragraph.

Because of the importance of preserving physical evidence, the officer should not enter the scene of a crime if it can be examined visually from one position and if no other pressing duty requires his presence there. There are some responsibilities, however, that take precedence over preservation of evidence. Some examples are as follows: rescue work, disarming dangerous persons, and quelling a disturbance. The officer should learn how to accomplish these more vital tasks while at the same time preserving as much evidence as possible. If he finds it necessary to enter the scene, he should quickly study the place of entry to learn if any evidence will suffer by his contact; then he should determine the routes to use in walking to the spot where his presence is required. Every place where a foot will fall or where a hand or other part of his body will touch should be examined with the eye. Objects should not be touched or moved unless there is a definite and compelling reason. For identification of most items of physical evidence at the initial investigation, it is seldom necessary to touch or move them.

37. When an officer feels it is essential for him to enter the immediate area where a crime has been committed, he should
(A) quickly but carefully glance around to determine whether entering the area will damage any evidence present.
(B) remove all objects of evidence from his predetermined route to avoid stepping on them.
(C) carefully replace any object immediately if it is moved or touched by his hands or any other part of his body.
(D) use only the usual place of entry to the scene to avoid disturbing any possible clues left on rear doors and windows.

38. The one of the following that is the least urgent duty of an officer who has just reported to the scene of a crime is to
(A) disarm the hysterical victim who is wildly waving a loaded gun in all directions.
(B) give first aid to a possible suspect who has been injured while attempting to leave the scene of the crime.
(C) prevent observers from attacking and injuring the persons suspected of having committed the crime.
(D) preserve from damage or destruction any evidence necessary for the proper prosecution of the case against the criminals.

39. An officer has just reported to the scene of a crime in response to a phone call. The best of the following actions for him to take with respect to objects of physical evidence present at the scene is to
(A) make no attempt to enter the crime scene if his entry will disturb any vital physical evidence.
(B) map out the shortest, straightest path to follow in walking to the spot where the most physical evidence may he found.
(C) move such objects of physical evidence as are necessary to enable him to assist the wounded victim of the crime.
(D) quickly examine all objects of physical evidence to determine which objects may he touched and which may not.

For questions 40 and 41, arrange the five sentences into a logical sequence to create your own coherent story.

40. 1. A body was found behind a clump of yucca.
2. A man proclaimed innocence.
3. Land Rover tracks were followed into a border village.
4. Fingerprints were found on a steering wheel.
5. The owner of the Land Rover was questioned.
(A) 1-3-4-5-2
(B) 1-4-3-5-2
(C) 1-5-4-3-2
(D) 1-2-3-4-5

41. 1. There was a sudden cloudburst in the mountains.
2. A rag-tag group of people walked along a dry riverbed.
3. The roar of rushing water was deafening.
4. A man snatched two small children to safety.
5. An old woman was drowned.

(A) 1-2-4-3-5
(B) 2-1-3-4-5
(C) 2-3-1-5-4
(D) 2-1-4-5-3

Complete the sentence.

42. After I talked with the witness, I ____.
(A) have wrote up the report.
(B) wrote the report.
(C) wrote what the witness told me had happened and handed in the herewith report.
(D) had written up the report.

43. Even before the wind had stopped, the rain ____.
(A) was slowed down.
(B) has been slowing down.
(C) had been slowing down.
(D) had been slowed down.

44. The dog was frothing at the mouth, snapping, and running in circles, so my partner ____.
(A) says, "He's rabid," and shoots it.
(B) said, "It's probably rabid," and shoots it in the head.
(C) said, "He's rabid," and shot it all dead.
(D) said, "It's rabid," and shot it.

45. Please tell the new recruits that they may park ____ cars over ____.
(A) they're…their
(B) there…they're
(C) their…there
(D) they're…there

46. There are ____ tollbooths at which tolls are collected especially ____ highway maintenance.
(A) for…fore
(B) four…for
(C) fore…four
(D) four…fore

47. On Thursday afternoon, Officers Byron and Birelli will lead a troop of Explorer ____ on a tour of the training facility.
(A) Scouts
(B) Scout's
(C) Scouts'
(D) Scouts's

Choose the best statement of the underlined portion.

48. Joe talked with the victim about the shooting. The victim said the weapon used was what the police officers have been using for years. Joe tells the sergeant that the victim says it was probably a 35 mm.

(A) Joe then told the sergeant the victim said the weapon was a 35mm.

(B) Joe tells to his sergeant that the weapon in that shooting could of been a 35mm.

(C) So Joe told his sergeant that the victim was thinking that the shooting weapon was most likely to be a 35mm.

(D) The sentence is correct as written.

49. The suspect, who was carrying a duffel bag at the time, was arrested. At the station house, the arresting officer dumped the contents of the duffel bag onto a table to inventory the contents. Contraband was discovered in the course of this reasonable inventory search.

(A) In the course of searching for contraband, an inventory was made.

(B) The officer was discovering contraband in the course of making a reasonable inventory search.

(C) Contraband was the discovery that was made in the course of the making of a reasonable inventory search.

(D) The sentence is correct as written.

50. The suspect was placed under arrest for driving while intoxicated. Over his objections, a blood sample was taken from him by a doctor at a hospital. The blood sample having been analyzed, the intoxicated suspect was placed under arrest.

(A) After the blood sample will be analyzed, the suspect will be found intoxicated.

(B) The blood sample was analyzed, and the suspect was found to have been intoxicated.

(C) The blood sample will be analyzed, and the suspect will be intoxicated.

(D) The sentence is correct as written.

ANSWER KEY

1. **D**	11. **C**	21. **D**	31. **D**	41. **B**
2. **C**	12. **A**	22. **C**	32. **C**	42. **B**
3. **A**	13. **C**	23. **A**	33. **B**	43. **C**
4. **D**	14. **C**	24. **A**	34. **B**	44. **D**
5. **D**	15. **D**	25. **B**	35. **A**	45. **C**
6. **A**	16. **C**	26. **C**	36. **C**	46. **B**
7. **C**	17. **A**	27. **C**	37. **A**	47. **A**
8. **B**	18. **D**	28. **D**	38. **D**	48. **A**
9. **B**	19. **B**	29. **A**	39. **C**	49. **D**
10. **B**	20. **B**	30. **B**	40. **A**	50. **B**

EXPLANATORY ANSWERS

1. **(D)** If you are driving south and make a U-turn, you will be heading north. A left turn when driving north results in heading west.

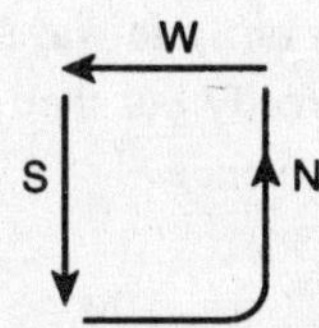

2. **(C)** If you are driving north and make a left turn, you will be heading west. A vehicle going in the other direction is going east.

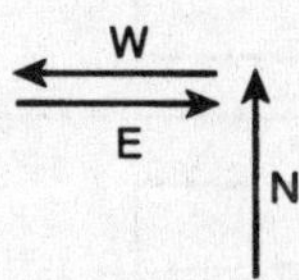

3. **(A)** If you are traveling east, a car approaching from your right is traveling north.

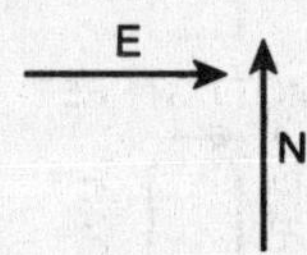

4. **(D)** Choice (A) incorrectly uses the singular verb form *is* with the plural subject *ways.* In (B), *in organizing* should be *to organize.* The inverted construction in sentence (C) is not as direct or as clear as the expression in sentence (D).

5. **(D)** Answer choice (A) contains the unacceptable expression *most all.* (B) incorrectly uses *which* to refer to persons. (C) includes the unacceptable expression *with regards to.*

6. **(A)** In (B), the subject of the second clause is *information,* which is singular. In (C), the adverb should be *really. Being that,* in (D), is not an acceptable form.

7. **(C)** $260 \times 3 = 780$.

8. **(B)** $24 - 4 - 5 - 5 = 10$.

9. **(B)** If 55 mph is 100 percent of the speed allowed, 28 percent more than the allowed is 128 percent of 55 mph. $55 \times 128\% = 70.4$ mph.

10. **(B)** The tank holds 18 gallons, so $\frac{3}{4}$ tank = 13.5 gal. The car gets 35 miles per gallon, so $13.5 \times 35 = 472.5$ miles to use $\frac{3}{4}$ tank. Odometer reading of $10{,}350 + 472.5$ miles = 10,822.5, the mileage at which the tank is down to $\frac{1}{4}$ full. The tank must be filled before this point, so 10,820 is the best answer.

11. **(C)** A.C. Wolf supervises two workers. Only one of these is named among the choices.

12. **(A)** The youngest person was born on 6/10/63. That person is a gunsmith.

13. **(C)** Just read across but read carefully.

14. **(C)** August 17 is a Thursday, and Roman Polski is in Group 1. Group 1 works in the North Quad on Thursday.

15. **(D)** Group 3 works in the South Quad on both Friday and Saturday. Tom Monk is the supervisor of Group 3.

16. **(C)** August 26 is a Saturday, and no group is scheduled for training on Saturday. The training supervisor, Captain Williams, should have the day off.

17. **(A)** C. Martens was arrested by Sgt. White. Sgt. White made only one arrest, and that arrest was for burglary. C. Martens must have been arrested for burglary.

18. **(D)** We know that Sgt. Liu made only one arrest, and that arrest was for murder. We know that B. Bailey was arrested for murder. However, there were two arrests for murder, and we do not know who the other murderer was. Therefore, we do not know if Sgt. Liu arrested Bailey or the other murder suspect.

19. **(B)** The only thing we know about Hynes is that Hynes lives alone. Hynes could have been arrested for drunk driving. Dragoon does not have a driver's license but could easily have been arrested for drunk driving (and other offenses) nonetheless. G. Farwell lives in Heights; as Farwell's roommate, P. Herman also lives in Height. The drunk drivers were arrested by Sgt. Wales, who did not arrest any residents of Heights, and Sgt. Gelb, who arrested only residents of Park.

20. **(B)** Put yourself in Mrs. Wagner's place. The right and left directions will be apparent.

21. **(D)** The answer should be clear from the diagrams. If your answer disagrees, look again.

22. **(C)** Choices (A) and (B) start right out going the wrong way on a one-way street; choice (D) starts out correctly but then goes the wrong way on 33rd Avenue.

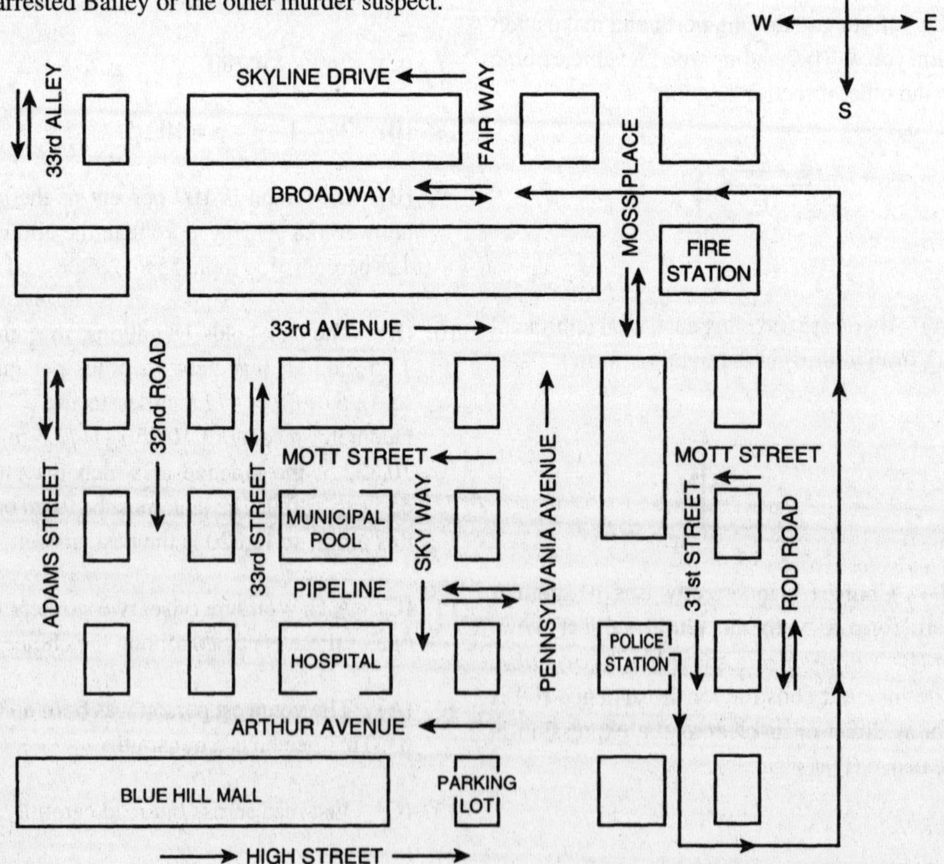

23. **(A)** Choice (B) is a perfectly legal route, but it is far longer than choice (A). Choices (C) and (D) are both quick and direct, but (C) sends you in the wrong direction on Arthur Avenue, and (D) requires wrong-way travel on both High Street and Sky Way.

24. **(A)** Focus on the years of birth. A person born in 1943 would be in elementary school in 1950. As years of birth, 1949, 1960, and 1924 make no sense at all.

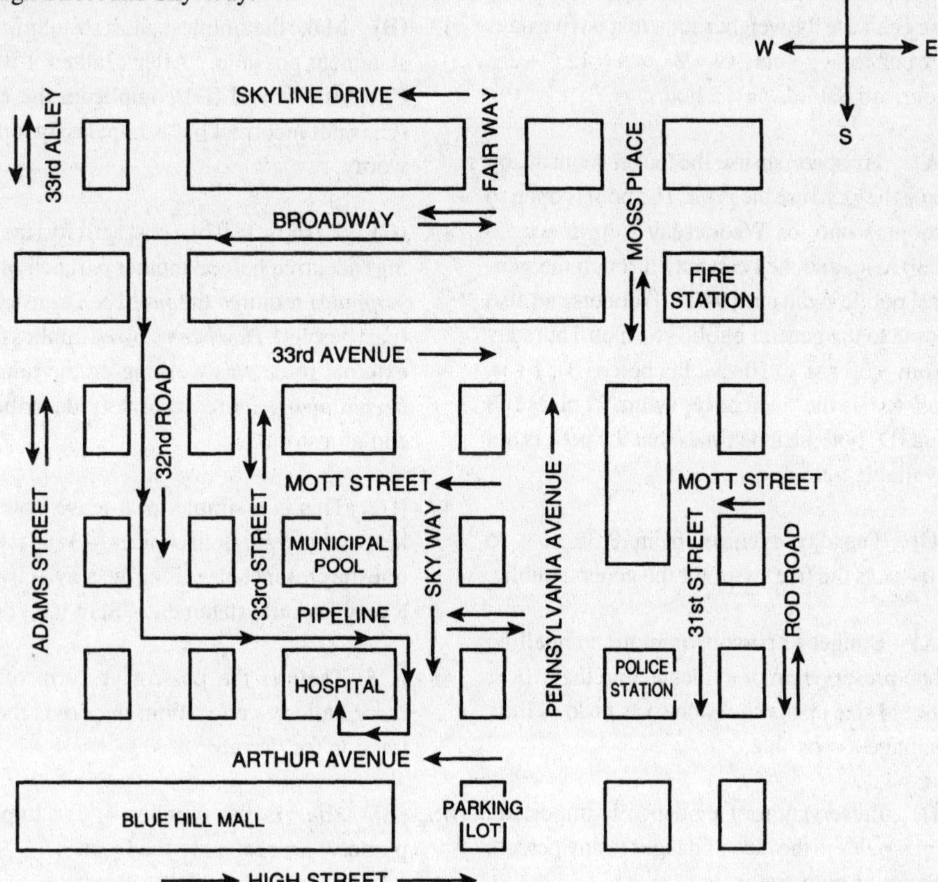

25. **(B)** A person who is 6'11" certainly should tower over the crowd.

26. **(C)** There are 26 letters in the alphabet. No first name could begin with the 35th letter.

27. **(C)** The driver has turned onto Route 23, so the top center number must be 23. The driver does not make a U-turn, so the next intersecting route cannot be the Route 46 from which he has just turned. Route 23 cannot intersect with itself, so (D) also cannot be correct.

28. **(D)** The number that designates the county has changed; the traveler has crossed a county line. The numbers in the bottom line indicate that the traveler has gone five miles.

29. **(A)** The trooper has made a U-turn. The trooper is still on Route 95, but the order of the locations between which mileage is calculated has been reversed. Distance is now being calculated from locality 38 to locality 11; on the earlier marker, it was calculated from locality 11 to locality 38.

30. **(B)** Just check against the illustration, number for number and letter for letter. Remember that Royals come in four-door sedan models.

31. **(D)** Eliminate choice (A) because hatchbacks are not assembled on Saturday; eliminate (B) because this is not a prototype; eliminate (C) because only sedans are assembled on the third shift.

32. **(C)** Check carefully, number by number and letter by letter.

33. **(B)** Vans are made in Gary.

34. **(B)** The troopers can use the gym at any time they can use the weight room, that is, five days a week for $2\frac{1}{2}$ hours @ $= 2\frac{1}{2} \times 5 = 12\frac{1}{2} + 2\frac{1}{2}$ hours on Saturday = 15 hours.

35. **(A)** Troopers can use the locker room at any time they can use the pool. The pool is open to troopers only on Wednesday from 6 A.M. to 7:30 A.M., and they can stay through the general public swim until 9 A.M. Troopers can also come to the general public swim on Thursday from 8:30 P.M. to 10 P.M. In choice (B), 1 P.M. to 3 P.M. is the "men only" swim. Choices (C) and (D) both include times that the pool is not available to troopers.

36. **(C)** Tuesday evening from 8:30 P.M. to 10 P.M. is the free swim for the general public.

37. **(A)** Danger to persons is more compelling than preservation of evidence, but the officer should size up the situation so as to do as little damage as possible.

38. **(D)** Preservation of evidence is important, but it pales in the face of danger to any person, victim or perpetrator.

39. **(C)** The same point is repeated. Save lives.

40. **(A)** 1-3-4-5-2

    First the body was found. Then Land Rover tracks were followed from the site where the body was found into a border village. In the logical sequence of events, once the Land Rover was located, finding fingerprints would be the next step whether or not the fingerprints were crucial to the story. Then the owner of the Land Rover was questioned and proclaimed his innocence.

41. **(B)** 2-1-3-4-5

    A rag-tag group of people, possibly illegal immigrants who had just entered the country, walked along a dry riverbed. There was a sudden cloudburst in the mountains, creating a flash flood. The roar of water rushing down the riverbed was deafening. A man from the group was able to snatch two small children to safety, but an old woman was drowned.

42. **(B)** Make the simplest, most straightforward statement possible. "After I talked, I wrote." Choices (A) and (D) complicate the tenses. (C) is not incorrect but is hopelessly long and wordy.

43. **(C)** To show that one past activity (the *slowing*) occurred before another past activity (the *stopping*) requires the *had been* construction (past perfect). *Had been slowed* implies that an external force was working on the rain. *Had been slowing* more accurately describes the end of a storm.

44. **(D)** This is a simple, past-tense statement; keep it that way. Both choices (A) and (B) shift into the present tense along the way. (C) makes a very juvenile statement: "Shot it all dead."

45. **(C)** *Their* is the possessive form of *they; there* indicates a location; *they're* is the contraction for *they are.*

46. **(B)** *Four* is the number 4; *for* implies a purpose; *fore* refers to the front.

47. **(A)** There is no call for a possessive form here; the simple plural *Scouts* will do just fine. If the plural of *Scouts* were to be used in the possessive, it would read *Scouts'*.

48. **(A)** Watch your tenses. The first two sentences of the passage are written in the past tense, so maintain consistency. In addition, in (B), *could of* is incorrect; *could have* is the grammatical form.

49. **(D)** "If it ain't broke, don't fix it." Choice (A) changes the meaning. (B) and (C) are wordy and convoluted.

50. **(B)** This already happened. Both (A) and (C) place the action in the future. The suspect was arrested in the first sentence, so the underlined portion is repetitious.

Federal Examinations

Federal law enforcement positions are filled through a number of different examinations. Most of these examinations have been developed over the years by the Office of Personnel Management (OPM), the government's overall personnel office. Some exams are administered by the OPM for the agencies at their request. Others are administered directly by the agencies. Some of these exams are known by their distinctive names such as the Treasury Enforcement Agent Exam (TEA), given to special agent candidates in a number of agencies and departments. Other OPM exams have descriptive titles such as the Federal Clerical Examination or are simply known by the job titles for which they test, as in the Border Patrol Agent Exam. Still other exams are tailor-made for specific positions. These exams tend to draw questions from the whole gamut of OPM exams as appropriate to the specific position. If you find yourself taking one of these tailor-made exams, you will surely recognize elements of exams described in these pages. Your best preparation for any unspecified exam is familiarity and competence with all exam question types represented in these pages.

The first examination that follows has no distinctive name; the Office of Personnel Management identifies it by number. This examination is administered to applicants for a variety of government jobs, not all of them in law enforcement.

This exam includes five different types of questions. The first, name and number comparisons, checks for detail-mindedness and speed and accuracy of observation and discrimination. The two verbal skills question types, reading comprehension and vocabulary, seek to measure the applicant's ability to understand directions and written materials and to communicate effectively. The last two types of questions, figure analogies and number series, are measures of reasoning, analytical ability, and creative thinking.

The sample questions that follow are the official sample questions distributed by the Office of Personnel Management. Try your hand at these questions to evaluate your skill with them and your chances for success on this exam. We have supplied a full set of explanations of the correct answers to help you understand the rationale behind the questions and to lead your thinking processes so you can answer such questions on your own.

The structure of a recent full-length exam was as follows:

Part I: Name and Number Comparisons
8 minutes; 50 questions
Questions were arranged in order of increasing difficulty so that toward the end of the section number groups consisted of 8 and 9 digits.

Part II Vocabulary and Reading Comprehension
25 minutes; 30 questions
15 vocabulary questions; 15 reading questions

Part III: Symbol Reasoning
20 minutes; 20 questions
Questions were based on curves and angles, on sizes of symbols, and on location of symbols within symbols rather than on quality of lines as in the sample questions.

Part IV: Numerical Sequence
20 minutes; 24 questions

ANSWER SHEET FOR SAMPLE QUESTIONS: OPM EXAM

1. Ⓐ Ⓑ Ⓒ Ⓓ Ⓔ	13. Ⓐ Ⓑ Ⓒ Ⓓ Ⓔ	25. Ⓐ Ⓑ Ⓒ Ⓓ Ⓔ	37. Ⓐ Ⓑ Ⓒ Ⓓ Ⓔ
2. Ⓐ Ⓑ Ⓒ Ⓓ Ⓔ	14. Ⓐ Ⓑ Ⓒ Ⓓ Ⓔ	26. Ⓐ Ⓑ Ⓒ Ⓓ Ⓔ	38. Ⓐ Ⓑ Ⓒ Ⓓ Ⓔ
3. Ⓐ Ⓑ Ⓒ Ⓓ Ⓔ	15. Ⓐ Ⓑ Ⓒ Ⓓ Ⓔ	27. Ⓐ Ⓑ Ⓒ Ⓓ Ⓔ	39. Ⓐ Ⓑ Ⓒ Ⓓ Ⓔ
4. Ⓐ Ⓑ Ⓒ Ⓓ Ⓔ	16. Ⓐ Ⓑ Ⓒ Ⓓ Ⓔ	28. Ⓐ Ⓑ Ⓒ Ⓓ Ⓔ	40. Ⓐ Ⓑ Ⓒ Ⓓ Ⓔ
5. Ⓐ Ⓑ Ⓒ Ⓓ Ⓔ	17. Ⓐ Ⓑ Ⓒ Ⓓ Ⓔ	29. Ⓐ Ⓑ Ⓒ Ⓓ Ⓔ	41. Ⓐ Ⓑ Ⓒ Ⓓ Ⓔ
6. Ⓐ Ⓑ Ⓒ Ⓓ Ⓔ	18. Ⓐ Ⓑ Ⓒ Ⓓ Ⓔ	30. Ⓐ Ⓑ Ⓒ Ⓓ Ⓔ	42. Ⓐ Ⓑ Ⓒ Ⓓ Ⓔ
7. Ⓐ Ⓑ Ⓒ Ⓓ Ⓔ	19. Ⓐ Ⓑ Ⓒ Ⓓ Ⓔ	31. Ⓐ Ⓑ Ⓒ Ⓓ Ⓔ	43. Ⓐ Ⓑ Ⓒ Ⓓ Ⓔ
8. Ⓐ Ⓑ Ⓒ Ⓓ Ⓔ	20. Ⓐ Ⓑ Ⓒ Ⓓ Ⓔ	32. Ⓐ Ⓑ Ⓒ Ⓓ Ⓔ	44. Ⓐ Ⓑ Ⓒ Ⓓ Ⓔ
9. Ⓐ Ⓑ Ⓒ Ⓓ Ⓔ	21. Ⓐ Ⓑ Ⓒ Ⓓ Ⓔ	33. Ⓐ Ⓑ Ⓒ Ⓓ Ⓔ	45. Ⓐ Ⓑ Ⓒ Ⓓ Ⓔ
10. Ⓐ Ⓑ Ⓒ Ⓓ Ⓔ	22. Ⓐ Ⓑ Ⓒ Ⓓ Ⓔ	34. Ⓐ Ⓑ Ⓒ Ⓓ Ⓔ	46. Ⓐ Ⓑ Ⓒ Ⓓ Ⓔ
11. Ⓐ Ⓑ Ⓒ Ⓓ Ⓔ	23. Ⓐ Ⓑ Ⓒ Ⓓ Ⓔ	35. Ⓐ Ⓑ Ⓒ Ⓓ Ⓔ	47. Ⓐ Ⓑ Ⓒ Ⓓ Ⓔ
12. Ⓐ Ⓑ Ⓒ Ⓓ Ⓔ	24. Ⓐ Ⓑ Ⓒ Ⓓ Ⓔ	36. Ⓐ Ⓑ Ⓒ Ⓓ Ⓔ	48. Ⓐ Ⓑ Ⓒ Ⓓ Ⓔ

SAMPLE QUESTIONS: OPM EXAM

Each question has several suggested answers lettered A, B, C, and so on. Decide which one is the best answer to the question. Then, on the sample answer sheet, find the answer space that is numbered the same as the number of the question and darken completely the circle that is lettered the same as the letter of your answer. Compare your answers with those given. Then study the explanations of the correct answers that follow the correct answer key.

Directions: *Sample questions 1 through 20 require name and number comparisons. In each line across the page, there are three names or numbers that are very similar. Compare the three names or numbers and decide which ones are exactly alike. On your sample answer sheet, mark the answer*

A if ALL THREE names or numbers are exactly ALIKE

B if only the FIRST and SECOND names or numbers are exactly ALIKE

C if only the FIRST and THIRD names or numbers are exactly ALIKE

D if only the SECOND and THIRD names or numbers are exactly ALIKE

E if ALL THREE names or numbers are DIFFERENT

1.	Davis Hazen	David Hozen	David Hazen
2.	Lois Appel	Lois Appel	Lois Apfel
3.	June Allan	Jane Allan	Jane Allan
4.	Emily Neal Rouse	Emily Neal Rowse	Emily Neal Rowse
5.	H. Merritt Audubon	H. Merriott Audubon	H. Merritt Audubon
6.	6219354	6219354	6219354
7.	2312793	2312793	2312793
8.	1065407	1065407	1065047
9.	3457988	3457986	3457986
10.	4695682	4695862	4695682
11.	Francis Ransdell	Frances Ramsdell	Francis Ramsdell
12.	Cornelius Detwiler	Cornelius Detwiler	Cornelius Detwiler
13.	Stricklund Kanedly	Stricklund Kanedy	Stricklund Kanedy
14.	Joy Harlor Witner	Joy Harloe Witner	Soy Harloe Witner
15.	R.M.O. Uberroth	R.M.O. Uberroth	R.N.O. Uberroth
16.	2395890	2395890	2395890
17.	1926341	1926347	1926314
18.	5261383	5261383	5261338
19.	8125690	8126690	8125609
20.	6177396	6177936	6177396

Sample questions 21 through 30 require verbal skills.

Directions: *Reading. In questions 21 through 25, read the paragraph carefully and base your answer on the material given.*

21. Probably few people realize, as they drive on a concrete road, that steel is used to keep the surface flat and even in spite of the weight of buses and trucks. Steel bars, deeply embedded in the concrete, provide sinews to take the stresses so that they cannot crack the slab or make it wavy.

The paragraph best supports the statement that a concrete road
(A) is expensive to build.
(B) usually cracks under heavy weights.
(C) is used exclusively for heavy traffic.
(D) is reinforced with other material.

22. The likelihood of America exhausting its natural resources seems to be decreasing. All kinds of waste are being reworked, and new uses are constantly being found for almost everything. We are getting more use out of our goods and are making many new byproducts out of what was formerly thrown away.

The paragraph best supports the statement that we seem to be in less danger of exhausting our resources because
(A) economy is found to lie in the use of substitutes.
(B) more service is obtained from a given amount of material.
(C) we are allowing time for nature to restore them.
(D) supply and demand are better controlled.

23. Through advertising, manufacturers exercise a high degree of control over consumers' desires. However, the manufacturer assumes enormous risks in attempting to predict what consumers will want and in producing goods in quantity and distributing them in advance of final selection by the consumers.

The paragraph best supports the statement that manufacturers
(A) can eliminate the risk of overproduction by advertising.
(B) distribute goods directly to the consumers.
(C) must depend upon the final consumers for the success of their undertakings.
(D) can predict with great accuracy the success of any product they put on the market.

24. What constitutes skill in any line of work is not always easy to determine; economy of time must be carefully distinguished from economy of energy because the quickest method may require the greatest expenditure of muscular effort and may not be essential or at all desirable.

The paragraph best supports the statement that
(A) the most efficiently executed task is not always the one done in the shortest time.
(B) energy and time cannot both be conserved in performing a single task.
(C) a task is well done when it is performed in the shortest time.
(D) skill in performing a task should not be acquired at the expense of time.

25. In the relations of people to nature, the procuring of food and shelter is fundamental. With the migration of people to various climates, ever-new adjustments to the food supply and the climate became necessary.

The paragraph best supports the statement that the means by which people supply their material needs are
(A) accidental.
(B) varied.
(C) limited.
(D) inadequate.

Directions: *Vocabulary. For questions 26 through 30, choose the one of the four suggested answers that means most nearly the same as the word in italics.*

26. *Flexible* means most nearly
(A) breakable. (C) pliable.
(B) flammable. (D) weak.

27. *Option* means most nearly
(A) use. (C) value.
(B) choice. (D) blame.

28. To *verify* means most nearly to
(A) examine. (C) confirm.
(B) explain. (D) guarantee.

29. *Previous* means most nearly
(A) abandoned. (C) timely.
(B) former. (D) younger.

30. *Respiration* means most nearly
(A) recovery. (C) pulsation.
(B) breathing. (D) sweating.

Directions: *Each of these reasoning questions, 31 through 35, consists of two sets of symbols. Find the one rule that explains the similarity of the symbols within each set and that also explains the difference between the two sets. Among the five suggested answers, find the symbol that can best be substituted for the question mark in the second set. In all these questions, you will find details that have nothing to do with the principle of the question: to find the similarity between the symbols within a set and the difference between the sets.*

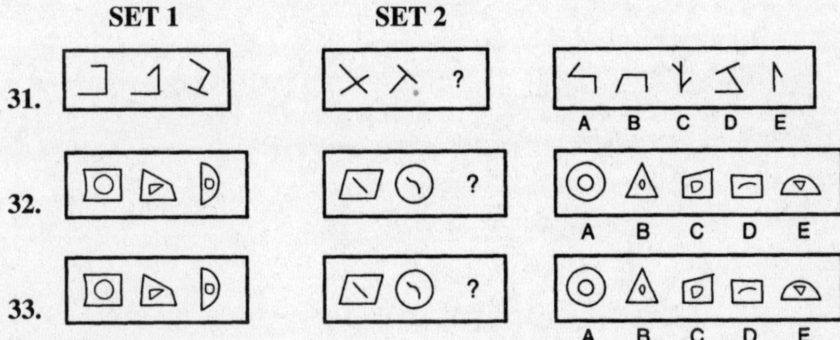

Directions: *Questions 36 through 48 require number reasoning skills. In each question, there is at the left a series of numbers that follow some definite order; at the right, there are five sets of two numbers each. You are to look at the numbers in the series at the left and determine what order they follow. Then, from the suggested answers at the right, select the set that gives the next two numbers in the series.*

36. 1 2 3 4 5 6 7 .... (A) 1 2 (B) 5 6 (C) 8 9 (D) 4 5 (E) 7 8

37. 15 14 13 12 11 10 9 .... (A) 2 1 (B) 17 16 (C) 8 9 (D) 8 7 (E) 9 8

38. 20 20 21 21 22 22 23 .... (A) 23 23 (B) 23 24 (C) 19 19 (D) 22 23 (E) 21 22

39. 17 3 17 4 17 5 17 .... (A) 6 17 (B) 6 7 (C) 17 6 (D) 5 6 (E) 17 7

40. 1 2 4 5 7 8 10 .... (A) 11 12 (B) 12 14 (C) 10 13 (D) 12 13 (E) 11 13

41. 21 21 20 20 19 19 18 .... (A) 18 18 (B) 18 17 (C) 17 18 (D) 17 17 (E) 18 19

42. 1 20 3 19 5 18 7 .... (A) 8 9 (B) 8 17 (C) 17 10 (D) 17 9 (E) 9 18

43. 30 2 28 4 26 6 24 .... (A) 23 9 (B) 26 8 (C) 8 9 (D) 26 22 (E) 8 22

44. 5 6 20 7 8 19 9 .... (A) 10 18 (B) 18 17 (C) 10 17 (9) 18 19 (E) 10 11

45. 91 01 11 12 2 13 .... (A) 2 14 (B) 3 14 (C) 14 3 (D) 14 15 (E) 14 1

46. 46 9 11 14 16 19 .... (A) 21 24 (B) 22 25 (C) 20 22 (D) 21 23 (E) 22 24

47. 8 8 1 10 10 3 12 .... (A) 13 13 (B) 12 5 (C) 12 4 (D) 13 5 (E) 4 12

48. 20 21 23 24 27 28 32 33 38 39 ..... (A) 45 46 (B) 45 54 (C) 44 45 (D) 44 49 (E) 40 46

Answer Key

1. **E**	9. **D**	17. **E**	25. **B**	33. **B**	41. **B**
2. **B**	10. **C**	18. **B**	26. **C**	34. **E**	42. **D**
3. **D**	11. **E**	19. **E**	27. **B**	35. **B**	43. **E**
4. **D**	12. **A**	20. **C**	28. **C**	36. **C**	44. **A**
5. **C**	13. **A**	21. **D**	29. **B**	37. **D**	45. **C**
6. **A**	14. **D**	22. **B**	30. **B**	38. **B**	46. **A**
7. **A**	15. **B**	23. **C**	31. **E**	39. **A**	47. **B**
8. **B**	16. **A**	24. **A**	32. **D**	40. **E**	48. **A**

Explanatory Answers

1. **(E)** In the first column, the first name differs from the first names in the other two columns. In the second column, the last name is different.

2. **(B)** In the first two columns, the two names are identical, but in the third column, the last name is different.

3. **(D)** In the second and third columns, the two names are identical, but in the first column, the first name is different.

4. **(D)** In the second and third columns, the names are identical, but in the first column, the last name is different.

5. **(C)** In all three columns, the initial and last names are identical, but in the second column, the middle name differs from the middle name in the first and third columns.

6. **(A)** All three numbers are identical.

7. **(A)** All three numbers are identical.

8. **(B)** In the first two columns, the last three digits are 407, but in the third column, they are 047.

9. **(D)** The number in the first column ends with 88, while the other two columns end with 86.

10. **(C)** Again, the difference occurs in the ending of the numbers. The numbers in the first and third columns end with 682, while the number in the second column ends with 862.

11. **(E)** In the first column, the last name differs from the last name in the other two columns. In the second column, the first name differs from that in the other two.

12. **(A)** All three names are identical.

13. **(A)** All three names are identical.

14. **(D)** The only difference is that, in the first column, the middle name differs from that in the other two columns.

15. **(B)** The names in the first two columns are identical, but in the third column, the second initial is different.

16. **(A)** All three numbers are identical.

17. **(E)** All the numbers differ from each other. In the first column, the last two digits are 41; in the second column, they are 47; in the third, they are 14.

18. **(B)** The first two columns end with 83, while the third ends with 38.

19. **(E)** There are differences in central digits and in final digits. The 66 in the middle of the number in the second column differs from the 56 in the middle of the other two. The 09 at the end of the number in the third column differs from the 90 at the end of the other two.

20. **(C)** The number in the second column ends with 936, while the numbers in the first and third columns end with 396.

21. **(D)** The steel bars that keep the concrete road from cracking are reinforcing it.

22. **(B)** The effect of recycling is to make greater use of resources so we do not need to constantly deplete fresh resources.

23. **(C)** If consumers don't buy, the manufacturers are stuck with excess stock.

24. **(A)** Many considerations must enter into an assessment of efficiency. Time, effort, energy, and money are all factors.

25. **(B)** The ability of people to adjust and adapt to changing climates and to changing circumstances implies that human beings are capable of varied responses and behaviors.

26. **(C)** *Flexible,* the opposite of rigid or stiff, means *easily bent, adjustable,* or *pliable.*

27. **(B)** An *option* is a *choice.*

28. **(C)** To *verify* is to *check the accuracy of* or to *confirm.*

29. **(B)** *Previous* means *occurring before in time or order,* hence *former.*

30. **(B)** *Respiration* is *breathing.*

31. **(E)** The simplest general rule that guides this question is that all the symbols are made up of lines that touch each other. In the first set, each of the symbols consists of three lines that touch. The second set contains symbols consisting of two lines that touch. Only choice (E) fulfills this requirement.

32. **(D)** The general rule governing this question is that all symbols are made up to two figures, one inside the other. The first set consists of a closed figure inside the outer figure. In the second set, there is a single line inside the outer figure. Only choice (D) conforms to this rule. Note that the shapes of the figures are irrelevant to the question.

33. **(B)** The general rule is that all symbols are made up of four lines. In the first set, all symbols consist of both straight and curved lines. In the second set, the symbols are made up of straight lines only. Of the choices, only (B) is made up of only straight lines. Whether or not lines within a symbol touch is irrelevant to the question.

34. **(E)** Each symbol is made up of three lines. In set 1, the lines that compose each symbol are of like quality, that is, solid, broken, or dotted. In set 2, the lines composing each symbol are not of the same quality. Of the choices, only (E) consists of straight and dotted lines. All the other choices are figures made up of lines of the same quality. The shapes of the lines are irrelevant.

35. **(B)** All symbols consist of a circle and a line. In the first set, the line is tangent to the circle. In the second set, the line is perpendicular or nearly perpendicular to the circle. Choice (B) best fits this requirement.

36. **(C)** You can see at a glance that the numbers in this series are increasing by 1. If the series were continued for two more numbers, it would read: 1 2 3 4 5 6 7 8 9.

37. **(D)** Clearly the numbers in this series are decreasing by 1. If the series were continued for two more numbers, it would read: 15 14 13 12 11 10 9 8 7.

38. **(B)** Each number in this series is repeated and then increased by 1. If the series were continued for two more numbers, it would read: 20 20 21 21 22 22 23 23 24. Your answer choice must include the repeat of the number and then the following number.

39. **(A)** This series is the number 17 separated by numbers increasing by 1, beginning with the number 3. If the series were continued for two more numbers, it would read: 17 3 17 4 17 5 17 6 17. Your answer must include the next number in the increasing series and the 17 that follows it.

40. **(E)** The numbers in this series are increasing, first by 1 and then by 2. If the series were continued for two more numbers, it would read: 1 2 4 5 7 8 10 11 13. In some more-difficult-to-visualize series, you may find it helpful to diagram the ongoing action. Thus, you could readily determine the correct answer to this question by writing:

+1 +2 +1 +2 +1 +2 +1 +2
1 2 4 5 7 8 10 11 13

41. **(B)** In this series, the number repeats and then decreases by 1. If the series were continued for two more numbers, it would read: 21 21 20 20 19 19 18 18 17. The answer includes the repeat followed by the decreased number.

42. **(D)** There are really two alternating series here. One series increases by 2, while the alternating series decreases by 1. If the first series were continued, it would read: 1 3 5 7 9; the other series continued would read: 20 19 18 17. Combined as a single series, the series would continue: 1 20 3 19 5 18 7 17 9. If you find this type of question difficult, consider the possibility of alternating series. The best solution of alternating series is a diagram:

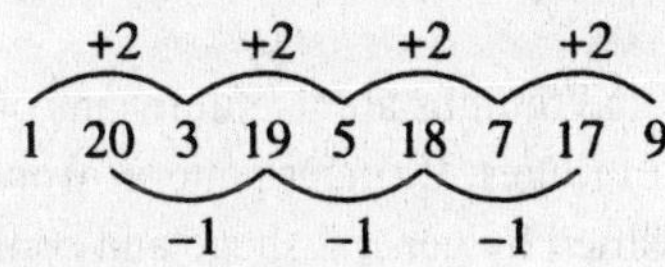

43. **(E)** Here we also have alternating series; the first series decreases by 2, while the alternating series increases by 2. Thus, one series would read: 30 28 26 24 22; the other would read: 2 4 6 8. Together, it would read: 30 2 28 4 26 6 24 8 22. Diagrammed, it looks like this:

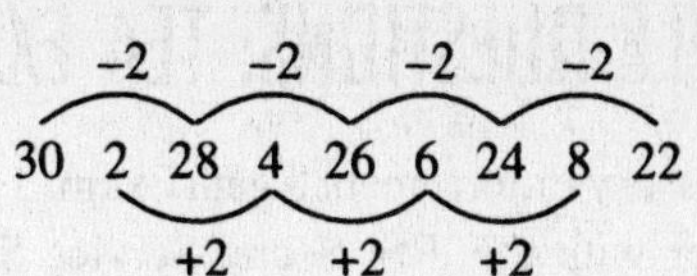

44. **(A)** This alternating series question has a slightly different rhythm, but after dealing with a few alternating series questions, you should easily see: 5 6 7 8 9 10 and 20 19 18. Once you recognize the pattern of alternation, you know that the continued series reads: 5 6 20 7 8 19 9 10 18.

45. **(C)** This series is similar to those in question 44; they just begin at different points. Continued, it reads: 9 10 1 11 12 2 13 14 3. In answering, you must be careful to pick up the total series at the proper place.

46. **(A)** This question involves a single series with alternating steps. Diagrammed, it looks like this:

+2 +3 +2 +3 +2 +3 +2 +3
4 6 9 11 14 16 19 21 24

47. **(B)** This series is similar to those in questions 44 and 45 except that all numbers increase by a factor of 2 instead of 1, and there is the repetition element. Continued, the series would read: 8 8 1 10 10 3 12 12 5.

48. **(A)** This is a single series with varying increasing steps. It is quite difficult to answer without a diagram, but it's very simple with one, as illustrated:

+1 +2 +1 +3 +1 +4 +1 +5 +1 +6 +1
20 21 23 24 27 28 32 33 38 39 45 46.

By the time you have diagrammed to the point of choosing an answer, you should have a clear understanding of the pattern and be able to continue with confidence.

SAMPLE QUESTIONS: TEA EXAM

The Treasury Enforcement Agent Exam (TEA) is given to candidates for the positions of Internal Security Inspector with the IRS; Secret Service Special Agent; Customs Special Agent; Bureau of Alcohol, Tobacco, and Firearms Special Agent; IRS Special Agent with the Criminal Investigation Division; Deputy U.S. Marshal; and a number of other positions as well. If you are a candidate for any of these positions, give careful attention to the official sample questions that follow. Even if you are applying for a local or state law enforcement position, you should give serious attention to all federal exam questions. Some of the same types of questions are likely to appear on whatever exam you must take.

The Treasury Enforcement Agent Exam (TEA) is divided into three parts: Part A, verbal reasoning; Part B, arithmetic reasoning; and Part C, problems for investigation. The official sample questions that follow are similar to the questions you will find in the actual test in terms of difficulty and form.

Part A—Verbal Reasoning Questions

In each of these questions, you will be given a paragraph that contains all the information necessary to infer the correct answer. Use only the information provided in the paragraph. Do not speculate or make assumptions that go beyond this information. Also, assume that all information given in the paragraph is true, even if it conflicts with some fact known to you. Only one correct answer can be validly inferred from the information contained in the paragraph.

Pay special attention to negated verbs (for example, "are *not*") and negative prefixes (for example, "*in*complete" or "*dis*organized"). Also pay special attention to quantifiers such as "all," "none," and "some." For example, from a paragraph in which it is stated that "it is not true that all contracts are legal," one can validly infer that "some contracts are not legal" or that "some contracts are illegal" or that "some illegal things are contracts," but one **cannot** validly infer that "no contracts are legal" or that "some contracts are legal." Similarly, from a paragraph that states "all contracts are legal" and "all contracts are two-sided agreements," one can infer that "some two-sided agreements are legal," but one **cannot** validly infer that "all two-sided agreements are legal."

Bear in mind that, in some tests, universal quantifiers such as "all" and "none" often give away incorrect response choices. That is **not** the case in this test. Some correct answers will refer to "all" or "none" of the members of a group.

Be sure to distinguish between essential information and unessential, peripheral information. That is to say, in a real test question, the preceding example ("all contracts are legal" and "all contracts are two-sided agreements") would appear in a longer, full-fledged paragraph. It would be up to you to separate the essential information from its context and then to realize that a response choice that states "some two-sided agreements are legal" represents a valid inference and hence the correct answer.

Sample questions 1 and 2 are examples of the reading questions on the test.

1. Impressions made by the ridges on the ends of the fingers and thumbs are useful means of identification since no two persons have the same pattern of ridges. If finger patterns from fingerprints are not decipherable, then they cannot be classified by general shape and contour or by pattern type. If they cannot be classified by these characteristics, then it is impossible to identify the person to whom the fingerprints belong.

The paragraph best supports the statement that

(A) if it is impossible to identify the person to whom fingerprints belong, then the fingerprints are not decipherable.

(B) if finger patterns from fingerprints are not decipherable, then it is impossible to identify the person to whom the fingerprints belong.
(C) if fingerprints are decipherable, then it is impossible to identify the person to whom they belong.
(D) if fingerprints can be classified by general shape and contour or by pattern type, then they are not decipherable.
(E) if it is possible to identify the person to whom fingerprints belong, then the fingerprints cannot be classified by general shape and contour or pattern.

The correct answer is response **B.** The essential information from which the answer can be inferred is contained in the second and third sentences. These sentences state that "if finger patterns from fingerprints are not decipherable, then they cannot be classified by general shape and contour or by pattern type. If they cannot be classified by these characteristics, then it is impossible to identify the person to whom they belong." Since response (B) refers to a condition in which finger patterns from fingerprints are not decipherable, we know that, in that circumstance, they cannot be classified by general shape and contour or by pattern type. From the paragraph, we can infer that, since they cannot be classified by these characteristics, it is impossible to identify the person to whom the fingerprints belong.

Response (A) cannot be inferred because the paragraph does not give information about all the circumstances under which it is impossible to identify the person to whom the fingerprints belong. It may be that the person is not identifiable for reasons other than the decipherability of the person's fingerprints.

Response (C) is incorrect because the paragraph does not provide enough information to conclude whether or not it would be possible to identify the person to whom the fingerprints belong from the mere fact of the decipherability of the fingerprints.

Response (D) is wrong because it contradicts the information in the second sentence of the paragraph. From that sentence, it can be concluded that, if fingerprints can be classified by general shape and contour or by pattern type, they are decipherable.

Response (E) is incorrect for a similar reason; it contradicts the information presented in the third sentence of the paragraph.

2. Law enforcement agencies use scientific techniques to identify suspects or to establish guilt. One obvious application of such techniques is the examination of a crime scene. Some substances found at a crime scene yield valuable clues under microscopic examination. Clothing fibers, dirt particles, and even pollen grains may reveal important information to the careful investigator. Nothing can be overlooked because all substances found at a crime scene are potential sources of evidence.

The paragraph best supports the statement that

(A) all substances that yield valuable clues under microscopic examination are substances found at a crime scene.
(B) some potential sources of evidence are substances that yield valuable clues under microscopic examination.
(C) some substances found at a crime scene are not potential sources of evidence.
(D) no potential sources of evidence are substances found at a crime scene.
(E) some substances that yield valuable clues under microscopic examination are not substances found at a crime scene.

The correct answer is response **B.** The essential information from which the answer can be inferred is contained in the third and fifth sentences. The third sentence tells us that "some substances found at a crime scene yield valuable clues under microscopic examination." The fifth sentence explains that "...all substances found at a crime scene are potential sources of evidence." Therefore, we can conclude that "some potential sources of evidence are substances that yield valuable clues under microscopic examination."

Response (A) cannot be inferred because the paragraph does not support the statement that all substances that yield valuable clues are found exclusively at a crime scene. It may be that valuable clues could be found elsewhere.

Responses (C) and (D) are incorrect because they contradict the fifth sentence of the paragraph, which clearly states that "all substances found at a crime scene are potential sources of evidence."

Response (E) is incorrect because the paragraph provides no information about the value of substances found somewhere other than at the crime scene.

Part B—Arithmetic Reasoning Questions

In this part, you will have to solve problems formulated in both verbal and numeric form. You will have to analyze a paragraph to set up the problem and then solve it. If the exact answer is not given as one of the response choices, you should select response E, "None of these." Sample questions 3 and 4 are examples of the arithmetic reasoning questions. The use of calculators will NOT be permitted during the actual testing; therefore, they should not be used to solve these sample questions.

3. A police department purchases badges at $16 each for all the graduates of the police training academy. The last training class graduated 10 new officers. What is the total amount of money the department will spend for badges for these new officers?

(A) $70
(B) $116
(C) $160
(D) $180
(E) None of these

The correct response is **C.** It can be obtained by computing the following:

$$16 \times 10 = 160$$

The badges are priced at $16 each. The department must purchase 10 of them for the new officers. Multiplying the price of one badge ($16) by the number of graduates (10) gives the total price for all of the badges.

Responses A, B, and D are the result of erroneous computations.

4. An investigator rented a car for six days and was charged $450. The car rental company charged $35 per day plus $.30 per mile driven. How many miles did the investigator drive the car?

(A) 800
(B) 900
(C) 1,290
(O) 1,500
(E) None of these

The correct answer is **A.** It can be obtained by computing the following:

$$6(35) + .30X = 450$$

The investigator rented the car for six days at $35 per day, which is $210; $210 subtracted from the total charge of $450 leaves $240, the portion of the total charge that was expended for the miles driven. This amount divided by the charge per mile ($240/.30) gives the number of miles (800) driven by the investigator.

Responses B, C, and D are the result of erroneous computations.

Part C—Problems for Investigation

In this part, you will be presented with a paragraph and several related statements. Sample questions 5 through 9 are based on the following paragraph and statements. Read them carefully and then answer questions 5 through 9.

On October 30, the Belton First National Bank discovered that the $3,000 it had received that morning from the Greenville First National Bank was in counterfeit $10, $20, and $50 bills. The genuine $3,000 had been counted by Greenville First National bank clerk Iris Stewart the preceding afternoon. They were packed in eight black leather satchels and were stored in the bank vault overnight. Greenville First National clerk Brian Caruthers accompanied carriers James Clark and Howard O' Keefe to Belton in an armored truck. Belton First National clerk Cynthia Randall discovered the counterfeit bills when she examined the serial numbers of the bills.

During the course of the investigation, the following statements were made:

(1) Gerald Hathaway, clerk of the Greenville bank, told investigators that he had found the bank office open when he arrived to work on the morning of October 30. The only articles that appeared to be missing were eight black leather satchels of the type used to transport large sums of money.

(2) Jon Perkins, head teller of the Greenville bank, told investigators that he did not check the contents of the black leather satchels after locking them in the vault around 4:30 P.M. on October 29.

(3) Henry Green, janitor of the Greenville bank, said that he noticed Jon Perkins leaving the bank office around 5:30 P.M., one-half hour after the bank closed on October 29. He said that Perkins locked the door.

(4) A scrap of cloth, identical to the material of the carriers' uniforms, was found caught in the seal of one of the black leather satchels delivered to Belton.

(5) Brian Caruthers, clerk, said he saw James Clark and Howard O' Keefe talking in a secretive manner in the armored truck.

(6) Thomas Stillman, Greenville bank executive, identified the eight black leather satchels containing the counterfeit money that arrived at the Belton First National Bank as the eight satchels that had disappeared from the bank office. He had noticed a slight difference in the linings of the satchels.

(7) Virginia Fowler, bank accountant, noticed two $10 bills with the same serial numbers as the lost bills in a bank deposit from Ferdinand's Restaurant of Greenville.

(8) Vincent Johnson, manager of Ferdinand's Restaurant, told police that Iris Stewart frequently dined there with her boyfriend.

5. Which one of the following statements best indicates that satchels containing the counterfeit bills were substituted for satchels containing genuine bills while they were being transported from Greenville to Belton?

(A) Statement (1)
(B) Statement (3)
(C) Statement (4)
(D) Statement (5)
(E) Statement (7)

The correct answer is **(C).** The armored truck carriers had the greatest opportunity to substitute counterfeit bills for real ones during the transportation procedure. The scrap of material from an armored truck carrier's uniform caught in the seal of one of the satchels strongly links the carriers to the crime.

6. Which one of the following statements best links the information given in statement (1) with the substitution of the counterfeit bills?
   (A) Statement (2)
   (B) Statement (3)
   (C) Statement (4)
   (D) Statement (5)
   (E) Statement (6)

The correct answer is **(E).** Statement (1) establishes that eight satchels were missing from Greenville Bank. Statement (6) identifies the satchels that arrived at the Belton Bank as the missing satchels.

7. Which one of the following statements, along with statement (7), best indicates that the substitution of the counterfeit bills casts suspicion on at least one employee of the Greenville bank?
   (A) Statement (1)
   (B) Statement (2)
   (C) Statement (3)
   (D) Statement (5)
   (E) Statement (8)

The correct answer is **(E).** Statement (7) establishes that two stolen $10 bills were spent at Ferdinand's Restaurant. Statement (8) identifies a bank employee as a frequent diner at Ferdinand's Restaurant. This statement "casts suspicion" on the bank employee but does not prove complicity.

8. Which one of the following statements would least likely be used in proving a case?
   (A) Statement (1)
   (B) Statement (3)
   (C) Statement (4)
   (D) Statement (5)
   (E) Statement (7)

The correct answer is **(D).** The fact that the bank clerk saw the armored truck carriers talking secretively may cast some suspicion, but it would not be useful in proving the case. People who work together may very likely exchange private jokes or share personal information.

9. Which one of the following statements best indicates that the substitution of the counterfeit bills could have taken place before the satchels left the Greenville bank?
   (A) Statement (1)
   (B) Statement (2)
   (C) Statement (3)
   (D) Statement (4)
   (E) Statement (7)

The correct answer is **(B).** The satchels were locked in the vault at 4:30 P.M. on one day and were not delivered until the following morning. Since we learn in statement (2) that the satchels were not checked after they were locked into the vault, the exchange could have taken place in the Greenville Bank.

SAMPLE QUESTIONS: BORDER PATROL AGENT EXAM

Applicants for the position of Border Patrol Agent must pass an OPM exam and qualify in the Spanish language. If the candidate feels comfortable speaking and understanding Spanish, he or she may choose to take an oral examination at the time of the interview for the position. If the candidate does not know any Spanish or if he or she is not certain of passing the oral exam, the candidate may elect to take a written multiple-choice test of ability to learn a foreign language. The multiple-choice language aptitude test must be requested and taken at the same time as the OPM exam. The candidate cannot choose the language aptitude exam after failing the oral Spanish exam at interview.

The following are official sample questions for the Border Patrol Agent Exam. This exam is administered by the Office of Personnel Management to candidates for other positions as well. The exam is a 65-question multiple-choice exam. It is divided into four parts, each of which is separately timed. The structure of the exam is as follows:

	Number of Questions	Timing (minutes)
Part A		25
Vocabulary	15	
Reading Comprehension	15	
Part B		
English Usage (Grammar)	15	7
Part C		
General Knowledge and Judgment	10	10
Part D		
Logical Reasoning	10	15
Total	65	57

When the exam is scored, you will receive credit for every correct answer but will suffer no penalty for a wrong answer. This means it is best to answer every question. A space left blank cannot raise your score, but even a wild guess could possibly help you. Choose the correct answer if you can. If not, eliminate obviously wrong answers and choose intelligently from the remaining choices or make a wild stab if you must. The official instructions that will be read to you in the examination room state: "It will be to your advantage to answer every question in this test that you can since your score will be the number of right answers only. If you don't know the answer to a question, make the best guess you can. You may write in the test booklet if you need to."

These official sample questions are just samples. They will give you a good idea of the kinds of questions that you must answer.

Directions: Each question has five suggested answers lettered A, B, C, D, and E. Decide which one is the best answer to the question. Then darken completely the space corresponding to the letter that is the same as the letter of your answer. Keep your mark within the space. If you have to erase a mark, be sure to erase it completely. Mark only one answer for each question.

Sample Answer Sheet

1. Ⓐ Ⓑ Ⓒ Ⓓ Ⓔ 6. Ⓐ Ⓑ Ⓒ Ⓓ Ⓔ 11. Ⓐ Ⓑ Ⓒ Ⓓ Ⓔ
2. Ⓐ Ⓑ Ⓒ Ⓓ Ⓔ 7. Ⓐ Ⓑ Ⓒ Ⓓ Ⓔ 12. Ⓐ Ⓑ Ⓒ Ⓓ Ⓔ
3. Ⓐ Ⓑ Ⓒ Ⓓ Ⓔ 8. Ⓐ Ⓑ Ⓒ Ⓓ Ⓔ 13. Ⓐ Ⓑ Ⓒ Ⓓ Ⓔ
4. Ⓐ Ⓑ Ⓒ Ⓓ Ⓔ 9. Ⓐ Ⓑ Ⓒ Ⓓ Ⓔ 14. Ⓐ Ⓑ Ⓒ Ⓓ Ⓔ
5. Ⓐ Ⓑ Ⓒ Ⓓ Ⓔ 10. Ⓐ Ⓑ Ⓒ Ⓓ Ⓔ 15. Ⓐ Ⓑ Ⓒ Ⓓ Ⓔ

Sample Questions 1 through 3. In each of the following sample questions, select the one of the five suggested answers that is closest in meaning to the word in italics. Then darken the proper space on the sample answer sheet.

1. The new training program is much better than any of the *previous* ones. *Previous* means most nearly
(A) abandoned.
(B) former.
(C) unused.
(D) recent.
(E) ineffective.

2. The officer made several phone calls in an attempt to *verify* the report. To *verify* means most nearly to
(A) examine.
(B) explain.
(C) confirm.
(D) believe.
(E) improve.

3. The driver's only *option* was to turn right at the intersection. *Option* means most nearly
(A) use.
(B) direction.
(C) hope.
(D) choice.
(E) opportunity.

Sample Questions 4 through 6. In each of the next three sample questions, select the one of the five suggested answers that is best supported by the paragraph. Then darken the proper space on the sample answer sheet.

4. Just as the procedure of a collection department must be clear-cut and definite, the steps being taken with the sureness of a skilled chess player, so too must the various paragraphs of a collection letter show clear organization, giving evidence of a mind that, from the beginning, has had a specific end in view.

The paragraph best supports the statement that a collection letter should always

(A) show a spirit of sportsmanship.
(B) be divided into several paragraphs.
(C) be brief but courteous.
(D) be carefully planned.
(E) be written by the head of the collection department.

5. To prevent industrial accidents, it is not only necessary that safety devices be used to guard exposed machinery, but also that mechanics be instructed in the safety rules they must follow for their own protection and that the lighting in the plant be adequate.

The paragraph best supports the statement that industrial accidents

(A) may be due to ignorance.
(B) are always avoidable.
(C) usually result from unsafe machinery.
(D) cannot be entirely overcome.
(E) usually result from inadequate lighting.

6. Through advertising, manufacturers exercise a high degree of control over consumers' desires. However, the manufacturer assumes enormous risks in attempting to predict what consumers will want and in producing goods in quantity and distributing them in advance of final selection by the consumers.

The paragraph best supports the statement that manufacturers

(A) can eliminate the risk of overproduction by advertising.
(B) distribute goods directly to the consumers.
(C) must depend on the final consumers for the success of their undertakings.
(D) can predict with great accuracy the success of any product they put on the market.
(E) are more concerned with advertising than with the production of goods.

Sample Questions 7 through 9. Each of the next three sample questions contains five sentences. Decide which one of the five sentences would be most suitable in a formal letter or report with respect to grammar and usage. Then darken the proper space on the sample answer sheet.

7. (A) The officer should of answered courteously the questions asked by the callers.
(B) The officer must answer courteously the questions of all them callers.
(C) The officer must answer courteously the questions what are asked by the callers.
(D) There would have been no trouble if the officer had have always answered courteously.
(E) The officer should answer courteously the questions of all callers.

8. (A) There are less mistakes in his work since he took the training course.
(B) The training course being completed, he makes very few mistakes in his work.
(C) Since he completed the training course, he has made few mistakes in his work.
(D) After taking the training course, his work was found to contain hardly any mistakes.
(E) After he completed the training course, he seldom ever made any mistakes in his work.

9. (A) If properly addressed, the letter will reach my supervisor and I.
   (B) The letter had been addressed to myself and my supervisor.
   (C) I believe the letter was addressed to either my supervisor or I.
   (D) My supervisor's name, as well as mine, was on the letter.
   (E) My supervisor and me will receive the letter if it is probably addressed.

Sample Questions 10 through 12. In each of these sample questions, use your judgment and general knowledge to select the best or most important answer from the five suggested answers. Then darken the proper space on the sample answer sheet.

10. From the standpoint of the prisoners, the *chief* advantage to be derived from a properly administered parole system is the
    (A) freedom from fear of being returned to prison.
    (B) opportunity to adjust themselves to release from imprisonment.
    (C) removal of the temptation to commit crime.
    (D) reduced cost of supervising prisoners.
    (E) opportunity to save whatever they are able to earn.

11. An officer of the law may arrest a person without a warrant upon reasonable suspicion that the person has committed a felony. The *chief* purpose of this rule is to
    (A) prevent the person's escape while his or her guilt is being investigated.
    (B) prevent the person from committing more crimes immediately.
    (C) give the person a chance to confess.
    (D) permit observation of the person's behavior.
    (E) increase the rate of arrest in proportion to the number of crimes committed.

12. Acquaintance with all types of ammunition commonly in use is extremely valuable to the worker in crime detection *chiefly* because
    (A) all criminals possess this knowledge.
    (B) a broad background is desirable for success in investigative work.
    (C) the worker's safety is thus ensured in time of danger.
    (D) the worker can thus eventually become a specialist in this line.
    (E) such knowledge often simplifies the problem of investigation.

Sample Questions 13 through 15. Each of these sample questions consists of five related events followed by five suggested orders in which the events could have occurred. Each suggested order represents the sequence in which the five sentences should be read. For example, 3-5-1-2-4 indicates that the third sentence should be read first, the fifth sentence second, the first sentence third, and so on. Select the one of the five suggested orders, lettered A, B, C, D, and E, in which the events most probably happened. Then darken the proper space on the sample answer sheet.

13. 1. The maid discovered the body and called the police.
2. The police found Mary at the home of her sister.
3. A man was shot while swimming in his private pool.
4. A gun was found in Mary's pocketbook and was identified as the murder weapon.
5. The police questioned the maid and discovered that the victim had had a heated argument with his wife, Mary, the night before.

(A) 1-3-5-4-2
(B) 3-5-1-4-2
(C) 3-1-5-2-4
(D) 1-5-2-4-3
(E) 3-1-2-4-5

14. 1. In addition to the paper, a printing press and a stack of freshly printed $10 bills were found in Mr. Hayes' basement.
2. A detective saw Mr. Hayes leave a printing shop with a large package.
3. Mr. Hayes was arrested for counterfeiting and taken to the station.
4. The owner of the shop said Mr. Hayes had bought very high-quality paper.
5. Mr. Hayes was under surveillance as a suspect in a counterfeiting case.

(A) 2-4-1-5-3
(B) 5-2-4-1-3
(C) 3-2-4-1-5
(D) 2-5-1.4-3
(E) 5-2-3-4-1

15. 1. The inspector realized that Ms. Smith was wearing a wig and had her searched.
2. The inspector decided to search Ms. Smith's luggage.
3. Although the inspector could not place the face, he knew that Ms. Smith looked familiar.
4. Narcotics were found sewn to the crown of Ms. Smith's wig.
5. The inspector found nothing in Ms. Smith's luggage, but her passport photograph revealed her identity as a suspected smuggler.

(A) 2-5-3-1-4
(B) 3-1-4-2-5
(C) 1-4-2-5-3
(D) 3-2-5-1-4
(E) 2-1-3-5-4

Answer Key

1. **B**	4. **D**	7. **E**	10. **B**	13. **C**
2. **C**	5. **A**	8. **C**	11. **A**	14. **B**
3. **D**	6. **C**	9. **D**	12. **E**	15. **D**

Explanatory Answers

1. **(B)** *Previous* means coming or occurring before something else.

2. **(C)** To *verify* means to prove or to determine the truth or correctness of something.

3. **(D)** *Option* means something that may be or is chosen.

4. **(D)** The correct answer, D, is supported by the paragraph's statement that a collection letter should show clear organization and should be written with a specific end in view. There is nothing in the paragraph to support alternatives A or E. Although the paragraph does imply that collection letters may contain several paragraphs (alternative B), it does not state that they should *always* be so divided. Also, the paragraph says nothing about the length or tone of a collection letter (alternative C); it only refers to the letter's clarity of thought and organization.

5. **(A)** The correct answer, A, is supported by the paragraph's statement that instructing mechanics in safety rules can help prevent industrial accidents, which implies that in some cases accidents may be due to ignorance of these rules. The paragraph does not support the statements that, in actual practice, industrial accidents are either *always* avoidable (alternative B) or cannot be entirely overcome (alternative D); it merely states the requirements of successful accident prevention. Although the paragraph does imply that industrial accidents can be caused by unsafe machinery (alternative C) and inadequate lighting (alternative E), it does not support the statements that such accidents *usually* result from these causes.

6. **(C)** The correct answer, C, is supported by the paragraph's statement that, although advertising gives manufacturers considerable control over the consumers' demands for their products, there are still big risks involved in producing and distributing their goods in advance of the consumers' final selection. This implies that manufacturers' ultimate success depends on the consumers. The paragraph's statement that there are such risks, in spite of advertising, contradicts alternatives A and D. There also is no support for the statements that manufacturers distribute goods *directly* to consumers (alternative B) or that they are more concerned with advertising than production (alternative E).

7. **(E)** Alternative A is incorrect because the word *have* should have been used instead of the word *of.* Alternative B is incorrect because the word *those* should have been used instead of the word *them.* Alternative C is incorrect because the word *that* should have been used instead of the word *what.* Alternative D is incorrect because the phrase *had have* is incorrect grammar; only the word *had* should have been used.

8. **(C)** Alternative A is incorrect because the word *fewer* should have been used instead of the word *less.* Alternative B is incorrect because poor word usage makes it seem as if *he* refers to the *training course.* Alternative D is incorrect because the word *few* should have been used instead of the phrase *hardly any.* Alternative E is incorrect because it is poor usage for the word *ever* to follow the word *seldom.*

9. **(D)** In alternative A, "my supervisor and *me*" is the object of the verb. In alternative C, "my supervisor and *me*" is the object of the preposition. In alternative B, the word *myself* should be replaced with the word *me.* In alternative E, "my supervisor and *I*" is the subject of the sentence.

10. **(B)** The *chief* advantage of a properly administered parole system from the prisoners' standpoint is the opportunity it provides them for information and assistance concerning their reentry into society. A parole system cannot guarantee that released prisoners will never return to prison in the future (alternative A), that they will not be tempted to commit crime (alternative C), or that they will have the opportunity to save whatever they earn (alternative E) because these possibilities are largely in the hands of the prisoners themselves. Although alternative D may be a result of the parole system, it is not the chief advantage from the standpoint of the prisoners.

11. **(A)** The *chief* purpose of arresting a person suspected of committing a felony is to ensure that the suspect does not escape while further investigation takes place. Although there may be some truth in all the other alternatives, none of them can be considered to be the primary reason for this rule.

12. **(E)** The *chief* advantage of familiarity with all types of ammunition for the worker in crime detection lies in the fact that such knowledge can be a valuable aid in discovering and following up clues during the process of investigation. Alternatives A and C are untrue, and although alternatives B and D may be true in some cases, neither one is the most important reason why acquaintance with ammunition is valuable to the worker in crime detection.

13. **(C)** The most logical order of the five events is that first the man was shot (3); second, his body was discovered by the maid, and the police were called (1); third, the police questioned the maid and learned of the couple's argument of the previous night (5); fourth, the police found Mary at her sister's home (2); and fifth, a gun was found in Mary's pocketbook and was identified as the murder weapon (4). The answer is not A because the maid could not have discovered the body (1) before the man was shot (3). The answer is not B because the police could not have questioned the maid (5) before she called them (1). The answer is not D because the first four events could not have taken place before the man was shot (3). The answer is not E because the police could not have looked for Mary (2) before learning from the maid that she was the victim's wife (5).

14. **(B)** The most logical order of the five events is that first Mr. Hayes was under surveillance (5); second, a detective saw him leave a printing shop with a large package (2); third, the shop owner said he had bought high-quality paper (4); fourth, a printing press and freshly printed bills were found in Mr. Hayes' basement along with the paper (1); and fifth, he was arrested for counterfeiting (3). The answer is not A or D because the detective would not have seen Mr. Hayes leave the printing shop (2) if he had not been under surveillance (5). The answer is not C or E because Mr. Hayes could not have been arrested for counterfeiting (3) before any evidence was discovered (1).

15. **(D)** The most logical order of the five events is that first the inspector saw that Ms. Smith looked familiar (3); second, he decided to search her luggage (2); third, he found nothing in her luggage but identified her from her passport photograph as a suspected smuggler (5); fourth, he realized that she was wearing a wig and had her searched (1); and fifth, narcotics were found in her wig (4). The answer is not A because the inspector would not have decided to search Ms. Smith's luggage (2) unless his suspicions were aroused by the fact that she looked familiar (3). The answer is not B, C, or E because the inspector would not have realized Ms. Smith was wearing a wig (1) before seeing her passport photograph (5).

If you choose to take the language aptitude exam, you will take this exam after a break on the same day that you take the OPM Exam just described. The language aptitude exam is an Artificial Language Exam. You must demonstrate your ability to learn a foreign language by manipulating vocabulary and grammar in an artificial language.

You will be presented with a booklet describing the artificial language. The booklet will include two vocabulary lists. One list, presented alphabetically by English word, gives the English word and its artificial-language equivalent (Example: alien = huskovy). The other list is alphabetized by artificial language and gives the English equivalent of each artificial-language word (Example: friggar = to work). The booklet includes a glossary of grammatical terms. Grammatical terms have the same meaning in both English and the artificial language. (Example: An adjective is a word that describes a noun.) Finally, the booklet sets out grammar rules for the artificial language. (Example: The feminine singular of a noun, pronoun, and adjective is formed by adding the suffix *ver* to the masculine singular form.)

The exam contains four different types of questions, 50 questions in all. The parts are *not* separately timed. You are allowed 1 hour and 45 minutes to study the accompanying booklet and answer the questions. The artificial language test is a test of your ability to reason and to manipulate the vocabulary and grammar of a foreign language. It is not a memory test. It does not test your ability to remember vocabulary or language. You may keep the booklet open in front of you and refer to it frequently as you answer the questions. You do not need to memorize any information.

The Office of Personnel Management does not provide official sample questions for the Artificial Language test. The following exam description can give you a feeling for the phrasing and style of questions, but without a vocabulary and grammar list, you cannot even attempt to answer these unofficial sample questions.

The first part consists of questions 1 to 20. In this part, you must identify correctly translated words. For example: You may be given an English sentence such as "He injured the man" followed by a sentence in the artificial language such as "Yer Zelet wir huskoy." You must then mark (A) if only #1 is translated
1 2 3 4
correctly, (B) if only #2 is correct, (C) if only #3 is correct, (D) if two or more are correct, and (E) if none are correct.

The second part consists of questions 21 to 30. In this part, you must choose which of five choices correctly translates an underlined word or group of words from English into the artificial language. [Example: There is the <u>lost boy</u>. (A) bex kapkoy, (B) wir kapvoy, (C) bex kapvoy, (D) wir kapkoy, (E) bex kapyok.]

The third part, questions 31 to 42, puts a slightly different spin on translation into the artificial language. You are given an incomplete sentence in the artificial language and must complete it with the correctly translated English word, being conscious not only of the vocabulary word but also the grammatical form. [Example: Synet bex avekoy (man). (A) ekapiko, (B) ekapiver, (C) kopiak, (D) ekapiak, (E) pokiver.]

The fourth part, questions 43 to 50, requires you to correct a sentence in the artificial language. You must change the form of the italicized word or words in the sentence according to instructions given in parentheses. [Example: Yer *bongar* wir broukon (present tense). (A) bongaro, (B) bonagar, (C) bongarara, (D) bongo, (E) bongit.]

SAMPLE QUESTIONS: POSTAL POLICE OFFICER EXAM

Sample Answer Sheet

1. Ⓐ Ⓑ Ⓒ Ⓓ Ⓔ	5. Ⓐ Ⓑ Ⓒ Ⓓ Ⓔ	9. Ⓐ Ⓑ Ⓒ Ⓓ Ⓔ	13. Ⓐ Ⓑ Ⓒ Ⓓ Ⓔ
2. Ⓐ Ⓑ Ⓒ Ⓓ Ⓔ	6. Ⓐ Ⓑ Ⓒ Ⓓ Ⓔ	10. Ⓐ Ⓑ Ⓒ Ⓓ Ⓔ	14. Ⓐ Ⓑ Ⓒ Ⓓ Ⓔ
3. Ⓐ Ⓑ Ⓒ Ⓓ Ⓔ	7. Ⓐ Ⓑ Ⓒ Ⓓ Ⓔ	11. Ⓐ Ⓑ Ⓒ Ⓓ Ⓔ	
4. Ⓐ Ⓑ Ⓒ Ⓓ Ⓔ	8. Ⓐ Ⓑ Ⓒ Ⓓ Ⓔ	12. Ⓐ Ⓑ Ⓒ Ⓓ Ⓔ	

Name and Number Comparisons

Directions: *In each of these questions, you will find listed across the page three names or numbers that are very similar. You should decide which ones are exactly alike. Choose the correct response from A, B, C, D, or E listed below.*

A if ALL THREE names or numbers are exactly ALIKE

B if only the FIRST and SECOND names or numbers are exactly ALIKE

C if only the FIRST and THIRD names or numbers are exactly ALIKE

D if only the SECOND and THIRD names or numbers are exactly ALIKE

E if ALL THREE names and numbers are DIFFERENT

Sample questions 1 through 10 are examples of the name and number questions in the test.

1.	Davis Hazen	David Hozen	David Hazen
2.	Lois Appel	Lois Appel	Lois Apfel
3.	June Allan	Jane Allan	Jane Allan
4.	Emily Neal Rouse	Emily Neal Rowse	Emily Neal Rowse
5.	H. Merritt Audubon	H. Merriott Audubon	H. Merritt Audubon
6.	6219354	6219354	6219354
7.	2312793	2312793	2312793
8.	1065407	1065407	1065047
9.	3457988	3457986	3457986
10.	4695682	4695862	4695682

The correct responses for questions 1 through 10 are:

1. **E**	3. **D**	5. **C**	7. **A**	9. **D**
2. **B**	4. **D**	6. **A**	8. **B**	10. **C**

Reading Questions

In each of these questions, you will be given a paragraph that contains all the information necessary to infer the correct answer. Use *only* the information provided in the paragraph. Do not speculate or make assumptions that go beyond this information. Also, assume that all information given in the paragraph is true, even if it conflicts with some fact known to you. Only one correct answer can be validly inferred from the information contained in the paragraph.

Pay special attention to negated verbs (for example, "are *not*") and negative prefixes (for example, "*in*complete" or "*dis*organized"). Also pay special attention to quantifiers such as "all," "none," and "some." For example, from a paragraph in which it is stated that "it is not true that all contracts are legal," one can validly infer that "some contracts are not legal" or that "some contracts are illegal" or that "some illegal things are contracts," but one *cannot* validly infer that "no contracts are legal" or that "some contracts are legal." Similarly, from a paragraph that states "all contracts are legal" and "all contracts are two-sided agreements," one can infer that "some two-sided agreements are legal," but one *cannot* validly infer that "all two-sided agreements are legal."

Bear in mind that, in some tests, universal quantifiers such as "all" and "none" often give away incorrect response choices. That is *not* the case in this test. Some correct answers will refer to "all" or "none" of the members of a group.

Be sure to distinguish between essential information and unessential, peripheral information. That is to say, in a real test question, the preceding above ("all contracts are legal" and "all contracts are two-sided agreements") would appear in a longer, full-fledged paragraph. It would be up to you to separate the essential information from its context and then to realize that a response choice that states "some two-sided agreements are legal" represents a valid inference and hence the correct answer.

Sample questions 11 and 12 are examples of the reading question in the test.

11. Impressions made by the ridges on the ends of the fingers and thumbs are useful means of identification since no two persons have the same pattern of ridges. If finger patterns from fingerprints are not decipherable, then they cannot be classified by general shape and contour or by pattern type. If they cannot be classified by these characteristics, then it is impossible to identify the person to whom the fingerprints belong.

The paragraph best supports the statement that

(A) if it is impossible to identify the person to whom fingerprints belong, then the fingerprints are not decipherable.

(B) if finger patterns from fingerprints are not decipherable, then it is impossible to identify the person to whom the fingerprints belong.

(C) if fingerprints are decipherable, then it is impossible to identify the person to whom they belong.

(D) if fingerprints can be classified by general shape and contour or by pattern type, then they are not decipherable.

(E) if it is possible to identify the person to whom fingerprints belong, then the fingerprints cannot be classified by general shape and contour or pattern.

The correct answer is response **B**. The essential information from which the answer can be inferred is contained in the second and third sentences. These sentences state that "if finger patterns from fingerprints are not decipherable, then they cannot be classified by general shape and contour or by pattern type. If they cannot be classified by these characteristics, then it is impossible to identify the person to whom they belong." Since response B refers to a condition in which finger patterns from fingerprints are not decipherable, we know that, in that circumstance, they cannot be classified by general shape and contour or by pattern type. From the paragraph, we can infer that, since they cannot be classified by these characteristics, it is impossible to identify the person to whom the fingerprints belong.

Response A cannot be inferred because the paragraph does not give information about all the circumstances under which it is impossible to identify the person to whom the fingerprints belong. It may be that the person is not identifiable for reasons other than the decipherability of the person's fingerprints.

Response C is incorrect because the paragraph does not provide enough information to conclude whether or not it would be possible to identify the person to whom the fingerprints belong from the mere fact of the decipherability of the fingerprints.

Response D is wrong because it contradicts the information in the second sentence of the paragraph. From that sentence, it can be concluded that, if fingerprints can be classified by general shape and contour or by pattern type, they are decipherable.

Response E is incorrect for a similar reason; it contradicts the information presented in the third sentence of the paragraph.

12. Law enforcement agencies use scientific techniques to identify suspects or to establish guilt. One obvious application of such techniques is the examination of a crime scene. Some substances found at a crime scene yield valuable clues under microscopic examination. Clothing fibers, dirt particles, and even pollen grains may reveal important information to the careful investigator. Nothing can be overlooked because all substances found at a crime scene are potential sources of evidence.

The paragraph best supports the statement that

(A) all substances that yield valuable clues under microscopic examination are substances found at a crime scene.
(B) some potential sources of evidence are substances that yield valuable clues under microscopic examination.
(C) some substances found at a crime scene are not potential sources of evidence.
(D) no potential sources of evidence are substances found at a crime scene.
(E) some substances that yield valuable clues under microscopic examination are not substances found at a crime scene.

The correct answer is response **B.** The essential information from which the answer can be inferred is contained in the third and fifth sentences. The third sentence tells us that "some substances found at a crime scene yield valuable clues under microscopic examination." The fifth sentence explains that "...all substances found at a crime scene are potential sources of evidence." Therefore, we can conclude that "some potential sources of evidence are substances that yield valuable clues under microscopic examination."

Response A cannot be inferred because the paragraph does not support the statement that all substances that yield valuable clues are found exclusively at a crime scene. It may be that valuable clues could be found elsewhere.

Responses C and D are incorrect because they contradict the fifth sentence of the paragraph, which clearly states that "all substances found at a crime scene are potential sources of evidence."

Response E is incorrect because the paragraph provides no information about the value of substances found somewhere other than at the crime scene.

Arithmetic Reasoning Questions

In this part of the test, you will have to solve problems formulated in both verbal and numeric form. You will have to analyze a paragraph to set up the problem and then solve it. If the exact answer is not given as one of the response choices, you should select response E, "None of these." Sample questions 13 and

14 are examples of the arithmetic reasoning questions in this test. The use of calculators will NOT be permitted during the test; therefore, they should not be used to solve these sample questions.

13. A police department purchases badges at $16 each for all the graduates of the police training academy. The last training class graduated 10 new officers. What is the total amount of money the department will spend for badges for these new officers?
(A) $70
(B) $116
(C) $160
(D) $180
(E) None of these

The correct response is **C**. It can be obtained by computing the following:

$$16 \times 10 = 160$$

The badges are priced at $16 each. The department must purchase 10 of them for the new officers. Multiplying the price of one badge ($16) by the number of graduates (10) gives the total price for all of the badges.

Responses A, B, and D are the result of erroneous computations.

14. An investigator rented a car for six days and was charged $450. The car rental company charged $35 per day plus $.30 per mile driven. How many miles did the investigator drive the car?
(A) 800
(B) 900
(C) 1,290
(D) 1,500
(E) None of these

The correct answer is **A.** It can be obtained by computing the following:

$$6(35) + .30X = 450$$

The investigator rented the car for six days at $35 per day, which is $210; $210 subtracted from the total charge of $450 leaves $240, the portion of the total charge that was expended for the miles driven. This amount divided by the charge per mile ($240/.30) gives the number of miles (800) driven by the investigator.

Responses B, C, and D are the result of erroneous computations.

SAMPLE QUESTIONS: THE FEDERAL CLERICAL EXAMINATION

The Federal Clerical Examination is administered in whole or in part to applicants for jobs in more than 60 different clerical fields. One of these is the position of Customs Aid, for which the full examination is used.

The first part of the examination is called the Verbal Tasks Test. This section includes questions in such areas as spelling, meaning, and relationship of words; recognition of sentences that are grammatically correct; and reading, understanding, and using written material. These test tasks relate to a variety of job tasks such as proofreading and correcting typed copy, using instruction manuals, organizing files of related materials, and carrying out written instructions.

The Verbal Tasks Test consists of 85 questions to be answered in 35 minutes. Of these:

- 25 are word-meaning questions in which you must choose the word that is closest in meaning to the given word.
- 10 are reading questions in which you must choose the statement that says the same thing as the short paragraph it follows.
- 10 are grammar questions in which you must choose the version of a sentence that is grammatically correct.
- 20 are spelling questions in which you choose which three given spellings of a word is correct or determine that none of the choices is the correct spelling.
- 20 are word-relationship questions in which you complete a relationship by choosing a word that is related to a given word in the same way as the second word in a presented pair is related to the first.

The second part of the Federal Clerical Examination is called the Clerical Tasks Test. This is a test of speed and accuracy on four clerical tasks. There are 120 questions to be answered within the very short time limit of 15 minutes. There are 30 questions of each of the four types. These are presented in cycles of five questions of each type. Since accuracy is an important consideration in the scoring of this test, there is a penalty for wrong answers. However, speed is also important, so you must move quickly from question to question without rechecking for perfection. The four types of questions are:

1. Name and number comparisons, in which you must determine which names or numbers in three columns are exactly alike. The answering code is repeated on every page, but you will find yourself working much more quickly if you can memorize the answering code.
2. Alphabetizing, in which you must place a given name into its proper location in a list of names. Alphabetize first by last names, disregarding capital letters in the middle of names and ignoring punctuation within names. Where two or more last names are identical, alphabetize by first names. If both last and first names are identical, consider initials.
3. Arithmetic, in which you choose the correct answer or decide that none of the given answers is correct. All answers are whole numbers; if you get a decimal, you made a mistake.
4. Letter and number inspection questions, in which you must choose which of the suggested answers contains only letters and numbers in the given question. The letters and numbers can appear in any order, but all letters and numbers in the answer must appear in the question.

Sample Answer Sheet

Verbal Tasks Test

1. Ⓐ Ⓑ Ⓒ Ⓓ Ⓔ 2. Ⓐ Ⓑ Ⓒ Ⓓ Ⓔ 3. Ⓐ Ⓑ Ⓒ Ⓓ Ⓔ 4. Ⓐ Ⓑ Ⓒ Ⓓ Ⓔ 5. Ⓐ Ⓑ Ⓒ Ⓓ Ⓔ

Clerical Tasks Test

1. Ⓐ Ⓑ Ⓒ Ⓓ Ⓔ	5. Ⓐ Ⓑ Ⓒ Ⓓ Ⓔ	9. Ⓐ Ⓑ Ⓒ Ⓓ Ⓔ	13. Ⓐ Ⓑ Ⓒ Ⓓ Ⓔ
2. Ⓐ Ⓑ Ⓒ Ⓓ Ⓔ	6. Ⓐ Ⓑ Ⓒ Ⓓ Ⓔ	10. Ⓐ Ⓑ Ⓒ Ⓓ Ⓔ	14. Ⓐ Ⓑ Ⓒ Ⓓ Ⓔ
3. Ⓐ Ⓑ Ⓒ Ⓓ Ⓔ	7. Ⓐ Ⓑ Ⓒ Ⓓ Ⓔ	11. Ⓐ Ⓑ Ⓒ Ⓓ Ⓔ	15. Ⓐ Ⓑ Ⓒ Ⓓ Ⓔ
4. Ⓐ Ⓑ Ⓒ Ⓓ Ⓔ	8. Ⓐ Ⓑ Ⓒ Ⓓ Ⓔ	12. Ⓐ Ⓑ Ⓒ Ⓓ Ⓔ	16. Ⓐ Ⓑ Ⓒ Ⓓ Ⓔ

Verbal Tasks Test

Directions: *Study the sample questions carefully. Each question has four suggested answers. Decide which one is the best answer. Find the question number on the Sample Answer Sheet. Show your answer to the question by darkening completely the space corresponding to the letter that is the same as the letter of your answer. Keep your mark within the space. If you have to erase a mark, be sure to erase it completely. Mark only one answer for each question. Do NOT mark space E for any question.*

1. *Previous* means most nearly

(A) abandoned.
(B) timely.
(C) former.
(D) younger.

2. Just as the procedure of a collection department must be clear-cut and definite, the steps being taken with the sureness of a skilled chess player, so too must the various paragraphs of a collection letter show clear organization, giving evidence of a mind that, from the beginning, has had a specific end in view.

The paragraph best supports the statement that a collection letter should always

(A) show a spirit of sportsmanship.
(B) be divided into several paragraphs.
(C) be brief but courteous.
(D) be carefully planned.

Directions: *Decide which sentence is preferable with respect to grammar and usage suitable for a formal letter or report.*

3. (A) They do not ordinarily present these kind of reports in detail like this.
(B) A report of this kind is not hardly ever given in such detail as this one.
(C) This report is more detailed than what such reports ordinarily are.
(D) A report of this kind is not ordinarily presented in this much detail.

Directions: *Find the correct spelling of the word and darken the proper answer space. If no suggested spelling is correct, darken space D.*

4. (A) athalete
(B) athelete
(C) athlete
(D) none of these

5. SPEEDOMETER is related to POINTER as WATCH is related to
(A) case.
(B) dial.
(C) hands.
(D) numerals.

Clerical Tasks Test

Directions: *In each line across the page, there are three names or numbers that are very similar. Compare the three names or numbers and decide which ones are exactly alike. On the Sample Answer Sheet mark the answer*

A *if ALL THREE names or numbers are exactly ALIKE*

B *if only the FIRST and SECOND names or numbers are exactly ALIKE*

C *if only the FIRST and THIRD names or numbers are exactly ALIKE*

D *if only the SECOND and THIRD names or numbers are exactly ALIKE*

E *if ALL THREE names or numbers are DIFFERENT*

1. Davis Hazen	David Hozen	David Hazen
2. Lois Appel	Lois Appel	Lois Apfel
3. June Allan	Jane Allan	Jane Allan
4. 10235	10235	10235
5. 32614	32164	32614

If you finish the sample questions before you are told to turn to the test, it will be to your advantage to study the code given above for A, B, C, D, and E. This code is repeated on every page.

Directions: *In the next group of sample questions, there is a name in a box at the left and four other names in alphabetical order at the right. Find the correct location for the boxed name so it will be in alphabetical order with the others, and mark the letter of that location as your answer.*

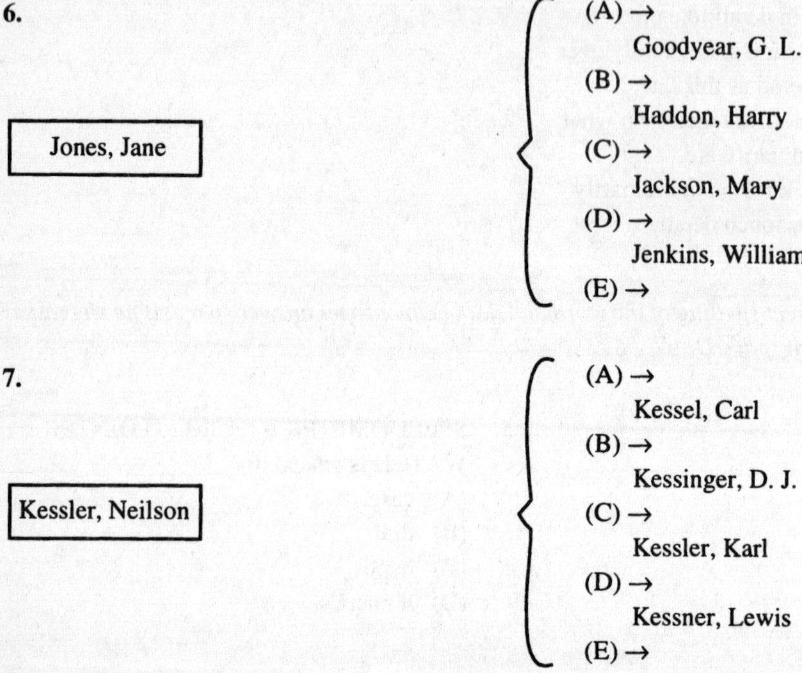

6. Jones, Jane

(A) →
Goodyear, G. L.
(B) →
Haddon, Harry
(C) →
Jackson, Mary
(D) →
Jenkins, William
(E) →

7. Kessler, Neilson

(A) →
Kessel, Carl
(B) →
Kessinger, D. J.
(C) →
Kessler, Karl
(D) →
Kessner, Lewis
(E) →

Directions: *In the following questions, solve each problem and find your answer in the list of suggested answers for that question. Mark the Sample Answer Sheet A, B, C, or D for the answer you obtained. If your answer is not among these, mark E for that question.*

8. Add:

$$\begin{array}{r} 22 \\ \underline{+\ 33} \end{array}$$

(A) 44
(B) 45
(C) 54
(D) 55
(E) none of these

9. Subtract:

$$\begin{array}{r} 24 \\ \underline{-\ 3} \end{array}$$

(A) 20
(B) 21
(C) 27
(D) 29
(E) none of these

10. Multiply:

$$\begin{array}{r} 25 \\ \times \underline{\ 5} \end{array}$$

(A) 100
(B) 115
(C) 125
(D) 135
(E) none of these

11. Divide:

$126 \div 6$

(A) 20
(B) 22
(C) 24
(D) 26
(E) none of these

Directions: *There is one set of suggested answers for the next group of sample questions. Do not try to memorize these answers because there will be a different set on each page in the test.*

To find the answer to a question, determine which suggested answer contains numbers and letters that all appear in the question. If no suggested answer fits, mark E for that question.

	Suggested Answers:
12. 8 N K 9 G T 4 6	(A) = 7, 9, G, K
13. T 9 7 Z 6 L 3 K	(B) = 8, 9, T, Z
14. Z 7 G K 3 9 8 N	(C) = 6, 7, K, Z
15. 3 K 9 4 6 G Z L	(D) = 6, 8, G, T
16. Z N 7 3 8 K T 9	(E) = none of these

Answer Key

Verbal Tasks Test

1. C 2. D 3. D 4. C 5. B

Clerical Tasks Test

1. E	5. C	9. B	13. C
2. B	6. E	10. C	14. A
3. D	7. D	11. E	15. E
4. A	8. D	12. D	16. B

Explanatory Answers

Verbal Tasks Test

1. **(C)** *Previous* means *former.* If you did not know the meaning of the word *previous* but remembered that the prefix "pre" usually means *before,* you could use that clue to choose an answer.

2. **(D)** Having a specific end in view is careful planning.

3. **(D)** Choice (A) incorrectly mixes singular and plural; choice (B) employs a double negative; choice (C) inappropriately inserts the word *what.*

4. **(C)** This is the correct spelling.

5. **(B)** Looking at the first pair of words, we see that there is a functional relationship between the two words. The function of the pointer on the speedometer is to indicate something (speed) at a particular moment. Likewise, the function of the hands on a watch is to indicate something (time) at a particular moment. The dial and numerals are involved in the telling of time, but they do not indicate a reading at a particular moment, so they do not really serve the same function. The watch case is quite clearly a wrong choice; it is even less related to indicating something at a given moment.

Clerical Tasks Test

1. **(E)** The name in the first column differs from those in the second and third columns because the first name is different; the name in the second column has a different last name.

2. **(B)** In the third column, the last name is different from the last name in the first and second columns.

3. **(D)** All three last names are alike, but the first name in the first column differs from the first names in the other columns.

4. **(A)** All three numbers are identical.

5. **(C)** The numbers in the first and third columns are identical, but in the second number, the third and fourth digits are reversed.

6. **(E)** O comes after E, so *Jones* comes after *Jenkins.*

7. **(D)** There are two identical last names, so you must alphabetize on the basis of first names. N comes after K, so *Kessler, Neilson* comes after *Kessler, Karl.*

8. **(D)**

$$\begin{array}{r} 22 \\ +\ 33 \\ \hline 55 \end{array}$$

ce (A). This choice
7. There is no 7 in
not be the answer.
other answer choices,
so eliminate that as
s a Z, which does not

13. **(C)** There is no G in question 13, so eliminate choice (A). There is no 8 in question 13, so eliminate choice (B). Choice (C) is correct; do not waste time looking at choice (D).

14. **(A)** Once you have found a correct answer, move immediately to the next question. You do not have time to check other options that cannot be correct.

15. **(E)** All the answer choices include either a 7 or an 8, but neither of these numbers appears in question 15, so (E) must be your answer.

16. **(B)** Eliminate choice (A) because there is no G in question 16. (B) is correct. Mark it and stop.

WHAT ABOUT ACWA?

If you have friends who have entered federal law enforcement service within the past few years, you have probably heard about ACWA, the Administrative Careers With America exam. At one time, OPM did nearly all the testing and hiring for federal agencies, and ACWA was an important component of the process. With the decentralization of hiring, the ACWA program has been discontinued. Some agencies may request that OPM administer the ACWA exam rather than a tailor-made exam for certain positions (the Bureau of Alcohol, Tobacco, and Firearms Inspector position comes to mind), but they are relatively few. While the ACWA exam itself is seldom used, ACWA-type questions have been liberally adopted by other examinations. The TEA exam, for instance, includes ACWA reading comprehension and mathematics. A number of exams make use of or adapt the self-rating section of ACWA known as the IAR, often without previous warning or sample questions. Since the bulk of the ACWA questions appear on other exams already described, the following official sample questions represent only a portion of the set. The Vocabulary and Tabular Completion sections may well be utilized in some tailor-made exams, so we offer them here for you to examine. They are not a part of the best-known named exams. You cannot prepare for the self-rating questions, but we are presenting a sampling for you here to spare you the possibility of disconcerting surprises.

Vocabulary

Law enforcement occupations require you to communicate well in both written and spoken language. Consequently, a good vocabulary is important for successful job performance. The questions present a key word and five suggested answers. Your task is to find the answer that is closest in meaning to the key word. Wrong answers may have some connection with the word, but their meanings will be essentially different from that of the key word. On the ACWA exam, there are 15 vocabulary questions. ACWA directions recommend spending no more than five minutes to answer the 15 vocabulary questions.

1. FRAUDULENT means most nearly
(A) suspicious.
(B) unproven.
(C) deceptive.
(D) unfair.
(E) despicable.

The word *fraudulent* means characterized by deceit or trickery, especially deliberate misrepresentation. Therefore, response C, *deceptive,* is the best synonym. Responses A, D, and E could be viewed as slightly related to the meaning of *fraudulent*. Response A, *suspicious*—sensing that something is wrong without definite proof—could describe a person's reaction to a *fraudulent* situation. Response D, *unfair,* and response E, *despicable,* could both be used to describe a *fraudulent* act. However, the basic meanings of these three words are completely different from the meaning of *fraudulent.* Response B, *unproven,* is clearly unrelated to the meaning of *fraudulent.*

2. ALLEGATION means most nearly
(A) denial.
(B) response.
(C) inquiry.
(D) assertion.
(E) revelation.

An *allegation* is a declaration that something is true, sometimes with little or no proof. An *assertion* is an affirmation that something is true, so the correct answer is response D. Response A, *denial,* is opposite in meaning to *allegation*—a declaration that something is false. Responses B, C, and E all share the general idea of a communicative statement but, on a specific level, are unrelated to *allegation.*

Tabular Completion Questions

These questions are based on information presented in tables. Only two sample questions of this type appear among the official sample questions distributed by the Office of Personnel Management. Because in the actual test you will have to find five unknown values in each table, we have expanded our sample table to include questions on all five unknowns and to thereby give you additional practice in calculating the values without a calculator. You must calculate these unknown values by using the known values given in the table. In some questions, the exact answer will not be given as one of the response choices. In such cases, you should select response E, "none of these."

The ACWA exam contains 10 tabular completion questions based on two tables. Instructions for ACWA recommend that test takers spend no more than 15 minutes to answer the tabular completion questions. Remember: Calculators are not permitted.

TABULAR COMPLETION
REVENUE (IN MILLIONS OF DOLLARS) OF ALL GOVERNMENTS BY SOURCE AND LEVEL OF GOVERNMENT FISCAL YEAR 1981*

Source	Total	Federal	State	Local
Total Revenue	1,259,421	660,759	310,828	V
Intergovernmental	184,033	1,804	70,786	111,443
From federal government	90,295	—	III	22,427
From state or local government	93,738	1,804	2,918	89,016
Revenue from Own Sources	1,075,388	II	240,042	176,391
General	820,814	487,706	187,373	145,735
Taxes	I	405,714	149,738	94,776
Property	74,969	—	2,949	72,020
Individual and corporate income	407,257	346,688	55,039	5,530
Sales and gross receipts	134,532	48,561	72,751	13,220
Other	33,470	10,465	18,999	4,006
Charges and miscellaneous	170,586	81,992	37,635	50,959
Utility and Liquor Stores	29,896	—	4,628	25,268
Insurance Trust	224,678	171,249	48,041	5,388
Employee and railroad retirement	36,962	6,580	IV	5,260
Unemployment compensation	18,733	162	18,443	128
Old age, disability, and health insurance	168,983	164,507	4,476	—

* Hypothetical data.

1. What is the value of I in millions of dollars?
   (A) 695,097
   (B) 616,758
   (C) 555,452
   (D) 254,574
   (E) none of these

The answer is **E.** The correct value (not given as an answer) can be calculated by subtracting the value for *Charges and miscellaneous* from the value for *General* under *Revenue from Own Sources.*

820,814 – 170,586 = 650,228

2. What is the value of II in millions of dollars?
   (A) 835,346
   (B) 662,563
   (C) 658,955
   (D) 417,433
   (E) none of these

The correct answer is **C.** It can be calculated by subtracting the value for *Intergovernmental* from the value for *Total Revenue.*

660,759 – 1,804 = 658,955

3. What is the value of III in millions of dollars?
   (A) 73,704
   (B) 68,868
   (C) 67,868
   (D) 67,978
   (E) none of these

The correct answer is **C.** Calculate the value of state revenues *From federal government* by subtracting the value of revenues *From state or local government* in the State column from the value of *Intergovernmental* revenues in the State column.

70,786 – 2,918 = 67,868

4. What is the value of IV in millions of dollars?
   (A) 43,565
   (B) 29,598
   (C) 25,122
   (D) 22,919
   (E) none of these

The correct answer is **C.** Calculate the value of state revenues from *Employee and railroad retirement* by subtracting the combined values of *Unemployment compensation* and *Old age, disability, and health insurance* in the State column from the value of *Insurance Trust.*

48,041 – (18,443 + 4,476) = 25,122

5. What is the value of V in millions of dollars?
   (A) 821,567
   (B) 464,175
   (C) 318,490
   (D) 287,834
   (E) none of these

The correct answer is **D.** To calculate total local revenue, add together *Intergovernmental* revenue in the Local column and *Revenue from Own Sources* in the Local column.

111,443 + 176,391 = 287,834

SELF-RATING QUESTIONS

The self-rating sections of federal examinations are set up to look like multiple-choice tests and are timed like tests, but they are not really tests at all. There are no right or wrong answers. You cannot study for the self-rating questions; your preparation consists only of gathering statistical records from your school years and thinking about what you achieved and when. On a typical self-rating section, you will find questions about your best and worst grades in school and about your favorite and least favorite subjects, questions about your extracurricular activities in school and college (if you went to college) and about your participation in sports, and questions about attendance, part-time jobs, and leadership positions. Other questions refer to your working life or school relationships. These questions ask what you think your peers think of you; others ask similar questions with respect to your supervisors or teachers. The questions ask how you think your teachers or employers might rate you on specific traits. Similar questions ask you to suggest what your friends might say about you. Still other questions ask how you rate yourself against others.

Some of these questions offer hard choices, but you do not have time to dwell on the answers. The self-rating sections are timed in the same manner as test questions. Just answer honestly and to the best of your ability. Do not try to second-guess and give the answers you think the examiners want. Some exams include two separate self-rating sections to check for honesty. Even where there is only one such section, it has built-in measures of general consistency.

There are no official self-rating sample questions. The following questions are representative.

1. My favorite subject in high school was
(A) math.
(B) English.
(C) physical education.
(D) social studies.
(E) science.

2. My GPA upon graduation from high school (on a 4.0 scale) was
(A) lower than 2.51.
(B) 2.51 to 2.80.
(C) 2.81 to 3.25.
(D) 3.26 to 3.60.
(E) higher than 3.60.

3. In my second year of high school, I was absent
(A) never.
(B) not more than 3 days.
(C) 4 to 10 days.
(D) more often than 10 days.
(E) an amount that I do not recall.

4. My best grades in high school were in
(A) art.
(B) math.
(C) English.
(D) social studies.
(E) music.

5. While in high school, I participated in
(A) one sport.
(B) two sports and one other extracurricular activity.
(C) three nonathletic extracurricular activities.
(D) no extracurricular activities.
(E) something other than the above.

6. During my senior year in high school, I held a paying job
(A) 0 hours a week.
(B) 1 to 5 hours a week.
(C) 6 to 10 hours a week.
(D) 11 to 16 hours a week.
(E) more than 16 hours a week.

7. The number of semesters in which I failed a course in high school was
(A) none.
(B) one.
(C) two or three.
(D) four or five.
(E) more than five

8. In high school, I did volunteer work
(A) more than 10 hours a week.
(B) 5 to 10 hours a week on a regular basis.
(C) sporadically.
(D) seldom.
(E) not at all.

If you did not go to college, skip questions 9 through 24. Go to question 25.

9. My general area of concentration in college was
(A) performing arts.
(B) humanities.
(C) social sciences.
(D) business.
(E) none of the above.

10. At college graduation, my age was
(A) under 20.
(B) 20.
(C) 21 to 24.
(D) 25 to 29.
(E) 30 or over.

11. My standing in my graduating class was in the
(A) bottom third.
(B) middle third.
(C) top third.
(D) top quarter.
(E) top 10 percent.

12. In college, I was elected to a major office in a class or in a club or organization
(A) more than six times.
(B) four or five times.
(C) two or three times.
(D) once.
(E) never.

13. In comparison to my peers, I cut classes
(A) much less often than most.
(B) somewhat less often than most.
(C) just about the same as most.
(D) somewhat more often than most.
(E) much more often than most.

14. The campus activities in which I participated most were
(A) social service.
(B) political.
(C) literary.
(D) I did not participate in campus activities.
(E) I did not participate in any of these activities.

15. My name appeared on the dean's list
(A) never.
(B) once or twice.
(C) in three or more terms.
(D) in more terms than it did not appear.
(E) I do not remember.

16. The volunteer work I did while in college was predominantly
(A) health-care related.
(B) religious.
(C) political.
(D) educational.
(E) I did not volunteer.

17. While a college student, I spent most of my summers
(A) in summer school.
(B) earning money.
(C) traveling.
(D) in service activities.
(E) resting.

18. My college education was financed
(A) entirely by my parents.
(B) by my parents and my own earnings.
(C) by scholarships, loans, and my own earnings.
(D) by my parents and loans.
(E) by a combination of sources not listed above.

19. In the college classroom, I was considered
(A) a listener.
(B) an occasional contributor.
(C) an average participant.
(D) a frequent contributor.
(E) a leader.

20. The person on campus whom I most admired was
(A) another student.
(B) an athletic coach.
(C) a teacher.
(D) an administrator.
(E) a journalist.

21. Of the skills I developed at college, the one I value most is
(A) foreign language ability.
(B) oral expression.
(C) writing skills.
(D) facility with computers.
(E) analytical skills.

22. I made my greatest mark in college through my
(A) athletic prowess.
(B) success in performing arts.
(C) academic success.
(D) partying reputation.
(E) conciliatory skill with my peers.

23. My cumulative GPA (on a 4.0 scale) in courses in my major was
(A) lower than 3.00.
(B) 3.00 to 3.25.
(C) 3.26 to 3.50.
(D) 3.51 to 3.75.
(E) higher than 3.75.

24. While in college I
(A) worked full-time and was a part-time student.
(B) worked 20 hours a week and was a full-time student.
(C) worked 20 hours a week and was a part-time student.
(D) was a full-time student working more than 10 but less than 20 hours a week.
(E) was a full-time student.

25. In the past six months, I have been late to work (or school)
(A) never.
(B) only one time.
(C) very seldom.
(D) more than five times.
(E) I don't recall.

26. My supervisors (or teachers) would be most likely to describe me as
(A) competent.
(B) gifted.
(C) intelligent.
(D) fast-working.
(E) detail oriented.

27. My peers would probably describe me as
(A) analytical.
(B) glib.
(C) organized.
(D) funny.
(E) helpful.

28. According to my supervisors (or teachers), my greatest asset is my
(A) ability to communicate orally.
(B) written expression.
(C) ability to motivate others.
(D) organization of time.
(E) friendly personality.

29. In the past two years, I have applied for
(A) no jobs other than this one.
(B) one other job.
(C) two to four other jobs.
(D) five to eight other jobs.
(E) more than eight jobs.

30. In the past year, I read strictly for pleasure
(A) no books.
(B) one book.
(C) two books.
(D) three to six books.
(E) more than six books.

31. When I read for pleasure, I read mostly
(A) history.
(B) fiction.
(C) poetry.
(D) biography.
(E) current events.

32. My peers would say of me that, when they ask me a question, I am
(A) helpful.
(B) brusque.
(C) condescending.
(D) generous.
(E) patient.

33. My supervisors (or teachers) would say that my area of least competence is
(A) analytical ability.
(B) written communication.
(C) attention to detail.
(D) public speaking.
(E) self-control.

34. In the past two years, the number of full-time (35 hours or more) jobs I have held is
(A) none.
(B) one.
(C) two or three.
(D) four.
(E) five or more.

35. Compared to my peers, my supervisors (or teachers) would rank my dependability
(A) much better than average.
(B) somewhat better than average.
(C) about average.
(D) somewhat less than average.
(E) much less than average.

36. In my opinion, the most important of the following attributes in an employee is
(A) discretion.
(B) loyalty.
(C) open-mindedness.
(D) courtesy.
(E) competence.

37. My peers would say that the word that describes me least is
(A) sociable.
(B) reserved.
(C) impatient.
(D) judgmental.
(E) independent.

38. My supervisors (or teachers) would say that I react to criticism with
(A) a defensive attitude.
(B) quick capitulation.
(C) anger.
(D) interest.
(E) shame.

39. My attendance record over the past year has been
(A) not as good as I would like it to be.
(B) not as good as my supervisors (or teachers) would like it to be.
(C) a source of embarrassment.
(D) satisfactory.
(E) a source of pride.

40. My peers would say that, when I feel challenged, my reaction is one of
(A) determination.
(B) energy.
(C) defiance.
(D) caution.
(E) compromise.

There are no "right" answers to these questions, so there is no answer key.

PART FIVE

Training

CONTENTS

TRAINING

No law enforcement agency will send a new recruit out into the field without appropriate training. All law enforcement agents are trained in self-defense, use of weapons, rules and regulations of the department, and of course, the specific duties of the job.

Local, county, and state police departments tend to have their own training programs. In some areas, these are very localized and individualized; in others, the programs are consolidated and regionalized. In a very small police department, this training may be on a one-to-one basis and may consist largely of on-the-job training by the side of a mentor. Larger jurisdictions have police academies at which recruits receive training in organized programs for a prescribed period of time.

Some state and local law enforcement agencies have made special arrangements for experienced officers to receive advanced, specialized training at the Federal Law Enforcement Training Center (FLETC) in Glynco, Georgia. This specialized training for seasoned officers includes subjects like Advanced Law Enforcement Photography, Cargo Theft, Advanced Arson for Profit Investigation, Advanced Explosives Investigative Techniques, Undercover Investigative Techniques, and Child Abuse and Exploitation Investigation, mostly in two-week programs.

With the exception of FBI Special Agents, who are trained at the FBI Academy at Quantico, Virginia, and Postal Inspectors, who are trained at the Postal Department's Inspector School in Potomac, Maryland, nearly all federal law enforcement officers receive their basic and specialized training at FLETC in Glynco, Georgia.

Some of the FLETC Basic Programs are:

- Police Training (mixed), 5- and 8-week programs
- Criminal Investigator (mixed), 8 weeks
- Police Integrated (Immigration Detention), 6 weeks
- Police Integrated (Federal Protective Service Physical Security Specialist), 6 weeks
- Police Integrated (Immigration Officer Basic Training Program), 14 weeks
- Police Integrated (U.S. Border Patrol), 18 weeks
- Police Integrated (U.S. Park Police), 18 weeks

Note: Mixed programs are those in which the participants are from several federal organizations. Following these programs, many organizations conduct follow-up basic programs for their agency's specific instructional material. Integrated programs are those in which instruction from the specific organization is provided along with instruction from the Center.

In all, students from 51 federal law enforcement organizations participate in training on the campus at FLETC. The training at FLETC is conducted in a college-like atmosphere; the students live in dormitories and eat in a central dining hall. Students attend classes for eight hours a day, Monday through Friday. A few agencies conduct training at night and on weekends as well. After classes are dismissed, students are free to come and go as they wish, but much free time must be given over to study, review, and practice. The Center does provide coordinated intramural sports activities throughout the year, and classes compete against one another for fun and physical fitness.

The FLETC campus was originally the Glynco Naval Air Station, and many facilities that were used by the Navy have been adapted by the Center. These include classrooms, dormitories, recreation facilities, the dining hall, and administrative and logistical support facilities. Supplementary construction since 1977 includes:

- a new classroom building that also houses various special-purpose areas including the library, a language laboratory, an interviewing-techniques complex, and various criminalistic teaching laboratories for rolling and lifting fingerprints and testing narcotics
- a new 96-point indoor firing range that provides eight separate ranges of 12 firing points each, classrooms, and weapons-cleaning areas
- a new driver-training complex that provides the ability to create more realistic situations for training in defensive driving, skid control, and highway driving
- additional physical specialties facilities
- an addition to the dining hall

(You will note that there are no facilities for dependents. Students are urged to leave their families at home during the training period. Transportation of dependents must be at the student's own expense. Housing in Brunswick, Georgia, is limited, and the program is so intensive that little visiting time remains.)

The training staff of the Center is made up of experienced instructors who have a minimum of five years of law enforcement experience. A portion of the instructors are federal officers and investigators on detailed assignment to the Center from their parent agencies. This mix of permanent and detailed instructors creates a balance of experience and fresh insight from the field.

The schoolday at FLETC is divided into classroom time, laboratories, and practical exercises. Part of the FLETC staff consists of professional role players who are able to give students very real training and experience in interviewing, pursuit, judgment in the use of firearms, and many other police techniques.

Each program at FLETC is geared to the specific needs of a specific type of law enforcement officer and to a specific agency. Nonetheless, the Criminal Investigator Training Program may be taken as typical. The Criminal Investigator Training Program consists of 38 training days. There are a total of 300 course hours in the program covered in eight weeks of training. The program begins on a Tuesday and ends on a Thursday to allow for travel time. All agencies pay for travel between the first duty station and Glynco, Georgia.

Here is the complete course of instruction for the Criminal Investigator Training Program.

POLICE/INVESTIGATOR BRANCHES

Course	Hours of Instruction			
	Lecture	Laboratory	Practical Exercise	Total
Behavioral Science				
Ethics and Conduct	2:00			2:00
Interpersonal Stress	6:00			6:00
Interviewing	7:00	—	6:00	13:00
Subtotal	15:00		6:00	21:00
Enforcement Operations				
Appraising Crowds and Mobs	2:00			2:00
Contemporary Law	2:00			2:00
Enforcement Situations				
Execution of a Search Warrant	6:00	2:00		8:00
Federal Firearms Violations	2:00			2:00
Felony Vehicle Stops	1:00	1:00		2:00
Firearms Policy	2:00			2:00
Informants	2:00			2:00

Course	Hours of Instruction			
	Lecture	Laboratory	Practical Exercise	Total
Officer Survival and Safety	2:00			2:00
Orientation to Federal Law Enforcement Agencies	2:00			2:00
Report Writing	6:00			6:00
Sources of Information	2:00			2:00
Surveillance	4:00		6:00	10:00
Undercover Operations	2:00			2:00
Subtotal	35:00	3:00	6:00	44:00
Enforcement Techniques				
Bombs and Explosives	4:00			4:00
Counterfeiting	2:00			2:00
Crime Scene Investigation	6:00		3:00	9:00
Description and Identification	3:00			3:00
Fingerprinting	2:00		4:00	6:00
Narcotics	3:00	2:00		5:00
Photography	6:00		1:00	7:00
Questioned Documents	2:00			2:00
Subtotal	28:00	2:00	8:00	38:00
Legal/Economic Crime				
Assault	1:00			1:00
Bribery	1:00			1:00
Civil Fraud Litigation	2:00			2:00
Civil Rights	2:00			2:00
Conspiracy	5:00			5:00
Constitutional Law	2:00			2:00
Court Testimony	2:00			2:00
Criminal Law	2:00			2:00
Detention and Arrest	6:00			6:00
Entrapment	1:00			1:00
Evidence	11:00			11:00
Federal Court Procedures	9:00			9:00
Link Analysis	2:00	2:00		4.00
Organized Crime/White-Collar Crime	4:00			4:00
Parties to Criminal Offenses	2:00			2:00
Privacy Act	1:00			1:00
RICO	1:00			1:00
Search and Seizure	21:00			21:00
Self-Incrimination	4:00			4:00
Subtotal	79:00	2:00		81:00
Police/Investigator Branches Total	157:00	7:00	20:00	184:00

SPECIAL TRAINING BRANCHES

Course	Hours of Instruction			
	Lecture	Laboratory	Practical Exercise	Total
Driver Specialties				
Defensive Driving	1:30		2:00	3:30
DECAT	:30	:30		1:00
Skid Control	1:30		2:00	3:30
Transporting Prisoners	1:00	1:00		2:00
Subtotal	4:30	1:30	4:00	10:00
Firearms Specialties				
Basic Marksmanship	1:00	6:00		7:00
Firearms Safety Rules	:30			:30
Judgment Pistol Shooting	1:30	2:00	:30	4:00
Practical Pistol Course	1:00	10:00	1:00	12:00
Reduced Light Course of Fire	1:00	1:00		2:00
Shotgun Course	:30	1:30		2:00
Shotgun Stress	:30	1:30		2:00
Weapons Maintenance and Cleaning	:30			:30
Subtotal	6:30	22:00	1:30	30:00
Physical Specialties				
Arrest Techniques	2:00	6:00	2:00	10:00
Cardiopulmonary Resuscitation	3:00	5:00	2:00	10:00
Defensive Tactics	3:00	7:00	2:00	12:00
Introduction to Physical Specialties	2:00			2:00
Physical Efficiency Battery			4:00	4:00
Subtotal	10:00	18:00	10:00	38:00
Special Training Branches Total	21:00	41:30	15:30	78:00

MULTI-BRANCH RESPONSIBILITY

Course	Hours of Instruction			
	Lecture	Laboratory	Practical Exercise	Total
Welcome and Orientation	2:00			2:00
Final Practice Exercise			24:00	24:00
Subtotal	2:00		24:00	26:00
All Branches Total	180:00	48:30	59:30	288:00

Administrative	Hours
Uniform and Equipment	1:00
Examination and Review	10:00
Graduation	1:00
Total	12:00

Total Program Length	Hours
Lecture	180:00
Laboratory	48:30
Practical Exercise	59:30
Administrative	12:00
Total	300:00

The fourth- and fifth-week schedules in the Criminal Investigator Training Program are typical of weekly scheduling in all programs.

FACULTY ADVISOR:
ASS'T FACULTY ADVISOR:
EDUCATIONAL AIDE:

FEDERAL LAW ENFORCEMENT TRAINING CENTER
CRIMINAL INVESTIGATOR TRAINING

ROOM NO. CLASS NO. AGENCY WEEK NO. 4

HOURS	MONDAY (13)	TUESDAY (14)	WEDNESDAY (15)	THURSDAY (16)	FRIDAY (17)
7:30 8:30 8:30 9:30	Firearms Specialties	Physical Specialties	Firearms Specialties	Physical Specialties	Firearms Specialties
9:30 10:30 10:30 11:30	514 Surveillance PE ENFORCEMENT OPERATIONS STAFF	219 Counterfeiting ENFORCEMENT TECHNIQUES STAFF	127 Organized Crime/ White-Collar Crime LEGAL/ECONOMIC CRIME STAFF	COMP EXAM I FACULTY ADVISOR EXAM REVIEW - 15 min.	209 Bombs and Explosives ENFORCEMENT TECHNIQUES STAFF
11:30 to 12:30	LUNCH	LUNCH	LUNCH	LUNCH	LUNCH
12:30 1:30 1:30 2:30	514 Surveillance PE ENFORCEMENT OPERATIONS STAFF	218 Questioned Documents ENFORCEMENT TECHNIQUES STAFF	506 Federal Firearms Violations ENFORCEMENT OPERATIONS STAFF	127 Organized Crime/ White-Collar Crime LEGAL/ECONOMIC CRIME STAFF	209 Bombs and Explosives (cont.) ENFORCEMENT TECHNIQUES STAFF
2:30 3:30 3:30 4:30		101 Search and Seizure (Pt 4) LEGAL/ECONOMIC CRIME STAFF	101 Search and Seizure (Pt 5) LEGAL/ECONOMIC CRIME STAFF	101 Search and Seizure (Pt 6) LEGAL/ECONOMIC CRIME STAFF	101 Search and Seizure (Pt 7) LEGAL/ECONOMIC CRIME STAFF

FACULTY ADVISOR:
ASS'T FACULTY ADVISOR:
EDUCATIONAL AIDE:

FEDERAL LAW ENFORCEMENT TRAINING CENTER
CRIMINAL INVESTIGATOR TRAINING

ROOM NO. CLASS NO. AGENCY WEEK NO. 5

HOURS	MONDAY (18)	TUESDAY (19)	WEDNESDAY (20)	THURSDAY (21)	FRIDAY (22)
7:30 8:30	Physical Specialties	Firearms Specialties	Physical Specialties	Firearms Specialties	Physical Specialties
8:30 9:30					
9:30 10:30	111 Evidence (Pt 1) LEGAL/ECONOMIC CRIME STAFF	111 Evidence (Pt 2) LEGAL/ECONOMIC CRIME STAFF	LEGAL EXAM II LEGAL/ECONOMIC CRIME STAFF	111 Evidence (Pt 4) LEGAL/ECONOMIC CRIME STAFF	111 Evidence (Pt 5) LEGAL/ECONOMIC CRIME STAFF
10:30 11:30			EXAM REVIEW - 15 min.		
11:30 to 12:30	LUNCH	LUNCH	LUNCH	LUNCH	LUNCH
12:30 1:30	520 Report Writing (Pt 2) ENFORCEMENT OPERATIONS STAFF	111 Evidence (Pt 2) (cont.) LEGAL/ECONOMIC CRIME STAFF	111 Evidence (Pt 2) (cont.) LEGAL/ECONOMIC CRIME STAFF	509 Informants ENFORCEMENT OPERATIONS STAFF	110 Assaults LEGAL/ECONOMIC CRIME STAFF
1:30 2:30		101 Search and Seizure (Pt 9)			505 Execution of a Search Warrant
2:30 3:30	101 Search and Seizure (Pt 8) LEGAL/ECONOMIC CRIME STAFF	LEGAL/ECONOMIC CRIME STAFF	Driver Specialties (Transporting Prisoners) Bldg. 210, Room B-6	515 Undercover Operations ENFORCEMENT OPERATIONS STAFF	ENFORCEMENT OPERATIONS STAFF
3:30 4:30					

Standard Daily Schedule at FLETC

Morning Session*	7:30 A.M. to 11:30 A.M.
Lunch	11:30 A.M. to 12:30 P.M.
Afternoon Session*	12:30 P.M. to 4:30 P.M.

*Classes are 50 minutes in length with breaks scheduled according to the subject matter being presented and the status of practical exercise activity.

Student Evaluation

The Criminal Investigator Training Program cognitive testing system consists of five examinations: three legal examinations and two comprehensive examinations. In addition, the student is expected to satisfactorily complete a series of practical exercises and/or homework assignments. Satisfactory completion of all examinations, practical exercises, and assignments is required for graduation from the Criminal Investigator Training Program.

Written Examinations

The student is required to achieve a score of at least 70% on each of the five written examinations. The student is allocated a total of one hour and 45 minutes to complete each examination. Immediately following each examination, a 15-minute examination review is conducted, allowing the students to assess their performance on the examination. Official results of examinations are posted as soon as possible after the completion of the examination. Each individual student's grade is maintained in confidentiality as far as fellow classmates are concerned. Student examination scores are available to the student's agency through official channels.

In the event that a student fails to achieve a score of at least 70% on any written examination, the student will be placed on probation. During this period, additional assistance will be made available to the student, upon request, in the form of counseling, out-of-class study assignments, and personal instructional sessions. The student will then take a remedial examination covering the same subjects as the original failed examination. The student must successfully pass this remedial examination to remain eligible for graduation.

A student may be placed on probation for failing a regularly scheduled examination on only two occasions. In the event that a student fails a third regularly scheduled examination (or fails to achieve a passing score on *any* remedial examination), the student will not be eligible for graduation from the Criminal Investigator Training Program.

Practical Exercises

The second component of the CITP evaluation system is the measurement of physical skills acquired during training. A student must satisfactorily complete *all* phases of the practical exercises to successfully complete the training program.

The practical exercises are designed to provide the student with as much individual attention and instruction as possible. This area involves the development of psychomotor skills and the basic knowledge needed to perform at least minimally in the occupational role. Each student is given a reasonable number of opportunities to meet the minimum standards of performance established by the learning objectives.

Evaluation of student performance is made during various practical exercises. Performance will be judged by the student's actual ability to satisfactorily complete the required tasks.

The Center encourages students to repeat the practical exercise portions of their training until mastery is achieved. Accordingly, a student who does not achieve mastery in any of these tasks is *not* placed on probation. However, if the student cannot demonstrate the ability to satisfactorily perform the tasks prior to the completion of the program, a certificate will *not* be awarded.

In addition to practical exercises in many specific areas, the student is required to successfully complete a final "single thread" practical exercise that lasts for three entire training days. The student, assigned to an investigative team, will be assigned a particular problem in which the tasks learned in prior training will be tested. Once assigned the problem, the student will employ techniques acquired in interviewing, surveillance, execution of search and arrest warrants, crime scene investigation, and testifying at trial. Grades will be based on the student's performance. In addition, each team member must contribute to a written case report documenting each individual's actions as well as the actions of the team in acquiring evidence during the exercise. The case report will be used as the basis for the mock trial and related court hearings pursuant to the trial.

Firearms Training

Marksmanship is evaluated on a point system. Each student must qualify with a minimum of 70% on the Practical Pistol Course. A student who does not achieve a satisfactory level of proficiency on the Practical Pistol Course (210 points out of 300 points = 70%) will be offered the opportunity to participate in remedial training to correct the deficiency. The total amount of scheduled firearms remedial training offered to a student will not exceed eight hours and two retests. Failure to qualify on this course will preclude the student from successful completion of the training program.

FINAL EXAM

The following is the final exam for the Criminal Investigator Training Program, the "single thread" exercise referred to earlier. The student who successfully completes this exam along with firearms training and physical training is exceedingly well equipped to enter the field as an effective Criminal Investigator.

COURSE: Final Practical Exercise (Continuous Investigative Case Problem)

LENGTH AND METHOD OF PRESENTATION:

Lecture	Laboratory	Practical Exercise	Total
		24:00	24:00

DESCRIPTION:

This graded practical exercise requires the student to demonstrate acceptable knowledge and proficiency in a variety of criminal investigative skills, procedures, and techniques in which training was received previously in the program. Under the scrutiny of faculty evaluators, the student teams will conduct a complete criminal investigation that will culminate in a realistic mock trial in which students will testify under direct and cross-examination to actual experiences encountered during the exercise. The exercise will include participating in surveillance; conducting an interview; handling informants; gathering evidence; preparing arrest and search warrants; making arrests and searches; handling and processing prisoners; using vehicles, weapons, and communications equipment; recognizing contraband; writing reports; demonstrating knowledge of federal court procedures; and other aspects of the criminal investigative process. In recognition of the diverse organizational backgrounds of CITP students, scenarios will encompass, to the extent possible, elements of activity common to all investigative personnel. Where common organizational affiliations exist within a class, the scenario will involve criminal violations pertinent to that organization.

OBJECTIVES:

At the conclusion of this practical exercise, the student will be able to:

1. Recognize and initiate logical investigative procedures.
2. Conduct productive interviews with witnesses and informants.
3. Conduct a proper surveillance and maintain a correct log.
4. Identify contraband including narcotics, counterfeit money, and/or illegal weapons.
5. Identify and contact appropriate sources of information (public records, computer sources, and so on).
6. Conduct a thorough crime scene investigation and search.
7. Collect and preserve evidence and transmit it to the laboratory, etc., as appropriate.
8. Identify and describe persons, things, and places in accord with Constitutional standards.
9. Recognize violations of 18 USC 111 (Assaults).
10. Demonstrate recognition of Constitutional restraints on law enforcement activity (Constitutional law and civil rights).
11. Recognize and develop all elements of a criminal offense.
12. Utilize effectively and safely the implements of law enforcement including vehicles, weapons, handcuffs, and communications equipment.
13. Prepare legally sufficient search and arrest affidavits (complaints) and warrants.
14. Demonstrate acceptable arrest techniques with or without arrest warrants.
15. Demonstrate legally acceptable entries to effect arrests or searches.
16. Conduct a proper search pursuant to an arrest or a search warrant.
17. Conduct a legally acceptable warrantless search.
18. Question suspects and/or arrestees demonstrating cognizance of Fourth, Fifth, and Sixth Amendment constraints.
19. Display correct judgment in "shoot–don't shoot" situations.
20. Demonstrate a proper felony vehicle stop.
21. Transport prisoners safely and in accord with prescribed procedures.
22. Demonstrate the ability to process prisoners including personal history, fingerprints, and mug shots.
23. Prepare a thorough and accurate report of investigation.
24. Demonstrate effective human relations skills in dealing with co-workers, witnesses, suspects, attorneys, and other contacts.
25. Provide direct testimony during court proceedings that is accurate and in accord with recommended techniques.
26. Demonstrate the ability to respond honestly and effectively to stringent cross-examination.
27. Facilitate the proper introduction of various types of evidence through appropriate testimony and custodial safeguards.
28. Demonstrate correct courtroom attire and demeanor.

PART

SIX

How to Choose

CONTENTS

HOW TO CHOOSE

Having read through this book, you are now aware of the many different law enforcement positions available. You are excited about the prospect of a law enforcement career, but you don't know quite where to begin. Your choice of a law enforcement career is narrowed by your own qualifications, your specific requirements, personal preferences, and the availability of openings.

Begin the narrowing process by looking carefully at the Comparison Charts on pages 211 through 216. With a red pencil, draw a line through positions that do not appeal to you at all. Then cross out positions for which you are disqualified because of age, education, physical condition, or experience. If one of the exams seems particularly intimidating to you, you might want to discount positions that require it, but do not rush to rule out a position just because of the exam. Check out working hours, travel and relocation requirements, starting pay, and opportunities for advancement. Then rank positions according to their desirability to you. Eliminate those positions that do not meet your personal requirements.

Consider and weigh carefully your personal needs, your personality characteristics, the surroundings you like best, and your long- and short-range goals.

- Do you have infirm parents who are going to need more and more time from you in the years ahead? If so, avoid a position that is likely to relocate you far from their home.
- Do you like to be home every night for dinner? Then choose a position with regularly scheduled hours like that of an Alcohol, Tobacco, and Firearms Inspector.
- Are you physically handicapped? There are a number of opportunities available to you including Import Specialist and Deportation Officer.
- Do you hate crowds? Do you enjoy solitude in the wide-open spaces? Border Patrol might be right for you.
- Did you drop out of scouting because you hated wearing a uniform? Avoid the uniformed services.
- Do you like to work closely with a few others? Criminal Investigators and Special Agents tend to work in teams.
- Do you feel strongly that every citizen should serve some time in the Armed Forces? Consider the Customs Service. Employees of the Customs Service can take leave from their positions to enter the Armed Forces, are assured that their jobs will await them when they return, and can earn promotions and raises during their absence. Employees of the Customs Service can also serve in the military reserves and collect regular pay while attending summer training.
- Do you have young children and feel that you should be around the house a good deal right now, yet you yearn for a more exciting life? A Postal Inspector must have postal experience. You might consider joining the Postal Service in a regularly scheduled position now and then plan to move into the position of Postal Inspector in the future.
- Do you enjoy rubbing elbows with the great and the famous? Perhaps you would like to be a Secret Service Special Agent despite the grueling hours and travel schedules.
- Do you thrive on long hours and look forward to lots of overtime pay? All law enforcement positions except Postal Inspector, which is paid at a higher annual rate, earn overtime pay for overtime work. The job descriptions tell you which positions demand greater overtime.
- Are you short on cash? Unless you can borrow startup money, you cannot be a Border Patrol Agent. Most of the uniformed services supply uniforms, but the Border Patrol Agent must buy his or her own uniforms, both rough duty and official, at a cost of over $1,200 and must pay for travel to the first duty station (but not to and from FLETC in Glynco, Georgia) as well.

Supplement the information in this book with personal information if possible. If you know anyone who holds a position in which you think you are interested, speak to that person. Ask about working conditions, special features of the job, and what the person likes most and least about the job. Evaluate the information in light of your own likes and dislikes and your own priorities. You might learn of low morale in a specific agency. This information might discourage you from applying, or you might seize the opportunity for rapid advancement because of turnover at the top. You must evaluate all information according to what is important to you. (Remember, however, that policies do change, and a condition described now may not exist by the time you are employed.) If you have no personal contacts in the agencies that interest you, check your phone book. If the agency has an office in your area, you might be able to arrange a meeting with an employee who would be willing to answer your questions. Such a person would undoubtedly be enthusiastic about the specific agency, but if you have prepared your questions well, you should be able to interpret the answers.

The final and crucial element in choosing your law enforcement career is *availability.* Positions at the local, county, and state law enforcement levels open with some frequency. Contact your municipal, county, or state police and ask for an application. You may receive immediate satisfaction, or you may be referred to an employment division or a department of personnel or human resources. Do not be discouraged if you are sent from one department to the next. Follow through. Even divisions that really want and need you are bound by bureaucracy. Don't let the runaround get you down. When you finally do reach a responsible party, ask lots of questions. Ask about filing dates, filing fees, exam dates, physical requirements, probationary periods, working conditions, pay scales, and benefits. All of these will vary from one local department to another, and you need all this information to choose intelligently and to file a timely and complete application.

If you are interested in a federal law enforcement position, you might find information at your State Employment Service. If the announcements you seek are not posted or filed at your State Employment Service, call, write, or go to a Federal Job Information Center. The most convenient Federal Job Information Center should be listed in the blue pages of your telephone directory under the heading "U.S. Government." A telephone call to this number may give you automated information pertinent to your own area or may direct you to a location at which you can pick up printed materials or conduct a search on a computer touch screen. Entry-level postal law enforcement openings should be posted on the bulletin board at your local post office.

One easy and efficient way to get information about federal law enforcement job openings throughout the country and to get application materials is to call the Career America Connection at 912-757-3000. This is a toll call, but it is a 24-hour automated service, so you can hold down costs by calling at night or on the weekend. You will need a touch-tone telephone to utilize the service. Allow yourself at least one-half hour to search job categories and geographical areas. The system is equipped to record your name and mailing address so you can be sent announcements and required forms through the mail. If you have a computer with a modem, you can access the same information from an OPM electronic bulletin board by dialing 912-757-3100.

A final, excellent source of information about the availability of federal law enforcement positions and application procedures is the agencies themselves. Call Washington, DC, information at 202-555-1212 and ask for the telephone number of the personnel office of the agency in which you are interested. Calls to government offices must be made during business hours, so prepare your questions ahead of time to hold down your phone bill.

Comparison Charts

AGE AT ENTRY • RETIREMENT • EDUCATION

Position	Age at Entry	Retirement	Education
Police Officer	20 to 35*	varies	HS plus (varies)
Deputy Sheriff	21 to 29*	varies	HS and some college (varies)
State Police Officer	21 to 29*	varies	HS plus (varies)
BATF Inspector	over 18	unspecified	college or experience
BATF Special Agent	21 to 37	eligible at 50 after 20 yrs.	college or experience
DEA Special Agent	21 to 37	eligible at 50 after 20 yrs.	bachelor's degree and experience
FBI Special Agent	23 to 37	mandatory at 55	advanced degree and experience
Federal Protective Officer	over 21	unspecified	2 yrs. college or experience
Border Patrol Agent	21 to 37	mandatory at 55	college or experience
Immigration Inspector	over 18	unspecified	college or experience
INS Criminal Investigator (Special Agents)	21 to 37	mandatory at 55	college or experience
Deportation Officer	21 to 37	mandatory at 55	college or experience
IRS Internal Security Inspector	21 to 37	eligible at 50 after 20 yrs.	college or experience
IRS Special Agent	23 to 37	eligible at 50 after 20 yrs.	bachelor's degree and advanced courses
Customs Aid	over 18	unspecified	2 yrs. college or experience
Customs Inspector	over 21	unspecified	college or experience

* Many localities have recently discarded the upper age limit. Check before eliminating yourself.

Position	Age at Entry	Retirement	Education
Import Specialist	over 20	unspecified	college or experience
Customs Special Agent	under 37	unspecified	college and 2 yrs. experience
Deputy U.S. Marshal	21 to 37	eligible at 50 after 20 yrs.	college or experience
Postal Police Officer	over 20	unspecified	no requirements
Postal Inspector	21 to 37	eligible at 50 after 20 yrs.	college or experience
Secret Service Uniformed Officer	over 21	eligible after 20 yrs. service	HS and police experience in large city
Secret Service Special Agent	21 to 37	mandatory at 55	college or experience

EXAM • PHYSICAL REQUIREMENTS • TRAINING

Position	Exam	Physical Requirements	Training
Police Officer	local	varies	varies
Deputy Sheriff	local	varies	varies
State Police Officer	local	varies	state training school
BATF Inspector	ACWA	not too strict	1 yr. on-the-job
BATF Special Agent	TEA	very strict; near perfect eyes	8 wks. FLETC and Special Agent School
DEA Special Agent	no written exam	very strict; near perfect eyes	12–15 wks. FLETC
FBI Special Agent	FBI's own	very strict	15 wks. FBI Academy
Federal Protective Officer	an OPM-developed exam	not too strict	8 wks. FLETC
Border Patrol Agent	Border Patrol Agent exam	very strict	17 wks. FLETC
Immigration Inspector	ACWA	not too strict	14 wks. FLETC
INS Criminal Investigator (Special Agent)	ACWA	very strict; perfect hearing	14 wks. FLETC
Deportation Officer	ACWA	certain handicaps allowed	FLETC
IRS Internal Security Inspector	TEA	not too strict	7 wks. FLETC and 2 wks. Internal Security (2×)
IRS Special Agent	TEA	very strict	20 wks. FLETC
Customs Aid	Federal Clerical exam	not too strict	on-the-job
Customs Inspector	no written exam	very strict	FLETC

Position	Exam	Physical Requirements	Training
Import Specialist	no written exam	lenient, but no colorblindness	classroom and on-the-job
Customs Special Agent	TEA	strict, but glasses allowed	11 wks. FLETC
Deputy U.S. Marshal	TEA	very strict	12 wks. FLETC
Postal Police Officer	Postal Police	very strict	8 wks. FLETC
Postal Inspector	PO's own	very strict	16 wks. at Potomac Management Academy
Secret Service Uniformed Officer	SS's own	very strict; near perfect eyes	FLETC
Secret Service Special Agent	TEA and SS's own	very strict; near perfect eyes	FLETC

SPECIAL SKILLS • TRAVEL • RELOCATION • HOURS

Position	Special Skills	Travel	Relocation	Hours
Police Officer	none for entry	no	no	rotating shifts and overtime
Deputy Sheriff	none for entry	some	unlikely	rotating shifts; emergency overtime
State Police Officer	none for entry	some	possible	rotating shifts; emergency overtime
BATF Inspector	none for entry	yes	yes	regular 40-hour week
BATF Special Agent	courses in Police Science	yes	yes	irregular 40-hour week plus overtime
DEA Special Agent	CPA, JD, or MS	yes	yes	irregular plus overtime
FBI Special Agent	advanced degree	yes	yes	40 hours plus overtime
Federal Protective Officer	none for entry	little	yes	rotating shifts
Border Patrol Agent	Spanish	yes	yes	60-hour week in irregular shifts
Immigration Inspector	none for entry	no	possible	long and irregular
INS Criminal Investigator (Special Agent)	none for entry	yes	yes	long and irregular
Deportation Officer	none for entry	some	possible	regular 40-hour week; probable overtime
IRS Internal Security Inspector	none for entry	yes	yes	40 irregular hours plus overtime
IRS Special Agent	accounting	yes	yes	40 irregular hours plus overtime
Customs Aid	none for entry	no	no	rotating shifts; 40-hour week

Position	Special Skills	Travel	Relocation	Hours
Customs Inspector	none for entry	no	once	rotating shifts; 40-hour week
Import Specialist	none for entry	no	once	rotating shifts; 40 hours plus overtime
Customs Special Agent	law or business	no	yes	rotating shifts; 40 hours plus overtime
Deputy U.S. Marshal	none for entry	yes	yes	long and irregular
Postal Police Officer	none for entry	no	no	shifts; 40-hour week with overtime and night differential
Postal Inspector	postal experience	yes	often	regular 48-hour week; emergency overtime
Secret Service Uniformed Officer	none for entry	no	possible	rotating shifts; 40 hours plus overtime
Secret Service Special Agent	none for entry	yes	yes	rotating shifts; much overtime